ROUTLEDGE LIBRARY EDITIONS:
17TH CENTURY PHILOSOPHY

Volume 4

SPINOZA IN SOVIET PHILOSOPHY

SPINOZA IN SOVIET PHILOSOPHY
A Series of Essays

Edited by
GEORGE L. KLINE

Taylor & Francis Group
LONDON AND NEW YORK

First published in 1952 by Routledge & Kegan Paul Ltd

This edition first published in 2020
by Routledge
2 Park Square, Milton Park, Abingdon, Oxon OX14 4RN

and by Routledge
52 Vanderbilt Avenue, New York, NY 10017

Routledge is an imprint of the Taylor & Francis Group, an informa business

© 1952 George L. Kline

All rights reserved. No part of this book may be reprinted or reproduced or utilised in any form or by any electronic, mechanical, or other means, now known or hereafter invented, including photocopying and recording, or in any information storage or retrieval system, without permission in writing from the publishers.

Trademark notice: Product or corporate names may be trademarks or registered trademarks, and are used only for identification and explanation without intent to infringe.

British Library Cataloguing in Publication Data
A catalogue record for this book is available from the British Library

ISBN: 978-0-367-27875-5 (Set)
ISBN: 978-0-429-29844-8 (Set) (ebk)
ISBN: 978-0-367-33099-6 (Volume 4) (hbk)
ISBN: 978-0-367-33100-9 (Volume 4) (pbk)
ISBN: 978-0-429-31798-9 (Volume 4) (ebk)

Publisher's Note
The publisher has gone to great lengths to ensure the quality of this reprint but points out that some imperfections in the original copies may be apparent.

Disclaimer
The publisher has made every effort to trace copyright holders and would welcome correspondence from those they have been unable to trace.

SPINOZA
IN SOVIET PHILOSOPHY

A SERIES OF ESSAYS
SELECTED AND TRANSLATED
AND WITH AN INTRODUCTION

BY

GEORGE L. KLINE

Ph.D. Instructor in Philosophy, Columbia University

ROUTLEDGE AND KEGAN PAUL LTD
Broadway House, 68–74 Carter Lane
London

*First published in 1952
by Routledge & Kegan Paul Limited
Broadway House, 68–74 Carter Lane
London E.C.4
Printed in Great Britain
by Butler and Tanner Limited
Frome and London*

PREFACE

QUOTATIONS from the works of Spinoza are based on the Hale-White translation of the *Ethics* and the Elwes translation of the *Theologico-Political Treatise, Political Treatise, On the Improvement of the Understanding,* and *Correspondence.* The Elwes translation of the *Ethics* and the Wolf translation of the *Correspondence* have also been consulted, together with the Latin original, in cases of doubtful interpretation or confusing terminology. Responsibility for the translation of one brief passage from the *Metaphysical Thoughts* and of certain passages from the untranslated Latin works of Descartes and Leibniz is mine; as is the responsibility for all translations from French and German sources, except where adequate English versions were available, in which case appropriate credit is given in references or bibliography.

In the spelling of Russian words and proper names I have followed the transliteration system adopted by Professor Ernest J. Simmons (cf. the 'Russian Transliteration Table' in his *Leo Tolstoy*, Boston, 1946, p. 776), which is a modified form of that used by the Library of Congress.

It is a pleasure to acknowledge my indebtedness to Professors Herbert W. Schneider and James Gutmann of Columbia University, and to the late Dr. Simon L. Millner, President of the Spinoza Foundation, for encouragement and helpful suggestions during the preparation of this work. Without the expert and generous assistance of librarians of many nationalities in New York, London, Paris, Vienna, and Belgrade, this project would scarcely have been possible.

My debt to my wife is greater than I can well express.

CONTENTS

PREFACE *page* v

INTRODUCTION
I. *Spinoza in Soviet Philosophy.*—II. *The Pre-Revolutionary Tradition.*—III. *Four Schools of Spinoza Interpretation among Russian Marxists.*—IV. *The Historical Setting of Spinoza's Philosophical Activity. Sources and Influences of Spinozism.*—V. *Spinoza's Ontology; the Problem of Hylozoism. The Concept of 'Substance.' Theory of Knowledge. Methodology. Cosmology.*—VI. *Spinoza and Religion.*—VII. *Ethics. Social and Political Philosophy.*—VIII. *General Marxist Appraisal of Spinozism.*—IX. *Concluding Critical Remarks.* 1

SPINOZA AND JUDAISM *by D. Rakhman* 48

SPINOZA AND MATERIALISM *by L. I. Akselrod (Ortodoks)* 61

SPINOZA'S WORLD-VIEW *by A. M. Deborin* 90

SPINOZA'S SUBSTANCE AND FINITE THINGS *by V. K. Brushlinski* 120

SPINOZA'S ETHICAL WORLD-VIEW *by S. Ya. Volfson* 131

SPINOZA AND THE STATE *by I. P. Razumovski* 149

THE HISTORICAL SIGNIFICANCE OF SPINOZA'S PHILOSOPHY *by I. K. Luppol* 162

BIBLIOGRAPHY
Literature on Spinoza in Russian—Non-Marxist 177
Literature on Spinoza in Russian—Marxist 179

INDEX 185

INTRODUCTION

I

SOVIET RUSSIA, during the past quarter century, has witnessed a remarkable renaissance of interest in the philosophy of Benedict Spinoza. During this period Spinoza has received more attention from Soviet writers than any other pre-Marxian philosopher with the possible exception of Hegel; and Russian Spinoza literature has exceeded, in quantity if not in quality, that of any country in the West. In the period from 1917 to 1938, 55,200 copies of Spinoza's works were published in the Soviet Union (as compared to 8,000 copies during the period from 1897 to 1916). These included: the *Principles of Descartes's Philosophy* (1926), the *Short Treatise* (1929), the *Correspondence* (1932), the *Ethics* (1933), *On the Improvement of the Understanding* (1934), and the *Theologico-Political Treatise* (1935). The only major work which has not been issued, the *Political Treatise*, is available in a pre-Revolutionary Russian edition dating from 1910. (Generally speaking, interest in Spinoza's political doctrines has been greater among non-Marxist than among Marxist writers in Russia.)

Available statistics on Soviet Russian Spinoza literature are incomplete, but the following minimum list will give some idea of its extent during the past thirty years: Nine books on Spinoza have been published, totalling some thousand pages; 46 articles in philosophical and literary journals, totalling over 600 pages; 19 chapters or sections of books (histories of philosophy, collections of philosophical essays, etc.), totalling about 450 pages. Many reviews of Russian and foreign Spinoza literature have been published, together with a few translations of foreign commentaries. Examples of the latter are Diderot's essay on Spinoza, and Feuerbach's 'Concluding Critical Remarks of 1847,' which appeared in *Pod znamenem marksizma* (*Under the Banner of Marxism*) in 1923 and 1939, respectively. These figures do not include material published in Ukrainian, Armenian, and other Soviet national languages, of which there is a small but significant amount. One of the more recent books on Spinoza (Moscow, 1940) is a semi-popular treatment written by Ya. A. Milner, general editor of the *Kratki filosofski slovar* (*Short Dictionary of Philosophy*) and a co-author of the three-volume *Istoriya filosofi* (*History of Philosophy*).

A large part of this material was published during the jubilee years 1927 and 1932 (the two hundred and fiftieth anniversary of Spinoza's death, and the tercentenary of his birth), both of which were widely celebrated in the Soviet Union. In 1927, special sessions of the various philosophical societies were held in Moscow, Minsk, Kiev, and other cities, and papers on Spinoza were read by A. M. Deborin (real name A. M. Ioffe), A. Thalheimer, S. Ya. Volfson, V. F. Asmus, and others. At the first All-Union Philosophical Conference, convened in Moscow on June 1, 1930, one of the four papers in the section on the History of Philosophy was devoted to Spinoza; it was read by I. K. Luppol.

On November 24, 1932 (the anniversary of Spinoza's birth), both *Pravda* and *Izvestia* devoted full pages, including large portraits, to material on Spinoza: articles by Luppol, M. B. Mitin, *et al.*, short biographical sketches, brief quotations from Spinoza's writings, and lists of his major works. On December 1, 1932, the Presidium of the Communist Academy in Moscow, in conjunction with the Institute of Philosophy, held a special Spinoza Tercentenary Celebration, at which M. A. Savelyev, President of the Academy, delivered the introductory address. Mitin read a paper on 'Spinoza and Dialectical Materialism,' and Luppol read a paper on 'The Historical Significance of Spinoza's Philosophy.' These papers, together with the introductory address, were published in *Pod znamenem marksizma*, No. 11–12, 1932. (See Bibliography.) A translation of Luppol's paper appears below, pp. 162–76.

On December 22, 1934, a panel discussion was held under the auspices of the Institute of Philosophy in Moscow, on the occasion of the publication of a new Russian edition of Spinoza's *Theologico-Political Treatise*. An abstract of this discussion was published in the *Vestnik kommunisticheskoi akademi* (*Bulletin of the Communist Academy*), No. 1–2, 1935.

That this development is generally unknown outside of Russia is to be explained largely by the fact that almost none of the Soviet literature in question has been translated into any Western European language, and none into English. One brief article by Deborin was reprinted in the *Chronicon Spinozanum* (The Hague, 1927) in the

INTRODUCTION 3

original Russian, with a German translation, and Deborin's major essay on Spinoza was included in a small German anthology which appeared in 1928.[1] These seem to be the only published translations of any Soviet interpretation of Spinoza's philosophy in a Western European language. The same condition prevails in the case of pre-Revolutionary and émigré Russian Spinoza scholarship, which has been entirely unavailable in English up to the present.

The Marxist view of Spinoza represents a break not only with the dominant traditions of Western scholarship, but also with those of pre-Revolutionary Russia. Nevertheless, significant points of contact remain, and a general acquaintance with the pre-Revolutionary Russian literature is helpful for a full understanding of the Spinoza of Soviet philosophy. The necessarily sketchy and incomplete survey which follows is intended primarily as a background to such understanding.

II

Pre-Revolutionary literature on Spinoza in Russian is for the most part critical and negative. Spinoza's philosophy is assailed on many counts, in a majority of cases from an idealistic or supernaturalistic viewpoint.[2] What non-Marxists consider his chief philosophical sins turn up later, in the Soviet Russian literature, as virtues and strong-points to be accepted and defended.

The first published work on Spinoza in Russian dates from 1819. That year was marked by the publication of the second volume of Professor A. I. Galich's *History of Philosophical Systems*, a derivative work based largely on German sources. The author adopted the prevalent eighteenth-century view of Spinoza's philosophy as an atheistic and immoral doctrine 'wholly incompatible with the moral sense.' 'That men greeted this system with loathing,' he wrote, 'that they saw in it a subverter of faith and morals, that they called it atheism, pantheism, Jewish cabala . . . shows that its falseness was quickly perceived by everyone.' Spinozism is too abstract and

[1] A. M. Deborin, 'Spinozizm i marksizm' ('Spinozism and Marxism'), *Chronicon Spinozanum*, V (1927), pp. 140–50; 'Die Weltanschauung Spinozas,' in *Spinozas Stellung in der Vorgeschichte des dialektischen Materialismus*, Berlin, 1928, pp. 40–74.

[2] During the late nineteenth and early twentieth centuries, Russian professional philosophy was strongly influenced by German idealism. In approaching Spinoza, Russian writers as a rule took the analysis and critique of Kant, Schelling, Hegel, and Schopenhauer as their point of departure.

difficult, Galich concludes, ever to find adherents among a wide public; nevertheless, for the thinker it remains 'a menacing . . . phenomenon which he cannot fail to view with alarm.'[1] Spinozism was in fact beginning to subvert traditional religious belief among certain of the Russian intelligentsia. The talented young members of the 'Philosophers' Society,' who met in Moscow between 1823 and 1825, studied Spinoza as well as Kant, Fichte, and Schelling, and one of them recalled later: 'Christian doctrine seemed to us suitable only for the masses, not for philosophers like us. We prized Spinoza particularly highly and valued his works much above the New Testament and other holy scriptures.'[2]

A strongly critical attitude toward Spinoza was also expressed in Archimandrite Gavriil's six-volume *History of Philosophy*, published at Kazan during the 1830's. The author attacks Spinoza's determinism and his equating of right and power in political philosophy. He charges that Spinoza failed to reconcile infinite substance and finite modes; and he is indignant over Spinoza's moral 'indifferentism.' For Spinoza, he writes, there is no difference between 'a learned academy and a madhouse, a judge and an outlaw, a devastating earthquake and the all-renewing spring'; they all follow with equal necessity from the one infinite substance. Gavriil concludes that Spinoza's system is pantheistic—but 'a pantheism of matter rather than an Eleatic pantheism.'[3]

The next Russian work on Spinoza of which we have a record appeared in 1862.[4] This was a prize-winning essay written by S. Kovner, then a student at Kiev, which was published in the University *Izvestiya* for that year. It comprised a biographical sketch, based on the accounts of Colerus and Auerbach and on Spinoza's correspondence, and an analysis of Spinozism patterned on that of Kuno Fischer. ('Spinozism is a species of the genus pantheism,' etc.) According to Kovner, Spinoza's philosophy is neither atheistic, nor fatalistic, nor a cabalistic doctrine of emanation, but essentially

[1] A. I. Galich, *Istoriya filosofskikh sistem* (*A History of Philosophical Systems*), Vol. II, St. Petersburg, 1819, pp. 47-8.
[2] A. I. Koshelev, *Zapiski* (*Journal*), 1889, p. 12. Besides Koshelev, the membership included Prince V. F. Odoyevski, I. V. Kireyevski (the celebrated Slavophile), and S. P. Shevyryov and M. P. Pogodin (who later became professors at Moscow University).
[3] *Istoriya filosofi* (*History of Philosophy*), Kazan, 1839, Part III, pp. 150 f.
[4] The first translation of Spinoza's *Ethics* into Russian was also made during the 1860's. However, this translation was destroyed, and the earliest surviving version dates from 1886.

INTRODUCTION 5

naturalistic: 'for Spinoza all is nature and all things are united in a chain of causal connection . . . there is no supernatural.'¹

Ten years later B. N. Chicherin in his *History of Political Theories* submitted Spinozism to a more critical analysis. He felt that, although Spinoza defended political and intellectual freedom, his system undermined the very foundation of such freedom since for him 'the individual is only a modification of universal substance. In the universe the individual is swallowed up by nature or Deity, in the state by the totality of social forces which dwarf the individual to insignificance.'² P. I. Linitski echoed this charge in 1874; Spinoza's rigidly formal attempt to overcome Cartesian dualism, he held, led to 'a denial of the freedom and independence, and even the individual being, of the spirit, in the name of an abstract idea of universal natural necessity.'³

In 1885, A. Volynski, writing in the Russian Jewish journal *Voskhod*, emphasized Spinoza's closeness to the tradition of medieval Judaism: 'All his life,' say Volynski, 'Spinoza remained a real Jew, a faithful son of his people.'⁴ But he rebukes Spinoza for his radical rationalistic approach to Jewish cult and ritual, and his recommendation that they be abolished.⁵ According to Volynski, this bold demand shows great philosophical consistency and forthrightness, but little insight and less faith in 'the historical mission of the Jewish people.'⁶ Spinoza's separation of philosophy and religion is regarded as a 'serious theoretical error, which distorted his interpretation of the faith of the Jewish people.' It is to

¹ S. Kovner, 'Spinoza, yevo zhizn i sochineniya' ('Spinoza: His Life and Works'), *Kiev. Univ. Izvestiya*, No. 11–12 (1862), p. 87.
² B. N. Chicherin, *Istoriya politicheskikh ucheni* (*History of Political Theories*), Part II, Moscow, 1872, pp. 135–36.
³ P. I. Linitski, *Obzor filosofskikh ucheni* (*Survey of Philosophical Doctrines*), Kiev, 1874, p. 177.
⁴ A. Volynski, 'Teologiko-politicheskoye ucheniye Spinozy' ('Spinoza's Theologico-Political Theory'), *Voskhod*, 1885, No. 10, p. 126.
⁵ A similar charge is made by G. B. Sliozberg in a brochure entitled *Mest Spinozy za 'kherem'* (*Spinoza's Revenge for his Excommunication*), published in Paris in 1933. Sliozberg accuses Spinoza of employing a double standard: of being formal, demanding, and negative toward Judaism, but forbearing and indulgent toward Christianity. Spinoza, he asserts, abstained from criticism of the New Testament and deliberately distorted the doctrines of the Old Testament, together with the philosophy of Maimonides. He was, the author tells us, 'an enemy of Judaism, a renegade, a vindictive and malicious slanderer, . . . an accuser of Judaism before the Christian world' (*op. cit.*, p. 48).
⁶ A. Volynski, *Voskhod*, 1885, No. 11, p. 146.

this faith, Volynski points out, that mankind is indebted for the 'greatest of all ideas, the idea of monotheism, which is of equal significance for morals and for philosophy.'[1]

Volynski feels that Spinoza's political doctrines derive from those of Hobbes, and he suggests that the Hobbes-Spinoza social-contract theory suffers from a serious inconsistency: How could men in the state of nature, led only by untamed passions and without any kind of morality, suddenly become capable of working out and setting up a rational socio-political contract?

N. Grot, in 1891, criticized Spinoza's God as abstract and lifeless, not a 'living God of living men,' but a kind of Buddhist nirvana of 'all and nothing.' Spinoza's *amor Dei intellectualis* he interprets psychologically as 'the love of agreement and unity among ideas . . . of the abstract plenitude of truth and knowledge.'[2] Spinoza's religious emotion is only a variant of the intellectual feeling of harmony—'the feeling of satisfaction which we experience when we achieve unity and agreement among all the ideas in our mind.'[3]

According to Grot, Spinoza is a pantheist but not a mystic: 'everywhere—in his doctrine of the world, of man, and even of God—he eliminated all that was dark, mysterious, imbued with emotion and faith.'[4] He rejected miracles, says Grot, 'and went to the ultimate limits of dry and cold abstraction,'[5] and what true mystic could do this?

Three years later A. Kirilovich came to the defence of Spinoza's religious reputation. Spinoza is indeed a mystic, he asserted, a monist and pantheist, to be sure, but a mystic nevertheless.[6] He is not in any case to be called a materialist. He does not identify God and nature absolutely; his substance is prior to nature, if not temporally, at least conceptually and causally. Kirilovich also restates Schopenhauer's critique of the identification of real and logical relations in Spinoza, a criticism which reappears more than once in the non-Marxist Russian literature on the subject.

The year 1897 was marked by the famous dispute between Pro-

---

[1] A Volynski, *Voskhod*, 1885, No. 11, p. 144.

[2] N. Grot, 'Osnovnyie momenty v razviti novoi filosofi' ('Basic Stages in the Development of Modern Philosophy'), *Voprosy filosofi i psikhologi*, No. 10 (1891), p. 15.

[3] *Ibid.*, p. 16.   [4] *Ibid.*, p. 14.   [5] *Ibid.*, p. 18.

[6] A. Kirilovich, 'Ontologiya i kosmologiya Spinozy v svyazi s yevo teoriyei poznaniya' ('Spinoza's Ontology and Cosmology in Relation to his Theory of Knowledge'), *Vera i razum*, No. 3 (1894), pp. 119-50.

fessor A. I. Vvedenski of the University of St. Petersburg and the poet-philosopher Vladimir Solovyov, which was carried on in the pages of the journal *Voprosy filosofi i psikhologi* (*Problems of Philosophy and Psychology*).[1] Vvedenski advanced the thesis that Spinoza's philosophy is neither theistic nor pantheistic, but essentially atheistic—'an atheistic monism of substance.' Admittedly, Spinoza uses the *word* 'God' on every page, but, Vvedenski maintained, he has gone beyond the permissible limits of the *concept* 'God' (a being characterized by free will and purposive activity) which is common to all religions. Vvedenski, an orthodox Kantian himself, was not concerned to further the cause of atheism, but he was convinced that the term 'God' in Spinoza's *Ethics* adds nothing that is not already conveyed by the term 'substance.' Why then did Spinoza use it? Certainly not to deceive his readers deliberately as to the fundamental atheism of his philosophy, says Vvedenski, since he was a highly moral and conscientious man, but perhaps to deceive himself, to conceal his own philosophical atheism from his essentially religious nature. This atheism, Vvedenski concludes, may be explained by the influence of the mechanistic philosophy of Descartes, in which God plays only a secondary and subsidiary role.

Solovyov replies that Vvedenski's definition of God is too narrow, and that not all of the historical religions have personal gods, evident exceptions being furnished by Southern Buddhism and Brahmanism. These faiths—as well as the philosophy of Spinoza —may legitimately be called pantheistic. All of them reject the concept of divine will and purpose. Furthermore, since Spinoza was deeply religious, he would not have seized upon the atheistic elements in Descartes's philosophy. Spinoza's system, Solovyov maintains, is essentially religious and contemplative, corresponding to the tenor of his mind. But Solovyov goes on to point out the theological inadequacies of Spinoza's world-view. His 'static pantheism,' according to Solovyov, satisfies neither religious nor philosophical requirements. 'God cannot be merely the God of geometry and

[1] A. I. Vvedenski, 'Ob ateizme v filosofi Spinozy' ('On the Atheism in Spinoza's Philosophy'), *Voprosy filosofi i psikhologi*, Bk. 37 (1897), pp. 157–84 (an abridged translation of this paper by the present writer is available in the Columbia University Library in New York); V. S. Solovyov, 'Ponyatiye o Boge; v zashchitu filosofi Spinozy' ('The Concept of God; in Defence of Spinoza's Philosophy'), *op. cit.*, Bk. 38, pp. 383–414. It is interesting to note that Solovyov himself, as a student, interpreted Spinoza's philosophy atheistically and materialistically, but later abandoned this interpretation. See L. M. Lopatin, 'The Philosophy of Vladimir Solovyov,' *Mind*, XXV (1916), pp. 425–60.

physics. He must be the God of history as well.'[1] This neglect of process and development is quite understandable in the light of the philosophical tradition in which Spinoza matured, but it remains a defect of his system. Nevertheless, this static pantheism was a necessary prerequisite to Hegel's historical pantheism and to true Christian philosophy.[2]

At the turn of the century Ernst Radlov continued the defence of Spinoza the mystic. In Spinoza's system, he asserted, 'rationalism was combined with a pantheistic mysticism, and modern philosophical views with those of the ancient Eleatics and Stoics.'[3] Radlov objected to the attempt to 'Kantianize' Spinoza, on the basis of his 'unknowable' infinity of attributes. Spinoza's whole system, he maintained, is characterized by objectivism and dogmatism. 'The basic difference between Kant and Spinoza is that, according to the former, reason knows only phenomena, while reality, the *Ding an sich*, remains unknown; but, according to Spinoza, reason grasps the very essence of being; there is nothing unknowable in the world.'[4]

The historian of law V. F. Zaleski, writing in 1902, criticized Spinoza's system on two main counts: (1) its axioms are questionable, and (2) many of its concepts are not clearly defined. An example of the former is the alleged 'law of causality,' which breaks down completely under the Humean critique. Spinoza's conception of causality is abstract, metaphysical, and absolute—causes and effects are conceived as links in an infinite chain—a view at odds with modern science. Furthermore, says Zaleski, the proposition that 'nothing can be destroyed except by a cause external to itself' (*Ethics*, III, 4), which Spinoza considers self-evident, is highly questionable: things do, in fact, perish from internal causes.

Zaleski feels that Spinoza's central ethical concept '*perfectio*' is not clearly defined; its definition rests on the empty concepts '*entitas*' and '*realitas*,' the latter in turn being identified with '*potentia agendi*.' And Zaleski concludes: 'Spinoza's system . . . interests us not as a deductive philosophy, for as such it does not withstand criticism, but as a magnificent surmise, which prophetically anticipated certain conclusions of contemporary science. There is no doubt that empirical data led him to many of his ideas . . . [through] unconscious inductive inference.'[5]

[1] Solovyov, *op. cit.*, p. 409.   [2] *Ibid.*, p. 411.
[3] E. L. Radlov, *Entsiklopedicheski slovar Brokgaus i Efron.*, Vol. 61, St. Petersburg, 1900, p. 219.   [4] *Ibid.*, p. 220.
[5] V. F. Zaleski, *Lektsi istori filosofi prava* (Lectures on the History of the Philosophy of Law), Kazan, 1902, p. 237.

INTRODUCTION 9

In the same year L. M. Lopatin, an idealist of strong religious conviction, acknowledged that there is a definite tendency toward materialism in Spinoza. 'Spinoza's God,' he wrote, 'is to a certain extent only universal matter.'[1] However, he preferred to call Spinoza a pantheist rather than a materialist; regarding Spinozism as a result of the impact of Hobbes' materialistic world-view upon Jewish pantheism, Cartesianism, and scholasticism. Following Schopenhauer, Lopatin criticized Spinoza for identifying '*ratio*' and '*causa*'—logical and real relations. He further criticized the passive role of thought in Spinoza's system. For Spinoza, he says, thought merely 'repeats and reproduces in the form of ideas that which is objectively given in the world of bodies. . . . Thus the role of active cause in the world process passes to the material nature of absolute substance; . . . hence the obviously materialistic colouring of Spinoza's world-view as a whole.'[2]

Lopatin is bothered by the problem of how God's extension can be reconciled with his absolute simplicity and inner unity. Despite Spinoza's positing of various modes of perceiving extension, Lopatin concludes, 'this single substance ceases to be a living unity; it disintegrates into an infinite multiplicity of bodies, becoming their abstract order, the abstract law of their multiform mechanical concatenation.'[3] Spinoza showed that it is not possible, Lopatin concludes, to reduce *creative* necessity to *logical* necessity. But he was not the last to try: Hegel made the same misguided attempt nearly two hundred years later.

I. I. Lapshin, G. F. Shershenevich, and N. M. Korkunov, writing in the early 1900's, agreed in considering Spinoza a pantheist. To this conventional epithet, Lapshin added 'mystic,' and Korkunov 'monist.' Shershenevich pointed out that, since the object of Spinoza's faith and reverence was the universe as a whole, he was rightly considered an 'atheist' by the dogmatic religions of his time. Lapshin interpreted Spinoza's '*amor Dei intellectualis*' as a purely mystical doctrine, which includes the elements of: '(1) the idea of constant values; (2) a concrete conception of the participation of others in the act of love to God; (3) emotion; (4) union with God; (5) an overcoming of the accidental circumstances of time; (6) a feeling of power and freedom.[4]

[1] L. M. Lopatin, *Istoriya novoi filosofi* (*History of Modern Philosophy*), Moscow, 1902, p. 211.   [2] *Ibid.*, p. 266.   [3] *Ibid.*, p. 267.
[4] I. I. Lapshin, *Zakony myshleniya i formy poznaniya* (*The Laws of Thought and the Forms of Knowledge*), St. Petersburg, 1906, pp. 63–5.

INTRODUCTION

N. A. Ivantsov, writing in 1906, continued the defence of Spinoza as a religious philosopher: although the object of Spinoza's religious reverence differs from the God of the Talmud, 'a deeply religious, even mystical feeling underlies his whole system.'[1] In political philosophy, Ivantsov suggests, Spinoza may be called a 'pan-anarchist' in the same sense in which we call him a 'pantheist' in metaphysics: 'Just as, in rejecting a God external to the world, he clothes nature with divine attributes, so, in rejecting external state power, he sees the basis of social order and state institutions in society itself.'[2] In this respect, Ivantsov concludes, Spinoza anticipates modern social theories.

Maxim Kovalevski, in the second volume of his massive history of political theories, which appeared the same year, focused attention on Spinoza as a political thinker whose doctrines were 'an essential link in the development of the theory of popular sovereignty,' anticipating Rousseau and the later social-contract theorists on many important points. Kovalevski praises Spinoza's eloquent defence of free thought and expression (in Chapter XX of the *Theologico-Political Treatise*), but finds an inconsistency in Spinoza's admission of the right of the state to persecute certain opinions on the ground that the mere professing of such opinions may be a criminal act. However, with this one reservation, according to Kovalevski, 'we must agree that very few seventeenth-century writers approached the contemporary conception of freedom of thought and speech as closely as did Spinoza.'[3]

E. V. Spektorski, in 1907, attempted to establish certain general correlations between the physical and social sciences of the seventeenth century: both were characteristically deductive, positive, and mechanistic. Spinoza's attempt to construct 'a moral geometry and a mechanics of social life'[4] was typical, but abortive. Spinoza tried to eliminate the distinction between ideal and real; but instead of positive science he produced a negative, critical idealism. 'His rationalistic theory,' says Spektorski, 'did not coincide with irrational reality'[5] (although it did lead him into philosophical atheism). In

---

[1] N. A. Ivantsov, 'Spinoza,' *Vestnik vospitaniya*, No. 9 (1906), p. 55.
[2] *Ibid.*, p. 88.
[3] M. M. Kovalevski, *Ot pryamovo narodopravstva k predstavitelnomu i ot patriarkhalnoi monarkhi k parlamentarizmu* (*From Direct to Representative Democracy and from Patriarchal Monarchy to Parliamentarianism*), Moscow, 1906, Vol. II, p. 458.
[4] E. V. Spektorski, *Ocherki po filosofi obshchestvennykh nauk* (*Essays in the Philosophy of the Social Sciences*), Part I, Warsaw, 1907, p. 145.   [5] *Ibid.*, p. 153.

INTRODUCTION 11

the face of this dichotomy, Spinoza 'moved from the world of moral reality to the world of the ideal, converting theoretical ethics into practical ethics.'[1] Spinoza set out to substitute descriptive ethics for normative ethics, excluding not only the supernatural, but also free will. Although he called his work *Ethics*, it actually provided not an ethics but a naturalistic physics of human conduct. 'In this book the physicism of seventeenth-century rational psychology reached its high point.'[2] The result, says Spektorski, was tautological definition and semi-scholastic dialectics. In reaction to this, the practical and normative tendency became dominant in Spinoza; and in the end he set up a 'practical programme for personal and public life, taught how the wise man-should conduct himself, and drafted constitutions.'[3] Spinoza, Spektorski concludes, was a systematic rather than a creative philosopher.

In 1912, Semyon Frank provided the first detailed analysis in Russian of Spinoza's theory of knowledge and doctrine of attributes. He held that Spinoza's 'epistemological monism'—the view that the content of consciousness is identical with objective reality—was the cornerstone of his system, and that it led to a psycho-physical monism—in which mind and body are regarded simply as 'knower' and 'known.' This, Frank feels, involves an illegitimate introduction of epistemological categories into psychology. 'The psychic correlate of physiological processes,' objects Frank, 'does not coincide with the cognitive "reflection" of the object in knowledge: for example, a sensation of toothache is not the same thing as an image of the bodily processes of decay which are going on in the ailing tooth.'[4] Spinoza identifies the epistemological concept 'knowledge' with the psychological concept 'thinking'; his self-consciousness (the idea of the mind) is an ambiguous concept: 'Man's mind bears the same relation to man as the idea of a circle to the circle itself as a physico-geometrical figure.'[5] Furthermore, Spinoza does not distinguish knowledge about knowledge from knowledge about objects; for him epistemology has no subject matter distinct from

[1] *Ibid.*, p. 154.
[2] Spektorski, 'Fizitsizm i svoboda v ratsionalnoi psikhologi XVII v.' ('Physicism and Freedom in the Rational Psychology of the Seventeenth Century'), *Voprosy filosofi i psikhologi*, No. 5 (1915), p. 495.
[3] Spektorski, *Ocherki po filosofi obshchestvennykh nauk* (*Essays in the Philosophy of the Social Sciences*), Part I, Warsaw, 1907, p. 165.
[4] S. L. Frank, 'Ucheniye Spinozy ob attributakh' ('Spinoza's Doctrine of Attributes'), *Voprosy filosofi i psikhologi*, No. 4 (1912), p. 531.
[5] *Ibid.*, p. 532.

that of ontology. Substance is the unity of knower and known, of subject and object.

Frank next proceeds to a discussion of Spinoza's mysticism. He distinguishes two kinds of truth in Spinoza's system: '(1) rational truth, expressed in logically fixed concepts, and (2) a truth which may be called mystical and which consists in the immediate contemplation of the highest unity of logically distinct concepts.'[1] Spinoza has been misunderstood, according to Frank, because his rationalistic terminology and mode of exposition do not adequately express the mystical essence of his ideas. In Spinozism we have 'a veneer of rationalism over a basic stratum of mysticism.'[2] Spinoza's infinite attributes are also to be understood in this mystical sense. 'No finite number of qualitative determinations . . . could exhaust the irrational plenitude of substance, the nature of all-perfect being.'[3]

Spinozism, according to Frank, is a form of 'objective ideal-realism,' and Spinoza's theory of knowledge represents 'the most rigorous logical realism.'[4] Basic to Spinoza's formulation of the ontological proof is 'the necessary connection of ideal and real being in the absolute, and, consequently, the correlative substitutibility of ideal and real necessity. . . .'[5]

The following year (1913), V. Polovtsova answered the charges of Frank and others in a long article, devoted largely to philological and historical considerations. She pointed out that many misunderstandings have arisen from ignorance of Spinoza's Latin terminology. For example, the word '*quatenus*' is a key term, indicating the particular field of knowledge referred to in a given context. It is especially important, Polovtsova held, to distinguish between Spinoza's use of Cartesian terms and expressions borrowed from common speech and his own terminology. Spinoza used the theological expressions of his time (such as '*creata*,' '*increata*,' '*Dei decreta*') to make himself understood by the people, not because he shared their opinions on theological matters. The critics who divide Spinoza's philosophical development into distinct 'phases' have confused these various kinds of terminology. In fact, says Polovtsova, Spinoza's philosophical views remained essentially the same throughout his life. He used the term '*Deus*' to distinguish his 'substance' from the 'substance' of

---

[1] S. L. Frank, 'Ucheniye Spinozy ob attributakh' ('Spinoza's Doctrine of Attributes'), *Voprosy filosofi i psikhologi*, No. 4 (1912), p. 537.
[2] *Ibid.*, p. 542.   [3] *Ibid.*, p. 547.   [4] *Ibid.*, p. 548.
[5] Frank, *Predmet znaniya (The Object of Knowledge)*, St. Petersburg, 1915, p. 484.

Descartes; but his *'Deus'* differs sharply from that of Descartes, as well as from the God of theology and ordinary usage.

Polovtsova takes sharp issue with Frank's interpretation of Spinoza's psychology and epistemology. The expression *'causa sive ratio,'* she maintains, does not imply an identification of real and logical relations; Spinoza uses this expression because for him 'a true idea must correspond with its ideate or object' (*Ethics*, I, ax. 6). Consequently, when, having true knowledge, we follow 'the order and connection of a system of [logical] grounds or ideas, *rationes*, we follow, at the same time, the order and connection of the causes or ideates which correspond to them.'[1]

Polovtsova also rejects Frank's interpretation of Spinoza's infinite attributes. In the first place, *'infinitas'* signifies not multiplicity but immeasurability. Spinoza's infinity, says Polovtsova, 'cannot be measured, and consequently cannot be expressed by any reference to number.'[2]

Similarly, Spinoza's *'natura'* is not modern 'naturalistic' nature, but 'essence.' *'Natura naturans'* is 'essence in the process of realization'; *'natura naturata,'* 'realized essence.' ' "Nature" in the naturalistic sense is for Spinoza . . . the limited aggregate of the imaginative, inadequate contents of the human consciousness,'[3]—and to call this nature *'Deus sive natura'* would amount to equating *'Deus'* and *'modus,'*—which from Spinoza's point of view would be absurd.

V. S. Shilkarski, in 1914, attempted to interpret Spinoza's system as a Parmenidean panlogism, with tendencies toward materialism. Spinoza's concepts *'ens absolute infinitum'* and *'causa sui,'* he finds, 'express only an abstract and purely negative characteristic of authentic being, its logical unconditionality.'[4] Shilkarski connects Spinoza's philosophical system with the logical realism of the Middle Ages, which *'hypostatizes* the logical acts of our mind *in reverse order* (the natural order being from less general to more general concepts),' and in which 'the highest reality belongs to the extreme product of abstraction, the most general of all ideas—the idea of being.'[5] But Spinoza is no more able than were the medieval realists to explain why or how this most abstract of concepts can provide the ground

[1] V. Polovtsova, 'K metodologi izucheniya filosofi Spinozy' ('On the Method of Studying Spinoza's Philosophy'), *Voprosy filosofi i psikhologi*, Vol. 24, No. 118 (1913), p. 363.
[2] *Ibid.*, p. 372.   [3] *Ibid.*, p. 381.
[4] V. S. Shilkarski, 'O panlogizme u Spinozy' ('On Spinoza's Panlogism'), *Voprosy filosofi i psikhologi*, No. 3 (1914), p. 243.
[5] *Ibid.*, p. 256.

from which all existence necessarily flows. There is no transition in Spinoza from the negative predicates of authentic being to the positive predicates of conditional being. Shilkarski sees Spinoza as advancing from *acosmism* in Part I of the *Ethics*, to *pantheism* in Part II, and finally to a definite *atheism* in the last three parts.

In the same year, V. A. Belyayev published a long book, *Leibnits i Spinoza* (*Leibniz and Spinoza*), which was intended as a refutation of Spinoza's pantheism from a theistic Leibnizian point of view. Because of the wide popularity of pantheism among the Russian intelligentsia, Belyayev considered this a particularly timely and important undertaking. Accepting Shilkarski's main criticisms, he went on to show that the fundamental and fatal errors of Spinoza's system resulted from his elevation of rational deduction into a unique and universal philosophic method. Spinoza conceived of God as a kind of logical pleroma, a 'universal plenum of premises,' from which the world 'follows' necessarily. The inevitable result, according to Belyayev, was ethical fatalism and metaphysical acosmism.

In general, although non-Marxist Russian writers vary widely in their approach to Spinoza, they exhibit certain recurrent themes, most of which reappear, in a new setting and with new emphasis, among Soviet writers. Chief of these is the charge of atheism, materialism, and naturalism, which is developed and defended, subject to certain qualifications, in present Soviet thought. The fusion of logic and ontology, the logical realism and epistemological monism, which are criticized by non-Marxists, are explicitly or implicitly accepted and defended by dialectical materialists. It is to a detailed examination of the career of Spinoza interpretation among Russian Marxists that we now turn.

III

In the historical fabric of Marxist Spinoza scholarship there are four readily distinguishable strands. The first of these is the tradition of G. V. Plekhanov (1856–1918), which had its beginnings in his writings of the 1890's and early 1900's. Starting from the few scattered references to Spinoza in Marx and Engels (notably in *Capital, Anti-Dühring,* and the *Dialectics of Nature,* first published in 1925), combined with his own keen interest in Spinoza and deep admiration for his philosophy, Plekhanov came to the conclusion that Spinozism, freed from its theological wrappings and interpreted as basically naturalistic and materialistic, was an historical forebear

INTRODUCTION   15

of dialectical materialism, that Marxism (as well as the philosophy of Diderot and Feuerbach) was a 'variety of Spinozism.' Plekhanov did not develop his views of Spinoza systematically, but embodied them in a number of scattered references, usually in connection with some other philosophic or historical problem. (See Bibliography.)

Marx and Engels had called French eighteenth-century materialism a 'reification of Spinoza's substance.' The latter they criticized as a passive 'phlegmatic thing,' but they held that Spinoza had solved correctly the fundamental ontological problem: the relation of consciousness to being, of thought to things.[1] This was emphasized by the continuers and elaborators of the Plekhanov tradition during the 1920's—Deborin (b. 1881), Karev, Luppol, Tymyanski, Dmitriev, and Mankovski, among others. Indeed, the Deborinites went so far as to speak familiarly of Spinoza as 'Marx without a beard.'[2]

But during this same period (1922–29) a reaction to the 'assimilation' of Marxism to Spinozism was growing among the so-called 'mechanists'—L. I. Akselrod (Ortodoks),[3] Varyash, Bykhovski, Tseitlin, -Sarabyanov, *et al.*—who emphasized and accepted the principle of mechanical conformity to law [*zakonomernost*] in Spinoza's system, but at the same time pointed out the predominantly metaphysical and religious character of his philosophy as a whole, and rejected the latter as dualistic and idealistic. Both groups took the problem of Spinozism very seriously. Akselrod, for example, asserted that 'a correct appraisal of the predecessors of dialectical materialism determines to a significant extent the correctness of our understanding of dialectical materialism itself.'[4] And Deborin held that 'the differences of opinion with regard to Spinoza concern our world-

[1] Plekhanov tells, in *Bernstein and Materialism* (1898), of a conversation which he had with Engels in London in 1889: ' "In your opinion," I asked, "was Spinoza right in saying that thought and extension are only two attributes of a single substance?"—"Certainly," Engels replied, "Spinoza was entirely right." ' (*Collected Works*, XI, Moscow, 1923, p. 22.)

[2] Cf. I. K. Luppol, 'Vyvody i uroki' ('Conclusions and Lessons'), *Pod znamenem marksizma*, No. 11 (1936), p. 183.

[3] Lyubov Isaakovna Akselrod (1868–1946)—not to be confused with Pavel Borisovich Akselrod, Russian Populist and Menshevik—adopted the pseudonym '*Ortodoks*' (Orthodox) during her pre-Revolutionary polemics against 'revisionist' Marxists who attempted to combine historical materialism with Kantian ethics and epistemology. Akselrod sank rapidly out of sight, publishing nothing after the mid-1930's. She was described in a recent official statement (*Bolshevik*, No. 15 (1950)) as a 'violent enemy of revolutionary Marxism.'

[4] L. I. Akselrod, 'Spinoza i materializm' ('Spinoza and Materialism'), *Krasnaya nov*, No. 7 (1925), p. 144.

view and involve the conception of materialism itself.'[1] In 1927, when the two hundred and fiftieth anniversary of Spinoza's death evoked a flurry of books and articles in the Soviet press, both the mechanists and the Deborinites were strongly represented, but the latter had clearly gained the upper hand. In 1929, the mechanist position was officially rejected and Deborin became for a brief period the philosophical leader of dialectical materialism in the Soviet Union.[2]

In January 1931, however, the Deborin group, who had come to be known as 'menshevising idealists,'[3] and had been criticized for divorcing theory from practice, and returning to an 'abstract scholasticism,' were in turn officially repudiated. Thus the Spinoza jubilee year of 1932 found both the extreme positions of 'mechanism' and 'Deborinism' out of favour, and an 'orthodox' middle position, represented by Mitin, Yudin, Vandek, Timosko, and Kryvelev, among others, in the ascendancy. The interpretation of Spinoza's philosophy which was adopted at that time has remained essentially unchanged to the present (1952). The orthodox view will be discussed in detail when we consider specific aspects of Spinoza's philosophy. In general, the orthodox Marxists insisted on Spinoza's essential materialism and atheism, but, recognizing the irreducible theological and metaphysical elements of his system as a whole, they refused to assimilate Spinozism completely into the materialist tradition.

The fourth strand in the thread of Russian Marxist Spinoza scholarship is shorter and more fragile than the others. It disappeared from the historical scene relatively early and has had but little influence on the subsequent course of Spinoza interpretation. This is the 'revisionist Marxism,' represented by Valentinov (real name Volski), Shulyatikov, *et al.*, which developed in Russia around

[1] A. M. Deborin, 'Mirovozzreniye Spinozy' ('Spinoza's World-View'), *Vestnik kommunisticheskoi akademii*, Bk. 20 (1927), p. 6.

[2] For a general account of the mechanist-Deborinite differences on other philosophical problems, see John Somerville, 'Pivotal Controversies in the History of Soviet Philosophy,' *Soviet Philosophy*, chapter VII, New York, 1946; also Gustavo A. Wetter, *Il Materialismo dialettico sovietico*, pp. 161–98, Turin, 1948. Deborin has published no philosophical works since the early 1930's, although he has continued to hold various minor editorial positions. He was until July 1951 assistant editor of the *Vestnik* of the Academy of Sciences of the U.S.S.R.

[3] This term was first used by Stalin in an interview granted to a representative of the Institute of Red Professors on December 9, 1930.

the turn of the century. The views of the Russian revisionists with regard to the history of philosophy in general and Spinoza in particular are now considered crude and oversimplified. These writers were 'vulgar' reductive materialists who saw in economic, social, and political conditions the direct and unique determinants of philosophical systems. We shall cite certain examples in the course of our detailed examination of the attitudes of the various schools toward specific aspects of Spinoza's philosophy. (See below, pp. 21 f.)

One 'revisionist,' however, deserves special mention. He is the philosopher-physician A. A. Bogdanov (real name A. A. Malinovski, 1873-1928), the principal object of Lenin's polemic in *Materialism and Empiriocriticism*, a brilliant and erudite writer, who exhibits very little of the 'vulgar materialist' tendencies of other revisionists. Bogdanov was highly critical of the attempts to interpret Spinoza as a materialist and Marxist, and as late as 1927 (the year before his death) he expressed his dissent in strong terms. In the first place, he pointed out, the value of the great philosophical systems of the past is historical and social rather than scientific; their empirical foundation is narrow and insecure. 'In these great systems,' he says, 'bridges of speculative reasoning were thrown across enormous gaps in knowledge and experience so that the result would be something whole. . . . They were theoretical utopias, *monistic* utopias, which presented an ideal of integrated, harmonious knowledge.'[1] But such systems as Spinoza's have become unnecessary, says Bogdanov, because the gaps in our knowledge and experience are incomparably smaller than were his; and to study such systems often does more harm than good. 'Not long ago,' he continues, 'it was discovered that Spinoza was a materialist, that Spinoza's substance is only a pseudonym for matter, as Plekhanov understands the term. . . . I doubt that Spinoza would have thought so; he did not foresee the contemporary concept of matter. Clearly, if the present generation has discovered that Spinoza's substance was "matter," the next generation will perhaps discover that this very "matter" was a pseudonym for God.'[2] Bogdanov's views on Spinoza are rather close to those of mechanists like Akselrod and Varyash, and for this he was duly rebuked by Deborin's followers. In fact, he was charged with

[1] A. A. Bogdanov, 'Predely nauchnosti rassuzhdeniya' ('The Limits of the Scientific Accuracy of Discursive Reasoning'), *Vestnik kommunisticheskoi akademi*, No. 21 (1927), p. 260.
[2] *Loc. cit.*

virtually all of the mechanists' philosophical sins, an accusation which, he complained, was hardly fair, and resembled the 'quotational shock-treatment and chain reaction' which Lenin had used in *Materialism and Empiriocriticism* to discredit his views by lumping them together with those of Lunacharski, Bazarov, *et al.*

The terms 'mechanist,' 'Deborinite' (or 'menshevising idealist'), 'revisionist,' and 'orthodox Marxist' (applied since 1931 to the Mitin-Yudin group), are far from adequately descriptive of the philosophical positions of the groups in question. However, these are the labels which tradition and the quirks of etymology and politics have affixed to these schools, so we shall employ them, somewhat reluctantly, for want of more accurate nomenclature. It should be pointed out that the views of these groups with regard to Spinoza's philosophy are not mutually exclusive or exhaustive, and that their differences are to a considerable extent differences of emphasis, although there are certain basically opposing interpretations, as we shall see. The four schools may be likened to overlapping discs whose outer extremities are separate, but whose central portions coincide in a substantial core of materialistic Marxist doctrine and attitude. The natural tendency of the various groups has been to emphasize their differences for reasons of polemical efficiency and clarity. In the following sections we shall attempt to exhibit both the common body of dialectical-materialistic interpretation and the characteristic differences of approach to Spinoza's philosophy.

IV

Marxist analysis of the history of philosophy and of individual philosophical systems proceeds not primarily by comparison with previous philosophies, but by reference to the concrete historical setting in which a given system was formed. This is succinctly set forth by Marx in the following passage from *Die deutsche Ideologie*: 'The actual content of all the epoch-making systems is determined by the needs of the time in which they arose. At the basis of each such system lies the whole previous development of a given nation, the historical form of class relations, with their political, moral, philosophical, and other consequences.'[1] This formula has been consistently applied to the philosophy of Spinoza, with results that may at first strike the Western reader as somewhat strange.

[1] Karl Marx, 'Die deutsche Ideologie,' *Marx-Engels Gesamtausgabe*, First Series, Vol. V, Berlin, 1932, p. 445.

It is emphasized, to begin with, that seventeenth-century Holland was, for a variety of economic and political reasons, the most advanced capitalist country of the period, and a thriving centre of art and science: Its cities boasted the best universities; its printing presses turned out more books than those of all the rest of Europe. Large ships for transoceanic navigation were first built on Dutch docks, and the Dutch merchant fleet was one of the greatest in existence. The chronometer, the telescope, the sextant, detailed geographical maps and charts, all were developed first in Holland.[1] The Dutch bourgeoisie had successfully thrown off the yoke of feudalism and was in substantial control of the Republican government headed by Jan de Witt, Spinoza's friend and protector.

Detailed studies have been made of the economic and political structure of the Netherlands and of Spinoza's relationship to leaders of the bourgeoisie.[2] Deborin and his followers stressed Spinoza's role as a member of and philosophical spokesman for the young revolutionary bourgeoisie in its struggle against clerical, aristocratic, and absolutist feudal society—as an intellectual revolutionist of the new bourgeois humanism, secularism, naturalism, and materialism. In philosophy, they maintain, this meant the overthrowing of medieval teleologism, idealism, otherworldliness, and mysticism; and enunciation of the universal laws of nature, strict causal determinism, and a monism of infinite and eternal substance.

If it be asked why the outstanding philosophical spokesman for a particular class should have been received with such suspicion and hostility by most of its members, the following answer is given: 'Spinoza expressed the interests of his class with such fulness and depth that his contemporaries, still immersed to a considerable extent in the ideology of feudal society, saw in him a dangerous heretic and fell upon him with all the strength they could command.'[3]

[1] Cf. G. F. Aleksandrov, *Istoriya zapadnoyevropeiskoi filosofi* (*History of Western European Philosophy*), Moscow, 1946, p. 244.
[2] A. V. Lunacharski, 'Barukh Spinoza i burzhuaziya' ('Baruch Spinoza and the Bourgeoisie'), *Novy mir*, Bk. 1 (1933), pp. 167–81; I. K. Luppol, 'Istoricheskoye znacheniye filosofi Spinozy' ('The Historical Significance of Spinoza's Philosophy'), *Pod znamenem marksizma*, No. 11–12 (1932), pp. 180–89; A. Thalheimer, 'Sootnosheniye klassov i klassovaya borba v Niderlandakh pri zhizni Spinozy,' ('Class Relations and Class Struggle in the Netherlands during Spinoza's Lifetime'), *Vestnik kommunisticheskoi akademii*, Bk. 20 (1927), pp. 30–49.
[3] G. S. Tymyanski, 'Teoriya poznaniya Spinozy' ('Spinoza's Theory of Knowledge'), introduction to a Russian translation of Spinoza's *On the Improvement of the Understanding*, Moscow, 1934, p. 21.

INTRODUCTION

Even Spinoza's stressing of mathematical thinking and the geometrical method is seen as ultimately conditioned by economic factors. 'This attitude toward mathematics,' writes Tymyanski, 'on the part of the majority of the greatest philosophers of the seventeenth century—Descartes, Spinoza, Leibniz, Hobbes, Newton, *et al.*—is determined basically by the problems of the economic development of the time, by the requirements of commerce, navigation, warfare, and also by the significance of mathematics for astronomy, and even painting.'[1]

Spinoza's excommunication by the Jewish community is considered an important factor in shaping his attitude toward organized religion and the relation of church and state, and in motivating his positive critique of religious prejudice and intolerance. However, at least one writer has warned against overemphasizing this factor, pointing out that excommunication was a relatively common occurrence in Jewish communities, and was often used as a disciplinary measure for minor or even trivial offences.[2]

The Deborinites emphasized the social, economic, and political conditioning of Spinoza's system to the virtual exclusion of the traditionally accepted 'philosophical' sources—neo-Platonism, medieval Jewish and Arabic philosophy, Christian scholasticism, Cartesianism, etc. They vigorously deny that Spinoza carried on and completed the philosophy of Descartes, insisting instead that Spinoza overcame Cartesian dualism with a materialistic monism, and that Descartes's influence was as much that of irritant as stimulant: Spinoza reacted against it rather than responded to it.

The present 'orthodox' position is that Descartes's philosophy had a very great influence on the young Spinoza, facilitating his break with religious tradition and directing his mind toward the working out of philosophical problems, but it is still maintained that Spinoza's relation to Cartesianism was marked more by friction than by assimilation.[3] Emphasis is placed on the influence of the pantheist Giordano Bruno and the English 'materialists' Bacon and Hobbes in determining the fundamentally materialistic direction of Spinoza's

---

[1] G. S. Tymyanski, 'Teoriya poznaniya Spinozy' ('Spinoza's Theory of Knowledge'), introduction to a Russian translation of Spinoza's *On the Improvement of the Understanding*, Moscow, 1934, p. 60.

[2] D. Rakhman, 'Spinoza i yudaizm' ('Spinoza and Judaism'), *Trudy instituta krasnoi professury*, Vol. I, Moscow, 1923, p. 86 (English translation, this volume, pp. 48–60).

[3] Cf. *Istoriya filosofi* (*History of Philosophy*), Vol. II, Moscow, 1941, p. 171.

thought. And the attempt to trace Spinoza's historical roots to Judaism is regarded as reactionary and un-Marxian.

Bogdanov, in 1920, offered an interpretation of Spinoza's substance as the 'universal necessity which is concealed in all phenomena,' that is, 'their *causality*, as this is understood in a trading society'[1]—a causality modelled on the economic necessity of the market. As a Jew Spinoza represented a nation skilled in trade, and he lived in a country which was a leader of commerce, with the result that 'he seized upon the nascent forms of commercial thought with a profundity unmatched in his time, applying them to the construction of a unified world-view.'[2]

V. Shulyatikov, one of the early revisionists, in a book entitled *The Justification of Capitalism in Western European Philosophy*, advanced a rather ingenious, if crudely oversimplified, hypothesis: The organizing function of the 'mind' in Spinoza's system, he says, corresponds to the organizing function of the manufacturing capitalist, while the body corresponds to the organized working class (organized, that is, by the capitalist in the process of production). Shulyatikov points out that Spinoza's circle of friends and acquaintances included many of the *fine fleur* of the Dutch bourgeoisie, and asserts that Spinoza was their ideologist who 'in his own special language characterized the internal structure of capitalist enterprise.'[3] 'Spinoza's philosophy,' he concludes, 'is the chant of triumphant capital—all-devouring, all-centralizing capital. Outside the single substance there is no being, no object: outside the large-scale manufacturing enterprise there can be no producer.'[4]

Such 'reasoning' by crude analogy is, let us hasten to add, extreme and atypical. And be it said to Lenin's credit that he was harshly critical of such 'vulgarization.' His marginal note to the passage just quoted is brief and eloquent: '*Childishness!*'[5] In general, Spinoza's philosophy, like the other great rationalistic systems, has been seen as a more or less 'sublimated,' rather than a direct or automatic, expression of class interests and class consciousness.

[1] A. A. Bogdanov, *Filosofiya zhivovo opyta* (*The Philosophy of Living Experience*), Moscow, 1920, p. 201.   [2] *Loc. cit.*
[3] V. Shulyatikov, *Opravdaniye kapitalizma v zapadnoyevropeiskoi filosofi* (*The Justification of Capitalism in Western European Philosophy*), Moscow, 1908, p. 40.
[4] *Ibid.*, p. 42.
[5] V. I. Lenin, 'Zametki na knigu Shulyatikova *Opravdaniye kapitalizma v zapadnoyevropeiskoi filosofi*' ('Notes on Shulyatikov's book *The Justification of Capitalism in Western European Philosophy*'), *Pod znamenem marksizma*, No. 6 (1937), p. 7.

However, views similar to those of Shulyatikov are occasionally to be found among orthodox Marxists. Thus, for example, Vandek and Timosko, in comparing the methodological approaches to knowledge of Descartes and Spinoza, assert that Descartes's scepticism and universal doubt were an expression of the precarious position of the bourgeoisie in France during the first half of the seventeenth century. Still deeply involved in its struggle with feudalism, and far from victory, the class which Descartes represented was filled with doubt and despair. In Holland, on the other hand, since the bourgeoisie was already well-established both economically and politically, and thus was psychologically stable and well-adjusted, Spinoza as its philosopher had no room for doubt or scepticism. He plunged directly into the business of knowing, confident that an external world exists and that the human mind can obtain adequate knowledge of it.[1] And A. Kazarin, writing in 1932, expressed himself as follows: 'Spinoza's teaching is more consistent than that of Bacon . . . ; it is better constructed and more revolutionary than the dualistic system of Descartes, better-constructed and more materialistic precisely because the Dutch bourgeoisie was much stronger than either the French or the English bourgeoisie. . . .'[2]

The mechanists as a group followed, or, as the Deborinites said, 'fell back into' the more traditional accounts of the sources of Spinoza's philosophy. Akselrod emphasized Spinoza's Jewish background, his training in the Hebrew school of Saul Morteira, and his thorough exposure to Hebrew religion and culture. Varyash stressed the influence of medieval Jewish philosophy. 'The pan-rationalistic philosophy of Maimonides and Ibn Ezra,' he wrote, 'overflows into mysticism, and it is clear that Spinoza never completely succeeded in breaking away from the powerful influence of this essentially pessimistic mysticism.'[3] At the same time, Varyash set himself the task of showing the connection of Spinoza's speculative system 'with the social soil on which it grew and from which it broke away.'[4] He offers a sociological analysis of the 'Collegiants' among whom Spinoza lived after his excommunication; he asserts that

[1] Cf. V. Vandek and V. Timosko, *Ocherk filosofi B. Spinozy* (*An Outline of Spinoza's Philosophy*), Moscow, 1932, p. 51.
[2] A. Kazarin, 'Benedikt Spinoza' ('Benedict Spinoza'), *Molodaya gvardiya*, No. 12 (1932), p. 147.
[3] A. Varyash, *Istoriya novoi filosofi* (*History of Modern Philosophy*), Part I, Moscow, 1926, p. 169. [4] *Ibid.*, p. 186.

INTRODUCTION 23

Spinoza's closest friends were members of the wealthy middle-class, and that his philosophical circle was an embryonic form of Free-Masonry—'the secular organization which was hostile to the principles of the feudal society of the time.'[1] 'Spinoza's view of society,' Varyash continues, 'and, in the final analysis, of substance, was conditioned by the development of the means of production, that is, the development of manufacturing production and markets, the condition of which is reflected in his theory of the state.'[2] The principle of universal causal dependence in Spinoza's system, according to Varyash, is both a 'powerful tool of science' and the 'most powerful ideological weapon' of the bourgeois revolution.

Tseitlin, another of the mechanists, maintained that Descartes rather than Spinoza was the real predecessor of the French materialists of the eighteenth century. He charged Plekhanov with ignorance of the history of science, and considered the latter's designation of Marxism as a 'variety of Spinozism' profoundly mistaken. Descartes's philosophy, he declared, was based on natural science, Spinoza's on 'logical speculations.' The Cartesian metaphysics is not essential to his system, being but a loose and artificial covering for it, but Spinoza's system is metaphysical through and through. This is natural, says Tseitlin, since great logicians easily become entangled in metaphysics.[3]

Luppol, who was at this time (1926) considered a menshevising idealist, but who has since been accepted (after recantation of his 'errors' in 1936) as an orthodox Marxist, answered Tseitlin in decisive terms.[4] He pointed out that if the metaphysical nature of Spinoza's substance lay in its separation from man, and if Spinoza's transition from infinite substance to finite things (modes) was unsatisfactory, exactly the same could be said of Descartes's philosophy. Motion for Spinoza was only an infinite mode, not an attribute; but so was it for Descartes. Time was real for Spinoza only in the world of modes, and not in relation to substance; but in Descartes time was likewise only a mode of thought. The dualism of the Cartesian

[1] *Ibid.*, p. 193.
[2] *Ibid.*, p. 207.
[3] Z. Tseitlin, 'Karl Marks o spinozizme i istochnikakh frantsuzskovo materializma XVIII veka' ('Karl Marx on Spinozism and the Sources of French Eighteenth-Century Materialism'), *Pod znamenem marksizma*, No. 11 (1926), pp. 214–20.
[4] I. K. Luppol, 'O sinitse, kotoraya ne zazhgla morya' ('The Titmouse that Failed to Set the Sea on Fire'), *Pod znamenem marksizma*, No. 11 (1926), pp. 221–33.

system was thoroughgoing and radical, Luppol maintained, whereas Spinoza overcame this dualism with a naturalistic monism.

Turning from the concrete historical setting and the factors which shaped Spinoza's philosophy to his position in the history of thought and his influence on the subsequent course of European civilization, we find a greater agreement among Marxist critics. The revisionist Valentinov, however, objected strongly to Plekhanov's attempt to relate Spinozism historically and philosophically to Marxism. Writing in 1908, he declared that Spinoza's system was much closer to the empiriocriticism of Avenarius and Mach than to Plekhanov's Marxism. 'Spinoza's appeal to Substance,' says Valentinov, 'is a pseudo-monistic attempt to solve the problem of Cartesian dualism. He gets rid of the dualism of *res extensa* and *res cogitans* by making them attributes of a third thing which he calls God, nature, substance.' However, Spinoza was writing in the seventeenth century; Plekhanov is writing in the twentieth. And what was valid two hundred and fifty years ago is no longer acceptable. 'Plekhanov,' Valentinov declares, 'in making experience monistic, reduces phenomena to matter as the *primary factor*. Such a solution was completely foreign to Spinoza, who was well aware of the irreducibility and mutual non-convertibility of the attributes of extension and thought.'[1] In other words, Valentinov considered Plekhanov's Marxism a reductive materialism, as opposed to the non-reductive naturalism of Spinoza.

The mechanists, as a group, admitted that Spinoza exercised a strong influence on La Mettrie and Holbach, but they insisted that, before Spinozism could be assimilated into the materialist tradition, it would have to be cleansed of its metaphysical and theological elements.

Deborin's followers gave Feuerbach credit for first disclosing the materialistic character of Spinoza's philosophy beneath its 'theological veneer'; and they emphasized the line of continuity which ran from Spinoza through the French materialists—La Mettrie, Holbach, Helvetius, and Diderot—through Hegel and Strauss to Feuerbach, Marx, and Engels.

Orthodox Marxists take a similar view. 'We may say without exaggeration,' writes Milner, 'that Spinoza's materialistic ideas lay

[1] N. V. Valentinov, *Filosofskiye postroyeniya marksizma* (*The Philosophical Constructions of Marxism*), Moscow, 1908, pp. 89–90.

at the basis of the European Enlightenment.'¹ The French materialists of the eighteenth century, according to Luppol, were neo-Spinozists in the sense that Feuerbach was a nineteenth-century neo-Spinozist, that is, they solved the fundamental ontological problem in the spirit of Spinoza—by the synthesis of extension and thought in a single material substance.² And he continues, quoting from Marx and Engels, 'In Hegel's system, Spinozism appeared as "metaphysically transformed nature in its separation from man." Seeking a way out of Hegel's system, the materialist Strauss "took Spinozism as his point of departure." And the materialist Feuerbach found a way out of Hegel's system "by turning absolute spirit into actual man, who is a part of nature." '³

Deborin went so far as to state that 'no other philosophical system can compare with Spinoza's in its direct or indirect influence upon the development of positive science';⁴ that 'the history of natural science from the time of Spinoza to our own day amounts to a detailed elaboration and application in science of the basic principles of Spinozism.'⁵ 'The history of materialism in the post-Spinozistic period,' he says in another place, 'is . . . only a further development and modification of Spinozism.'⁶ Dialectical materialism, according to Deborin, is a synthesis of materialistically reworked Hegelian dialectics and Feuerbachian materialism. And, since Feuerbach's materialism is a modification of Spinozism, the latter is an essential component in Marxist philosophy. Deborin is careful, however, not to identify Marxism with Spinozism; he points out that Plekhanov's formula ('Marxism is a variety of Spinozism') applies only to the problem of the relation of thought to existence.

Despite this precaution, Deborin's opponents accused him of 'virtually equating Spinozism and Marxism,' of assuming that the more highly he and his followers valued a philosopher and the more closely they related him to Marxism, the better. The Deborinites, it was said, thought that in capturing Spinoza from the idealists and converting him into a dialectical materialist they were performing a praiseworthy service. But, in fact, they were rendering both Spinoza and Marxism a serious disservice. The orthodox Marxist Isakov characterized a work of Mankovski (a student and follower of

¹ Ya. A. Milner, *Benedikt Spinoza* (*Benedict Spinoza*), Moscow, 1940, p. 243.
² Luppol, *op. cit.* ³ *Ibid.*, p. 228.
⁴ Deborin, 'Benedikt Spinoza' ('Benedict Spinoza'), *Pod znamenem marksizma*, No. 2–3 (1927), p. 10.
⁵ *Ibid.*, p. 11. ⁶ *Ibid.*, p. 20.

Deborin) as 'remarkable for its anti-Marxist, abstract scholasticism.' And this, according to Isakov, is characteristic of Deborin's whole group, as is the 'inability to approach Spinozism concretely and historically,' and 'an attempt to avoid the difficult problems connected with it.'[1] Deborin's 'menshevising idealists' were further accused of over-emphasizing the dialectical elements in Spinoza's philosophy, just as the mechanists were accused of neglecting the few genuinely dialectical elements which his system contains.

V

Turning now to Spinoza's system as a whole, we shall examine first the basic problems of ontology, methodology, and epistemology which have been the source of much philosophical discussion in the Marxist tradition. Marxists consider the relation of thought to existence, of consciousness to being, as the fundamental problem of philosophy. And Spinoza's popularity in Soviet Russia rests to a considerable extent on what is regarded as his correct, and essentially materialistic, solution of this problem. The orthodox Marxist position is close to that of Spinoza (interpreted naturalistically), as may be seen from the following quotation from Stalin's *Anarchism or Socialism*: 'Consciousness and being, idea and matter, are two different forms of a single phenomenon, which is called, generally speaking, nature. Consequently, they do not contradict each other, but at the same time they do not represent a single phenomenon.'[2] Spinoza's famous proposition that 'the order and connection of ideas is the same as the order and connection of things' (*Ethics*, II, 7) is deeply congenial to dialectical materialists.

Although the mechanists tended to emphasize the principle of causality as the criterion for dividing idealism from materialism, both Deborinites and orthodox Marxists have insisted that the line of demarcation lies rather in the solution of the ontological problem —the relation of matter to consciousness. Materialism, they point out, makes matter primary and basic, whereas idealism gives priority to mind and consciousness. And by this test, Spinoza was a materialist. As compared to Descartes, Spinoza is not plagued by 'methodological doubt'; he 'categorically repudiates Descartes's well-

[1] P. Isakov, 'K voprosu o "teologicheskom priveske" v učeni Spinozy ('On the Question of the "Theological Trappings" in Spinoza's Doctrine'), *Antireligioznik*, No. 11-12 (1932), pp. 16-17.
[2] Quoted by Milner, *op. cit.*, p. 237.

known idealistic *cogito*; he does not begin his philosophizing with thought as immediately and obviously existing. Spinoza begins with being, with nature. His initial assertion is: nature is, it exists. Nature is primary, existing before all philosophizing, before all doubt and reflection.'[1] To be sure, Spinoza expresses this 'givenness' of nature in a rationalistic and speculative form, which distinguishes it from the concrete, historical givenness of dialectical materialism. Nevertheless, it is held, Spinoza's position is truly materialistic.

The orthodox Marxist view modifies the above interpretation of Spinoza's ontology and theory of knowledge in one important point. Deborin, following Plekhanov, had accepted uncritically the element of hylozoism implicit in Spinoza's definition of thought as an infinite and eternal attribute of nature (God). Plekhanov, it is held, was essentially a hylozoist himself and for this reason tacitly approved of Spinoza's hylozoism. Quotations to support this charge can be multiplied. For example, Plekhanov, in a conversation with P. N. Lepeshenski (reported by the latter), stated that 'thought is complex motion and is made up of those same elements of motion which determine the state of energy of a stone. And if anyone wishes to accept "thought" as a substantial property of matter, he must ascribe this property to the stone as well.'[2] Plekhanov's hylozoism seems to have resulted from his inability to explain on any other hypothesis how 'in a living cell, sensation (the basic element of psychic life) can appear suddenly, like a revolver shot.' We must conclude, says Plekhanov, 'that there is inherent in inorganic bodies a minimal and simple psychic process, which grows and becomes complex as we ascend the scale of living beings.'[3] This view is now regarded as a mechanistic reduction of quality to quantity, which in fact eliminates the category of quality and ignores 'leaps' in nature.

Certain writers have maintained that Plekhanov's views were shared by Lenin and Engels, and even by Marx. Thus Tseitlin attributed to Lenin the view that 'the internal state of all matter in motion is psychic.'[4] In another place Tseitlin asserted that on the question of hylozoism Lenin shared the viewpoint of his teacher, Plekhanov,

---

[1] G. Dmitriev, 'Filosofiya Spinozy i dialekticheski materializm' ('Spinoza's Philosophy and Dialectical Materialism'), *Pod znamenem marksizma*, No. 9–10 (1926), p. 37.
[2] P. N. Lepeshenski, *Na povorote (At the Turning Point)*, 1925, p. 155.
[3] G. V. Plekhanov, 'Bernshtein i materializm' ('Bernstein and Materialism'), *Collected Works*, Vol. XI, pp. 14–15.
[4] Tseitlin, *Chto takoye materiya? (What is Matter?)*, p. 115.

and that Plekhanov in turn shared the viewpoint of Diderot, La Mettrie, and Spinoza.¹ G. I. Chelpanov held that Marx himself was a 'Spinozistic materialist, that is, a hylozoist.'² Berdyaev in 1932 characterized orthodox Soviet philosophy as hylozoistic. The 'matter' of which Soviet philosophers speak, he points out, is alive with sensation, thought, and freedom. 'It is evident,' Berdyaev concludes, 'that such a system is not materialism but hylozoism.'³

That Lenin at least did come rather close to hylozoism may be inferred from such quotations as these: 'In the foundation of the structure of matter one can only surmise the existence of a faculty akin to sensation';⁴ 'it is logical to assert that all matter possesses a property which is essentially akin to sensation, the property of reflection.'⁵

In order to set off the views of Lenin and Engels from those of Plekhanov, an Aristotelian distinction has been introduced: Plekhanov, it is maintained, regards sensation as an *actual* property of matter; for Lenin and Engels it is *potential*, and becomes actual only when 'the conditions necessary for it are present.'⁶ And this sets off the orthodox Marxist view from that of Spinoza, who assumed the presence of consciousness wherever there is extension.⁷ For Spinoza, it is held, matter is *logically* prior to thought, but for dialectical materialism this priority is *historical* as well as logical.

Spinoza's hylozoism is regarded as a result of his static, non-temporal approach to such problems, which in turn was conditioned by the primitive level of biological science in the seventeenth century. Without the knowledge that man had developed from lower animal forms and that life had arisen from inorganic motion, the problem of the emergence of consciousness could not even be formulated, let alone solved. Spinoza was thus faced with a dilemma: 'He could not deny thought to man. But to recognize thought as an

---

¹ Tseitlin, 'O chuvstvitelnosti materi' ('On the Sensitivity of Matter'), *Ateist*, No. 27 (1928), p. 51.

² G. I. Chelpanov, *Psikhologiya i marksizm* (*Psychology and Marxism*), p. 19. Cf. also: Chelpanov, *Spinoza i materializm* (*Spinoza and Materialism*), Moscow, 1927, p. 43.

³ N. A. Berdyaev, *Generalnaya liniya sovetskoi filosofi* (*The General Line of Soviet Philosophy*), Paris, 1932, pp. 16–17.

⁴ Lenin, 'Materialism and Empiriocriticism,' *Selected Works*, XI, New York, 1943, p. 113.

⁵ *Ibid.*, p. 157.

⁶ This phrase is from Engels' *Dialectics of Nature*, New York, 1940, p. 228.

⁷ Cf. 'Spinoza,' *Bolshaya sovetskaya entsiklopediya*, Vol. 52 (1947), p. 423.

exclusive property of man would have meant returning to the dualism of Descartes. . . . Therefore Spinoza chose the only correct path: he declared thought an attribute, an eternal property of nature.'[1]

The mechanist Akselrod followed the lead of Höffding in interpreting Spinoza's substance as 'the order of nature'—'the law of causality'—a non-material conformity to law, abstracted from natural phenomena. Varyash pointed out that confusion results from the fact that Spinoza 'did not draw a sharp distinction between relations (all laws of nature are relations between things) and the idea of these relations.'[2] 'For Spinoza,' he wrote in another place, 'law is not only the universal real relation of the parts (modes) of the material universe, but also their productive principle, the mediator between universal substance and individual modes.'[3]

This mechanistic interpretation has been severely criticized by both Deborinites and orthodox Marxists as an attempt to turn Spinoza into an idealist and dualist. The charge is substantiated by references to the mechanists' connection, through Höffding, to the idealistic tradition of Spinoza interpretation. Spinoza's nature-substance-God, says Dmitriev, is real, objective, material nature—not a 'pale shadow,' a mere abstract law or orderliness.

Akselrod points out that Spinoza's metaphysics is parallelistic and static, but she stresses that this parallelism evaporates into pure materialism in his treatment of knowledge, in his psychology, and in his investigation of the sources of morality. 'Where Spinoza is an investigator,' she says, 'he stands on firm materialistic ground, that is, he persistently seeks the material basis of events, and he finds it *to the extent permitted by the level of knowledge of his time*.'[4] Chuchmarev goes so far as to call Spinoza's rejection of empirical science an 'invention of the idealistic historians of philosophy.'[5]

According to the present interpretation, 'Spinoza considers that empirical investigation provides material which can direct the reason to the knowledge of the essences of things, so that the connection

[1] V. Raltsevich, 'Ideolog peredovoi burzhuazi XVII veka' ('An Ideologist of the Progressive Bourgeoisie of the Seventeenth Century'), *Problemy marksizma*, No. 11–12 (1932), p. 24.
[2] Varyash, *op. cit.*, p. 218.
[3] *Ibid.*, Part II, p. 225.
[4] Akselrod, *op. cit.*, p. 167.
[5] Cf. V. I. Chuchmarev, *Materializm Spinozy (Spinoza's Materialism)*, Moscow, 1927.

between sensory knowledge and logical knowledge is preserved.'[1] But he remains basically a rationalist and thus, from the point of view of dialectical materialism, seriously undervalues empirical knowledge and experimental science. However, it is emphasized that Spinoza as a materialist makes greater use of experience than his rationalistic denial of its role in cognition would consistently permit.[2] And he is emphatically *not* a psycho-physical parallelist or dualist, as Varyash and Akselrod maintained, but a thoroughgoing monist.

The Deborinites are charged with attempting to make Spinoza into a dialectical materialist, with overlooking or glossing over the mechanistic, metaphysical, and contemplative character of his materialism and the idealistic elements in his system. Among the latter, it is pointed out, is Spinoza's deductive, mathematical method, which is not merely a form of exposition, as the Deborinites maintained, but is basic to his whole methodology.[3] Both the mechanists and the Deborinites, it is felt, glossed over or ignored the intuitivism and extreme rationalism of Spinoza's theory of knowledge, and his central doctrine of the 'knowledge of essence.' It is emphasized that Spinoza distinguished in principle between the knowledge of substance and the knowledge of modes. The former is purely rational and intuitive, the latter empirical, partial, and imperfect. Spinoza is wrong, the Marxists hold, in placing the ultimate criterion of truth within the human mind, rather than beyond it in the external world.

Vandek and Timosko sum up the present position in regard to Spinoza's epistemology in these words: 'Making rationalistic knowledge absolute, Spinoza as a metaphysician was not able to find a transition from the knowledge of finite things to the knowledge of the infinite, from sensation to thought, from the particular to the universal; for the universal, the essence, according to Spinoza, is not perceived through the senses, but is accessible only to supersensory

---

[1] Tymyanski, *op. cit.*, p. 58.

[2] *Istoriya filosofi* (*History of Philosophy*), Vol. II, p. 189.

[3] Interestingly enough, this view, which was first put forward by Polovtsova in 1913, is defended in the introduction to Spinoza's *Ethics* published in 1932—nearly two years after Deborin's group had been officially repudiated. 'It is quite absurd,' writes the editor, A. K. Toporkov, 'to assume that Spinoza, in working out his world-view, actually proceeded from finished definitions and axioms to his final propositions. Clearly, the reverse is true: these axioms and definitions were formulated after he had done all of his work . . . and was faced with the task of developing his world-view "in the geometrical order." ' (Introduction to the *Ethics*, p. vii.)

INTRODUCTION 31

intuition, which is the only reliable way of knowing.'[1] They go on to list the principal defects of Spinoza's methodology of knowledge as follows: 'A rationalistic doctrine of knowledge, the predominance of "pure intellect," a separation of reason from sense experience, the lowering of the latter to the level of confused "imagination," a contemplative criterion of truth, and a mystical supersensory intuition.'[2] Spinoza, they point out, 'takes nature, comprehended by nonsensory intuition, as primary, and then deduces from nature, as from an axiom, the knowledge of all other finite things.'[3]

Tymyanski, in his detailed study of Spinoza's theory of knowledge, softens these judgments somewhat. Spinoza's clear and distinct knowledge, he says, is not an *act* but a *path*; his intuition is an 'intellectual contemplation which includes both the element of immediate clarity and self-evidence, and the comprehension of universal causal connection. . . .'[4] The intuition that substance necessarily exists is 'the presupposition of all knowledge. The knowledge of substance is intuitive because the existence of nature cannot be logically inferred; it is perceived as given.'[5] Spinoza's intuition, Tymyanski concludes, is only the point of departure for his theory of knowledge; the whole process of his thought is basically one of formal deductive logic.

Aleksandrov in 1946 repeated the observation which Semyon Frank had made in 1912: 'For Spinoza knowledge of things is not distinguished in principle from knowledge about knowledge.'[6] 'Furthermore,' he continues, 'since ideas themselves are, according to Spinoza, a property of matter, ideas of ideas cannot precede ideas of bodies, but rest on the study of things.'[7]

The objective quality of natural law is an element of Spinozism which is warmly received by dialectical materialists. Spinoza follows the Greeks, as Engels remarked, in being 'convinced from the outset that nature cannot be unreasonable or reason contrary to nature.'[8] 'The laws of the world of things are also the laws of the world of thought, and only because of this is knowledge possible. . . . If the laws of cognition were of one kind—if thought were subject to certain laws—and the laws of the world of things were entirely different, then our consciousness, the totality of our ideas, could not

[1] Vandek and Timosko, *op. cit.*, p. 65. [2] *Ibid.*, p. 67.
[3] *Ibid.*, p. 66.
[4] Tymyanski, *op. cit.*, p. 68. [5] *Ibid.*, p. 72.
[6] Aleksandrov, *op. cit.*, p. 253. [7] *Ibid.*, p. 254.
[8] Engels, *op. cit.*, p. 178.

provide a reflection of what occurs in the world of things.'[1] These lines from Luppol recall Lenin's 'theory of reflection'—a point of contact with Spinozism which will be examined in detail below. (Cf. pp. 42 f.)

The static, metaphysical (i.e. non-dialectical) character of Spinoza's system, according to the present view, made it difficult for him to solve the problem of the connection of infinite substance and finite things, of nature as producer (*natura naturans*) and nature as product (*natura naturata*).[2] Recognizing only being and not-being, and lacking an organic conception of growth and development, Spinoza refers motion only to *natura naturata*. The problem of how the manifold movement and change of finite things can be brought about by a substance which is absolute and immovable remains unsolved. It is emphasized that Spinoza's thinking, here as elsewhere, is spatial and non-temporal, his analogies geometrical and static.

However, in this as in other 'contradictions,' a skilful dialectical materialist can find elements of acceptable 'dialectics.' Thus Deborin points out that Spinoza's substance is uncreated and uncaused; yet individual modes are strictly and necessarily caused. Formal logic, says Deborin, would require that the law of causality be extended to nature as a whole, but 'the dialectical meaning of Spinoza's doctrine is that the category applied to a *part* of nature cannot be extended to the *whole of nature*.'[3] Deborin even asserts that Hegel's dialectics, in so far as it is concerned with finite and infinite, freedom and necessity, is only a further development and deepening of Spinoza's dialectical ideas.

Profound dialectical significance is also seen in Spinoza's '*omnis determinatio est negatio*,' a phrase which Lenin considered of 'enormous importance.'[4] This is interpreted not as 'every (logical) *definition* is a negation,' but rather, 'every *limitation* (real determination) is a negation.' And, Luppol says, 'we must agree with Spinoza that every limitation of his infinite substance is a negation of this substance as infinite.'[5]

Another aspect of Spinoza's metaphysics which is generally

---

[1] Luppol, 'Filosofskaya sistema Spinozy' ('Spinoza's Philosophical System'), in *Istoriko-filosofskiye etyudi*, Moscow, 1935, p. 82.

[2] 'Spinoza,' *Bolshaya sovetskaya entsiklopediya*, Vol. 52 (1947), p. 422.

[3] Deborin, 'Mirovozzreniye Spinozy' ('Spinoza's World-View'), *Vestnik kommunisticheskoi akademi*, Bk. 20 (1927), p. 21 (English translation, this volume, pp. 90–119).

[4] *Leninski sbornik*, IX, p. 67.   [5] Luppol, *op. cit.*, p. 74.

INTRODUCTION 33

accepted by Soviet writers is his conception of the universe as an organic, interconnected whole. This is close to the conception of universal dialectical interrelation—derived from Hegel's doctrine of internal relations—which lies at the basis of Marxist monism. As Stalin tells us, 'nature' for dialectical materialists is 'a connected and integral whole, in which things, phenomena, are organically connected with, dependent on, and determined by, each other.'[1] Beside this we may place Spinoza's statement (in Letter XV to Oldenburg) that 'all bodies are surrounded by others, and are mutually determined to exist and to act in a definite and determined manner. . . . Every body, in so far as it exists modified in a certain way, must be considered to be a part of the whole universe, to be in accord with the whole of it, and to be connected with the other parts.' Brushlinski comments on this passage as follows: 'Spinoza's fundamental idea of the continuity of universal being and the universal connection and union of all things fully corresponds to . . . the views of dialectical materialism.'[2]

We should perhaps stress at this point a basic element of Spinoza's ontology which has found general acceptance and admiration among Marxist critics of all schools. That is the doctrine of nature as self-caused (*causa sui*), infinite and eternal, first singled out for comment by Engels in his *Dialectics of Nature* (p. 173). The acceptance of nature as the ultimate 'given,' without limits in time or space, is basic to dialectical materialism, and in this doctrine Marxist philosophers find a strong central tie to Spinozism. According to Aleksandrov, this doctrine has its historical roots in seventeenth-century natural science. 'The works of Copernicus, Kepler, Galileo, and Huyghens,' he writes, 'had prepared the way for the conclusion that the universe is infinite in time and space. . . . In the 1640's Descartes's thesis concerning the preservation of the quantity of motion in nature was already finding many adherents among scientists—and this favoured the assertion . . . that nature is one and eternal.'[3]

The view of the universe as infinite and eternal is strongly defended by present-day Soviet cosmologists in the face of such 'reactionary' doctrines as Einstein's 'finite, unbounded universe.' Questions as to the 'origin of matter' or the 'origin of the universe' can have no

[1] J. V. Stalin, *Dialectical and Historical Materialism*, New York, 1940, p. 7.
[2] V. K. Brushlinski, 'Spinozovskaya substantsiya i konechniye veshchi' ('Spinoza's Substance and Finite Things'), *Pod znamenem marksizma*, No. 2–3 (1927), p. 58 (English translation, this volume, pp. 120–30).
[3] Aleksandrov, *op. cit.*, p. 249.

meaning, it is held, for, as Engels put it, 'Nothing is eternal but eternally changing, eternally moving matter and the laws according to which it moves and changes.'[1] Spinoza's rejection of an act of creation and of continuing intervention in the governance of the world by a supernatural being is regarded as a basically materialistic and atheistic doctrine, of bold and revolutionary import in the seventeenth century. The essential truth of Spinozism, Marxists feel, is in its atheism and materialism, in the consistent attempt to explain the world through itself alone.

VI

Marxist interpreters distinguish two separate aspects of Spinoza's relation to religion: (1) his critique of historical religions, religious prejudice and superstition,[2] his biblical criticism, and his treatment of the problem of church and state, of theology and philosophy; and (2) the basic philosophical atheism of Spinoza's system as a whole, when stripped of its theological veneer and remnants of scholasticism.

As to the first aspect there is general agreement. It is pointed out by the mechanist Akselrod, by the 'menshevising idealists' Deborin and Volfson, and by orthodox writers such as Milner and Mitin, that Spinoza 'destroyed the most important support of medieval ideology, the teleological conception of the world, and deposed the religious myth to which the scientific thought of his time had been subordinated,' that he was 'an enemy of all the transcendental tendencies which dominated the philosophy of his time,'[3] that he was the first thinker in history to treat religion as an historical and social phenomenon, and that the *Theologico-Political Treatise* established him as 'the founder of scientific biblical criticism.'[4] Spinoza, it is emphasized, saw in 'religious ceremonies and rites a special form of obedience, a fraud by which "monarchical government" screens itself.'[5] He accepted institutional religion only to the

[1] Engels, *op. cit.*, p. 24.

[2] The Spinoza jubilee edition of *Pravda* (November 24, 1932) included several brief quotations from the *Theologico-Political Treatise* and the *Ethics*, under the heading 'Spinoza on Religion.'

[3] S. Ya. Volfson, *Eticheskoye mirosozertsaniye Spinozy* (*Spinoza's Ethical World-View*), Minsk, 1927, p. 3 (English translation, this volume, pp. 131–48).

[4] A. B. Ranovich, 'B. Spinoza kak rodonachalnik bibleiskoi kritiki' ('Spinoza as the Founder of Biblical Criticism'), *Anti-religioznik*, No. 21–2 (1932), p. 22.

[5] I. P. Razumovski, 'Spinoza i gosudarstvo' ('Spinoza and the State'), *Pod znamenem marksizma*, No. 2–3 (1927), p. 68 (English translation, this volume, pp. 149–61).

INTRODUCTION 35

extent that it did not conflict with sound judgment or the interests of the state, since, as he says in the *Theologico-Political Treatise*, it is 'such a comfort to those whose reason is comparatively weak.'[1]

Deborin's group contented itself with pointing out the essentially anti-theological direction of Spinoza's polemic—his rejection of revelation, miracles, and personal immortality, and his designation of fear and ignorance as the foundations of religious superstition— praising these elements as progressive and atheistic. However, the present position is that Spinoza's conflict with established religion and traditional theology was purely defensive, an attempt to preserve the freedom of philosophy and scientific investigation from theological censorship. Spinoza felt that religious superstitions could be adequately dispelled by philosophical enlightenment, whereas dialectical materialists insist that the social and economic function of organized religion in the class struggle makes genuine atheism possible on a broad scale only in a socialist society. They thus regard Spinoza's atheism as of a bourgeois and limited character. He was not a militant atheist; his atheism was intended for the enlightened few rather than for the masses.

But what of Spinoza's specific denial in his correspondence of the charge of atheism? Both Spinoza and his accusers, according to the Marxists, were using the term in its seventeenth-century sense of 'immorality, licence'; and Spinoza quite naturally denied such accusations. But this is an 'atheism' quite different from that which is ascribed to him by dialectical materialists.—Is Spinoza then a consistent philosophical atheist in the precise sense of the term? To this question the various schools have given widely differing answers.

The mechanists, especially Akselrod, regarded Spinoza as a sensitive, poetic philosopher whose profound religious feeling was directed toward the infinite and immutable order of the universe rather than toward a personal, anthropomorphic God, with the result that this order—the *Logos*—was hypostatized above the material world.[2] To this it is replied that Spinoza's substance is not *Logos*—nature's conformity to law—because conformity to

---

[1] B. Spinoza, *Theologico-Political Treatise*, ch. XV, §§ 26–43.
[2] This is the view which Akselrod developed during the 1920's. In 1903 she considered Spinoza an atheist and 'the founder of the mechanistic world-view.' 'The esteem which the atheist Spinoza mistakenly enjoys among contemporary philosophizing theologians,' she wrote, 'must be blamed in part on the philosopher himself, who, out of infinite love for his atheism, called it God.' (*O 'Problemakh idealizma*' (*On 'The Problems of Idealism*'), Geneva, 1903, p. 7n.)

law cannot itself have the attribute of extension, which Spinoza's substance clearly possesses.

Lunacharski regards Spinoza's philosophy as a pantheistic 'mathematical mysticism,' strongly influenced by Maimonides and the Cabbalists. Both mechanists and orthodox Marxists agree that Spinoza took his doctrine of infinite attributes from the theologians. If he had ascribed to substance (God) only the two attributes of thought and extension, he would have destroyed the theological conception of God, which his terminology and mode of expression tended to preserve. This inconsistency in Spinoza's atheism, which was emphasized by the mechanists, the contradiction between the materialistic content and the theological form of his philosophy, was glossed over by the Deborinites in various ways. Mankovski, a disciple of Deborin, saw in this theological veneer a deliberate deception. 'Spinoza,' he says, 'quite consciously, taking into account the conservative character of public opinion, did everything that was necessary to deceive readers of a certain type.'[1] Deborin himself felt that Spinoza was aware of the inadequacy of his theological terminology, but 'considered it necessary to speak in a language that would be intelligible and accessible to his contemporaries.'[2] These views have been decisively rejected. 'The theological "trappings" of Spinoza's philosophy,' writes Isakov, 'are not a deliberately invented form for the deception of reactionary public opinion, but represent a unique stage in the history of seventeenth-century materialism and atheism.'[3]

Mankovski also attempted to interpret the doctrine of infinite attributes in a dialectical and evolutionary sense. At present we know only the attributes of thought and extension, he says, but in the course of nature's development other attributes will manifest themselves. This interpretation has been rejected as contrary to the obvious intention of Spinoza's philosophy. For, if additional attributes appear at a specific time, they cannot be eternal; yet Spinoza defines them as 'expressing eternal and infinite essence.' Mankovski is accused of distorting historical fact in attributing to Spinoza a theory of the infinite evolution of substance; for it is just such a theory of natural growth and development that Spinoza's system conspicuously lacks.

How then are Spinoza's infinite attributes to be explained? The

[1] L. A. Mankovski, *Spinoza i materializm* (*Spinoza and Materialism*), Moscow, 1930, p. 46.
[2] Deborin, *op. cit.*, p. 16.   [3] Isakov, *op. cit.*, p. 21.

INTRODUCTION 37

present Marxist position is that their motivation is psychological rather than logical, that they have all the characteristics of the infinite attributes (whose function was primarily honorific) of the God of the medieval schoolmen. It was the scholastic conception of an '*ens realissimum*' which led Spinoza to posit an infinity of attributes. As he himself remarks (*Ethics*, I, 9): 'The more reality or being a thing has, the greater the number of its attributes.'

The concepts 'infinite intellect,' 'infinite will,' and 'eternity of the mind' were explained away, to a certain extent, by the Deborinites. Thus Luppol: 'The intellect as an infinite mode is only the aggregate of all finite intellects; similarly, the will as an infinite mode is only the aggregate of all finite wills.'[1] He goes on to deny religious significance not only to Spinoza's infinite will and intellect, but to his doctrine of the mind's eternity and immortality: 'The latter,' he writes, 'flows from the cognitive love of substance-God. In so far as this latter is timeless, according to Spinoza, its intuitive contemplation unites man to timelessness.'[2]

However, the orthodox Marxist position is that these concepts entered Spinoza's system together with the terms 'God,' 'natural light,' etc., none of which is an integral or positive element in Spinoza's philosophy. They are its priestly vestments, the traces of scholasticism and theology which Spinoza did not completely overcome.

On the question of Spinoza's pantheism and religious feeling, the present position is substantially that of Plekhanov and Deborin. The view of Spinoza as a genuine pantheist—which was defended by Lunacharski, Bogdanov, and Akselrod—is decisively rejected; even the word 'pantheism' is considered self-contradictory. The alleged pantheist, writes Isakov, 'either pronounces the world an illusion and dissolves it in "God", or he causes "God" to disappear in the world. In the first case the result is idealism, in the second materialism.'[3] The latter, needless to say, is considered to be the case with Spinoza. Toporkov refutes Spinoza's alleged pantheism by an additional argument: 'Spinoza,' he declares, 'differs sharply from every kind of pantheist, in as much as pantheism necessarily presupposes acceptance of a mystical teleology.'[4]

According to Plekhanov, 'religious feeling' cannot be isolated

[1] Luppol, *op. cit.*, p. 80.   [2] *Ibid.*, pp. 86–7.
[3] Isakov, *op. cit.*, p. 14.
[4] A. K. Toporkov, Introduction to Russian edition of Spinoza's *Ethics*, Moscow, 1932, p. xiv.

from the 'more or less orderly system of ideas, dispositions, and actions' which make up religion.[1] If it is so isolated, as the mechanists claim it to be in Spinoza, it loses its theological meaning and ceases to be religious. Without God and animism, says Plekhanov, religion cannot exist. God, identified with nature, loses his character as deity. Spinoza's system, it is maintained, is marked neither by animism nor religious feeling in any significant degree. Indeed, Spinoza's great contribution, Plekhanov asserts, is to have banished all animism from philosophy.

VII

Spinoza's ethical and social philosophy is regarded by Marxist interpreters as of central importance to his system as a whole. The determinism and naturalism of his ethical theory is especially congenial to dialectical materialism, as is his relativizing of the concepts 'good' and 'evil.' 'Spinoza,' says Volfson, 'included man in a single system of the world—of nature—and subjected him to an iron-clad, deterministic law.'[2] Spinoza was a destroyer of the anthropocentric fiction, who 'knew that man is subject to the laws which reign throughout the universe, that the world's conformity to law controls man's actions and fate, that to regard man as outside this law is to create illusions unworthy of a scientist.'[3] It is emphasized that Spinoza 'approached the solution of ethical problems with what he considered the one and only scientific method; that is, he investigated morality "by means of the general laws and rules of nature." '[4]

He is looked upon as the founder of 'scientific ethics' and an unqualified opponent of the transcendental, supernatural ethics of the idealistic tradition.

The mechanists, however, stressed the contemplative and stoical character of Spinoza's ethical ideal. 'Concentrating all of his philosophical attention,' says Akselrod, 'on inner "stoical freedom," identified with the knowledge of universal necessity, Spinoza naturally came to the culminating point of his system—the intellectual love of God. True—that is, adequate—knowledge, freedom, and supreme happiness coincide. The ultimate attainment of this ideal leads in the final analysis to the complete dissolution of individuality. Beginning with freedom and the perfection of individuality, Spinoza ends by seeking the dissolution and annihilation of the

---
[1] G. V. Plekhanov, *Collected Works*, XVII, Moscow, 1923, p. 197.
[2] Volfson, *op. cit.*, p. 3.   [3] *Ibid.*, p. 5.   [4] *Ibid.*, p. 6.

latter in deity.'¹ The strong traces of fatalism, stoicism, and mysticism in Spinoza's ethics, according to the mechanists, are reflected in his doctrine of 'inner freedom.' Spinoza's freedom is an inner mastery of emotion by reason; whereas the freedom of dialectical materialism leads to creative activity, based on the knowledge of natural necessity. The former results in passive contemplation, the latter in the active changing of the external environment. For the Marxist, who follows in the tradition of Bacon, knowledge is not an end in itself, but a necessary means for extending 'man's dominion over nature.'

Lunacharski, whose views on this subject are close to those of the mechanists, although he is not formally identified with that group, emphasizes the passive character of Spinoza's ethical ideal, speaking of him as 'the great voice calling men to acquiescence, to peace.'² He criticizes Spinoza for failing to recognize the existence of suffering, and for maintaining that we are wrong to regard anything as evil, because from the highest point of view, from the point of view of the whole, apparent evil is true good.³ Such a doctrine Lunacharski sees as an integral part of Spinoza's 'mathematical mysticism.'

The Deborinites, according to the present view, over-emphasized the activistic and dialectical character of Spinoza's ethical views (the dialectics of freedom and necessity, for example) and under-emphasized his metaphysical opposition of chance and necessity, his limitation of chance to a subjective category. 'We call those things chance,' says Spinoza, 'whose cause we do not know.' This denial of the objective nature of chance, it is now felt, gives a fatalistic colouring to Spinoza's determinism. The present interpretation is · that Spinoza's activity is not activity in the Marxist sense, but rather an active condition of the mind—a conscious passive condition. It is recognized that Spinoza, like Aristotle, regards *activity* as the highest human good, but that he qualifies this doctrine, as Aristotle does, by pointing out that *knowing* is the highest and most genuinely human activity.

Tymyanski emphasizes the close connection between Spinoza's ethical and political theories: 'Spinoza,' he writes, 'like other great thinkers of the young seventeenth-century bourgeoisie, did not set

[1] Akselrod, *op. cit.*, p. 164.
[2] Lunacharski, *Ot Spinozy do Marksa (From Spinoza to Marx)*, Moscow, 1925, p. 20.
[3] *Ibid.*, p. 18.

out to find a quiet haven for himself. He was a revolutionary, faced with the political problem of finding a way to bring about a new state of society in which men would be happy, at a time when the economic and political foundations of the past were breaking up. But in the conditions of the seventeenth century, social happiness could be conceived only as the sum of the happinesses of separate individuals. Therefore the problem of social welfare had to be reduced to the welfare of the individual. Spinoza followed the general path of his time and restricted the problem of politics to an ethical problem.'[1]

Deborin was rebuked for finding in Spinoza 'a prophetic anticipation of socialist society,' based on the latter's advocacy of community of property among friends, and his insistence on the responsibility of the state toward its needy citizens. Spinoza's social and political theory, it is emphasized, was 'determined by the political temper of seventeenth-century bourgeois society. On the one hand there was a tendency to consolidate the absolute power of the state in order to secure the foundations of "civil society," and the fear of a return to the feudal "state of nature" and mutual conflict. On the other hand, apprehension was felt at such excessive strengthening of the state, which, in a majority of cases, still had a plainly feudal character; an apprehension for the freedom of the bourgeois individual, a tendency to set certain boundaries to the rights and powers of the government.'[2]

According to orthodox Soviet Marxism, Spinoza's theoretical approach to society and the state is metaphysical and static. 'Man—biological man—is the foundation of Spinozism.... Spinoza did not recognize the viewpoint of socio-historical man.'[3] He regards society as unchanging and neglects class structure and class conflict. For him society and the state coincide. Marxists also emphasize that Spinoza defended private property, opposed political revolution, and was closely connected with the ruling oligarchy of Holland. In view of these facts, Deborin's attempt to assimilate Spinoza's political and social views to those of dialectical materialism is considered illtaken. Spinoza, it is held, was a politically enlightened philosopher, a direct link between Machiavelli and Hobbes, on the one hand, and Montesquieu, Rousseau, and the French materialists, on the other; but his approach to politics and society was conditioned by the state

[1] Tymyanski, *op. cit.*, p. 27.
[2] Razumovski, *op. cit.*, p. 73.
[3] Toporkov, *op. cit.*, p. ix.

INTRODUCTION 41

of seventeenth-century science and by the interests of the revolutionary bourgeoisie for which he was a philosophical spokesman.

VIII

The essential limitations of Spinoza's system are authoritatively summed up by one of the leading figures in contemporary Soviet philosophy, M. B. Mitin, under the following four heads:

'(1) Spinoza's materialism is enclosed in a theological wrapping. This is not entirely external in relation to his whole system, but expresses a very serious inconsistency in his philosophy, . . . which is a mixture of materialism and theology.

'(2) Spinoza's materialism is an abstract and contemplative materialism. It is abstract in the sense that his nature (substance) is not sensuous nature, given in all its living concrete form; it is contemplative in the sense that Spinoza's philosophy does not include the actual, active, concretely-historical subject. . . .

'(3) Spinoza does not recognize the category of motion. Motion is, according to him, one of the infinite modes; it is not an attribute of substance. This gives Spinoza's substance a lifeless, immobile character, despite the elements of dialectics which are present in his philosophy.

'(4) From Spinoza's treatment of thought as an attribute of substance flows the theory of the universal animation of matter. This theory indicates a materialistic view of the problem of the relation of thought to being, in that the basis of the unity is being. However, only the dialectical materialism of Marx, Engels, and Lenin, applying the historical view to nature as a whole and thus to the problem of the origin and development of thought and its relation to being, provides a genuinely scientific solution of this problem.'[1]

These limitations are serious in Marxist eyes and substantially qualify the Marxist evaluation of Spinoza's total philosophical achievement. Nevertheless, they are recognized as necessary consequences of the historical setting in which Spinoza's philosophy was formed. In the broad perspective of history, the movement and direction of Spinoza's thought is seen as essentially materialistic and naturalistic, and his great positive contributions, his consistent attempts to apply the scientific method of his day to the solution of

[1] M. B. Mitin, 'Spinoza i dialekticheski materializm' ('Spinoza and Dialectical Materialism'), *Pod znamenem marksizma*, No. 11–12 (1932), p. 173.

philosophical problems, are seen as overshadowing the 'historically transient and class-bounded in his philosophy.'[1] As Aleksandrov puts it: 'Only as the result of a profound insight into the state of the natural sciences of his time and the perspectives of their development could Spinoza see the unity of the world when science for the most part still divided that world into parts, prove the eternity of nature when science recognized a First Impulse as a principle, . . . affirm that necessity and conformity to law reign in nature at a time when only a few isolated discoveries in this direction had been made by science.'[2]

'Spinoza's very great role in the history of thought,' concludes Milner, 'consists in the fact that he made a truly grandiose attempt to explain the world completely through itself alone;

'That, having created a profoundly thought-out materialistic philosophy, he anticipated with genius and formulated with brilliance a whole series of dialectical propositions which found their development in the works of Hegel, and subsequently in those of the great founders of scientific communism;

'That he was the first in the history of science to provide a fully developed philosophical basis for atheism, and that he subjected religious views to positive criticism.

'Spinoza, in the very dawn of the modern period, raised the sacred banner of the battle for science and reason against darkness and obscurantism, and in the course of his whole brief life he held high this great banner of human progress.'[3]

IX

There are certain points of contact between Spinoza's philosophy and contemporary dialectical materialism which have not been emphasized by Russian Marxists, but seem nevertheless to warrant some comment. In the first place, both systems are deterministic monisms, characterized by strict conformity to law, a law which is conceived as objectively existing in nature. Spinoza does not stress the objective character of natural law as consistently as do Engels and Lenin, but this assumption seems to underly the bulk of his writing. For Engels and Lenin the laws of dialectics are laws of ontology: contradiction is objectively present in nature, etc. In fact, Lenin uses the terms 'objective logic' and 'subjective logic' (in the *Philosophical Notebooks*) to designate what are usually referred to as

[1] Razumovski, *op. cit.*, p. 75.   [2] Aleksandrov, *op. cit.*, p. 249.
[3] Milner, *op. cit.*, pp. 242–3.

'ontology' and 'logic,' respectively. He comments that in Aristotle 'objective logic is combined with subjective logic in such a way that the former is everywhere evident.' And he continues, in words that could be applied equally to Spinoza and to dialectical materialists, '[In Aristotle] there is no doubt as to the objectivity of knowledge; —a naïve faith in the power of reason, in the strength, force, objective truthfulness of knowledge.'[1]

According to both Engels and Lenin, logical relations are *reflections* of relations which exist objectively in nature: and this view (a thoroughgoing logical realism) appears to be substantially shared by Spinoza. He expresses this most unequivocally in the *Short Treatise*, where he comes close to a Platonic view of the being of ideas: 'They are and will be just the same, though neither I nor any other human being ever thinks of them.' (I, 1, App. 2.) As Gebhardt remarks: 'Plato and Spinoza meet in an *absolute conceptual realism*. . . . Spinoza's ideas are not transcendental essences, being immanent in particular things, but they remain completely real.'[2] And Ueberweg supports this judgment: 'We are landed at once,' he says, 'in a crude realism (in the medieval sense of the term), the scientific legitimacy of which is simply presupposed, but not demonstrated, by Spinoza.'[3] It seems clear at least that Spinoza differed sharply from the nominalists: for him true universals (*'notiones communes'*) exist *in re* as well as *post rem*. And this is essentially the view of Engels and Lenin. In the course of his remarks on Aristotle, Lenin speaks of the 'explanation of the leap from *the universal in nature* to the mind, from object to subject . . .'[4] (italics mine). And in another place he goes so far as to assert that 'the particular exists only in the connection that leads to the universal,'[5] thus suggesting a Platonic realism for which universals exist *ante rem*.

A recent Soviet writer, in the course of a bitter attack on modern 'neo-nominalists' (semanticists and logical positivists), expressed the Leninist view as follows: 'Scientific abstraction, the process in which universal concepts are formed, . . . is a reflection of objective reality, reflecting it more profoundly, accurately, and completely than mere sensation could do. Abstraction, if it is truly scientific,

[1] Lenin, *Filosofskiye tetrady* (*Philosophical Notebooks*), Moscow, 1936, p. 291.
[2] Carl Gebhardt, 'Spinoza und der Platonismus,' *Chronicon Spinozanum*, I (1921), p. 208.
[3] Friedrich Ueberweg, *History of Philosophy*, II, New York, 1873, p. 67.
[4] Lenin, *op. cit.*, p. 276.
[5] *Ibid.*, p. 327.

... leads us into the depths of objective reality, revealing to thought the essential conformity to law, the internal structure of the material world, which is inaccessible to direct perception. *Universal concepts ... reflect real universals, existing in things themselves*'[1] (italics mine).

B. Rudayev has even attempted to interpret Marx as a Platonic realist, for whom concepts exist 'in a certain sense' *ante rem*. He bases his conclusion on Marx's assertion that existence is relational ('man is a complex of social relations,' etc.), and points out that 'in order to dissolve existence into relations without destroying it altogether, it is necessary that we should have knowledge of relations themselves ... as existing.'[2]

Aleksandrov seems to be the only Soviet writer who has explicitly noted Spinoza's closeness to dialectical materialism on this point. 'The logical connection of ideas,' he writes, 'was for Spinoza only an expression of the real connection of things. Thus the question not only of the logic of ideas, but of the logic of things themselves, was decisively formulated.'[3]

This brings us to the theory of truth, in which Spinozism and Marxism–Leninism exhibit certain important similarities. Spinoza made *good* and *evil*, *beauty* and *ugliness*, *order* and *confusion* relative to human desire and judgment, thus depriving these categories of fixed metaphysical status. But not so with *truth*, which remained objective and absolute. Dialectical materialists have carried their relativization as far as, but no farther than, Spinoza: ethical and æsthetic categories they recognize as relative, but *truth* remains objective and absolute, fully accessible, as Lenin puts it, to 'genuine, powerful, omnipotent, objective, absolute human knowledge.'[4] Objective truth, in the words of a recent writer, is 'that content of our ideas and concepts which depends neither on man nor on humanity, but reflects the properties and laws of objective reality.'[5] 'Human thought,' Lenin says in another place, 'by its nature is capable of giving, and does give, absolute truth, which is compounded of a sum-total of relative truths. Each step in the development of science adds new grains to the sum of absolute truth. . . .'[6] "The existence of such truth is

[1] B. E. Bykhovski, *Marazm sovremennoi burzhuaznoi filosofi* (*The Marasmus of Contemporary Bourgeois Philosophy*), Moscow, 1947, p. 9.
[2] B. Rudayev, *Na putyakh k materializmu XX veka* (*On the Road to Twentieth-Century Materialism*), Kharkov, 1927, p. 268.
[3] Aleksandrov, *op. cit.*, pp. 255–6.
[4] Lenin, 'On Dialectics,' *Selected Works*, XI, New York, 1943, p. 85.
[5] Ya. Betyayev, *Bolshevik*, No. 6 (1947), p. 61.
[6] Lenin, 'Materialism and Empiriocriticism,' *op. cit.*, p. 197.

INTRODUCTION 45

unconditional, and the fact that we are approaching nearer to it is also unconditional.'¹ And again: 'The mastery of nature manifested in human practice is a result of an objectively correct reflection within the human head of the phenomena and processes of nature, and is proof of the fact that this reflection (within the limits of what is revealed by practice) is *objective, absolute*, and *eternal* truth'² (italics mine).

The immediate target of Lenin's polemic in this section of *Materialism and Empiriocriticism*, it will be remembered, was the 'revisionist' doctrine of Bogdanov and Bazarov, who held that: 'Marxism entails a denial of the unconditional objectivity of any truth whatsoever, a denial of all eternal truths, . . .'³ 'since every ideology, and thus all formulations of knowledge, depend on the changing and developing practices of production. Thus it is evident that the assertion of a given truth's "eternity" cannot be verified [or falsified] so long as the enlargement of experience does not show it to be inadequate. This means that the recognition of its "eternity" is based on simple faith; and this rests, as always, on some authority or other that decides which truths in particular are eternal, and which are not.'⁴ Such a procedure, Bogdanov concludes, is at odds not only with dialectical materialism, but with modern science generally, which rejects all absolutes in knowledge and insists on continuous and unrestricted criticism of its findings.

Bogdanov went on (in 1906) to formulate his own theory of truth, a theory very close to that of American pragmatism. 'Truth,' he says, 'is a vital organizing form of experience; it *leads* us somewhere in our activity and provides a point of support in the struggle of life.'⁵ Lenin recognized the similarity of Bogdanov's doctrine to that of William James, and attacked them both with equal intensity. 'From the standpoint of materialism,' he wrote, 'the difference between Machism and pragmatism is as insignificant and unimportant as the difference between empiriocriticism and empiriomonism.'⁶

Thus the pragmatist James, and more recently the instrumentalist Dewey—whose philosophy is characterized as 'a variety of reaction-

---

[1] *Ibid.*, p. 198.
[2] *Ibid.*, p. 250.
[3] Bogdanov, *Empiriomonism*, Bk. III, Moscow, 1906, pp. iv, v.
[4] Bogdanov, *Filosofiya zhivovo opyta* (*The Philosophy of Living Experience*), Moscow, 1920, p. 203.
[5] Bogdánov, *Empiriomonism*, Bk. III, p. viii.
[6] Lenin, *op. cit.*, p. 392.

ary idealism'[1]—have both been attacked by Soviet Marxists for relativizing the concept of 'truth.' That Spinoza, who wrote two hundred years before Darwin, cultural anthropology, and Wissenssoziologie, did not entertain the possibility of a relativistic or instrumental theory of truth, is hardly to be wondered at. But it seems strange that contemporary dialectical materialists should cling to a theory of absolute and objective truth which—as Bogdanov showed clearly more than forty years ago—is incompatible not only with the conclusions of modern science but with the theoretical assumptions of historical materialism.

The dialectical doctrine of universal, never-ending growth and development offers a kind of cosmic consolation very close to that which many students have found in the philosophy of Spinoza. L. Rudas of the Marx-Engels-Lenin Institute, taking as his point of departure a passage in Engels' introduction to the *Dialectics of Nature*, expresses this in the following words: 'What passes away at one point of the universe, develops anew at another. Our solar system passes away, new ones develop. Life passes away from the earth, it arises elsewhere anew. In this sense, dialectical materialism asserts an eternal development; what exists evolves. It evolves because the dialectical self-movement of everything which exists is a driving force towards development. Decay holds in general for every special case, the endlessness of development holds only for the infinite universe *sub specie æternitatis*.'[2] The specific terminology, as well as the general mood, of the passage is Spinoza's.

One further point should perhaps be clarified. Does the term 'matter,' as used by Spinoza and by modern dialectical materialists, mean the same thing in both cases? Bogdanov answered this question with a strong negative. 'It is clear,' he said, 'that the word "matter" had a quite different meaning in Spinoza's time, and that Spinoza's experience differed vastly from contemporary experience. . . . It is simply absurd to attempt to translate his terms into contemporary language. . . . All of Spinoza's terms have lost their former meaning.'[3]

[1] G. Aleksandrov, 'Filosofstvuyushchiye oruzhenostsy amerikanskoi reaktsi' ('Philosophizing Henchmen of American Reaction'), *Bolshevik*, No. 11 (1947), p. 26.

[2] L. Rudas, 'Dialectical Materialism and Communism,' *The Labour Monthly*, No. 9 (1933), pp. 575–6.

[3] Bogdanov, 'Predely nauchnosti rassuzhdeniya' ('The Limits of the Scientific Accuracy of Discursive Reasoning'), *Vestnik kommunisticheskoi akademii*, No. 21 (1927), p. 260.

It seems clear that Plekhanov's definition of matter as 'that which directly or indirectly acts, or may, under certain conditions, act on our external senses,'[1] or Lenin's definition—'Matter is a philosophical category designating the objective reality which is given to man by his sensations'[2]—differs from Spinoza's conception of matter as 'mass or corporeal, extended substance.' The Marxist definitions are broader, including much that Spinoza would not have regarded as 'mass or corporeal substance' (for example, various kinds of radiant energy: light, heat, etc.). It would thus be less accurate to call Spinoza a materialist in his own sense of the term than in the Marxist sense.

If in these last pages I have digressed from a strict examination of Spinoza's position in Soviet thought to a general discussion of Soviet philosophy, it is because I feel that the present work is peculiarly adapted to an illumination of the labyrinths of contemporary dialectical materialism, as revealed in its relation to a great philosopher of the past. We may study with profit not only Spinoza in Soviet philosophy but Soviet philosophy through Spinoza.

[1] Plekhanov, *Collected Works*, XVII, p. 123.
[2] Lenin, *op. cit.*, p. 192.

D. Rakhman

SPINOZA AND JUDAISM [1]

I

WE understand by an investigation of the ideological origins of Spinoza's doctrine neither an indication of the authors from whom Spinoza borrowed his teaching nor a searching out of the fragments which make up his system. In treating an original thinker like Spinoza such an approach is incorrect. Here the question can only be one of indicating the raw materials which provided the philosopher with nutriment, with matter to be elaborated and transformed. The most diverse instruments may be employed for this purpose, and the results of the process may be quite different from its point of departure, but their connection should not be forgotten.

It is not at all difficult to indicate Spinoza's connection with Judaism from such a point of view. Indeed, the facts speak for themselves. To be the foremost student in a model school in the most cultured Jewish community of the time—to remain in this traditional environment until the age of twenty-two—is in itself sufficient to bind one to Judaism with a thousand ties, despite the influence of the outside world and of alien doctrines, and even despite a personal desire to emancipate oneself decisively and finally from all influences.

For this reason we find it strange when certain scholars try zealously to show that Spinoza, an exile from the Jewish community, had nothing in common with Judaism, that he was rather a Christian, that he definitively effaced from his life the early years of his Jewish education, that he drew exclusively from new, outside sources, etc. Without going into detail as to precisely where these 'new sources'

[1] A translation of 'Spinoza i yudaizm,' *Trudy instituta krasnoi professury*, Vol. I, Moscow, 1923, pp. 85–95.

are to be found, and without intending to deny categorically the possibility of such sources, I should like merely to point out that there was in Judaism itself a great variety of trends and a wealth of philosophical motifs which, in an extreme case, could by themselves have nourished Spinoza's powerful intellect and furnished him with a fixed and stable point from which to make a complete turn.

Furthermore, we should not forget that from his earliest youth Spinoza applied himself to a thorough study of the natural sciences and mathematics, and this doubtless protected him from both the sophistries of the Talmud and the nonsense of cabala. But on the other hand, the Talmud and cabala, as well as all subsequent religious and philosophical Jewish thought, did their work in secret and not only furnished the point of departure, the beginning of Spinoza's philosophizing, but also left their traces in his finished system.

Since I wish to be brief, I shall not quote from Spinoza's works, but shall confine myself to citing a number of passages from Jewish sources which in one way or another remind us of the teachings of Spinoza.

First, however, a few words about Spinoza's famous excommunication. It seems to me that some Soviet scholars do not have an adequate conception of the meaning of this anathema. I should say that excommunication is not at all a rare event among the Jews, nor is it as dreadful as some scholars portray it in speaking of Spinoza's excommunication. According to the Talmud, the following offences are punishable by excommunication: criticizing the actions of a rabbi (even after his death), stigmatizing a companion with an offensive nickname, violating the rules of social morality, keeping a vicious dog in one's house, taking the Lord's name in vain, etc.

In more recent times excommunication has served chiefly as a means of maintaining discipline and morality among the Jews. Thus in the eleventh century the following were forbidden under penalty of anathema: (1) polygamy, (2) compulsory divorce, (3) reading other people's letters (Rabbenu Gershon). It is interesting that whatever the offence or admonition the text of the anathema was virtually the same, and included expressions such as these: 'Let great and incurable ulcers plague him, maladies numerous and extraordinary. . . .' 'Let the earth swallow him up . . . and let heaven's thunder smite him with death.' Yet this procedure did not mark excommunication from Judaism but merely excommunication from a particular community.

Spinoza left Judaism not because of any anathema but because there was no longer any place for him there. Rather the reverse was true. The Jewish community expelled him because he had already departed from it too far. This happens at the present time as well. A political party hastens to expel a member as soon as it realizes that the member in question wishes to leave the party. But all this is by the way. Let us return to our original point.

The fundamental characteristic of Spinoza's philosophy is its monism, or in his own words: 'the knowledge of the unity of the mind with the whole of nature.' This motif of unity, though not, to be sure, in such a broad sense of the word, is a fundamental principle of Judaism. Religious Jews repeat daily: 'I believe that God is one and beyond comparison. He was, is, and shall be one.' No less well known are the sacred words which have been uttered by many Jews as they died a martyr's death at the stake: 'Hear thou, Israel, our God is one.' The prayer '*Aleinu*' ('It is upon us'), with which every service of worship concludes, speaks of the coming of the glorious day when all peoples will understand that there is on earth the kingdom of but one *God*.

The struggle against every kind of anthropomorphism is another fundamental motif of Judaism. Thus Jews repeat daily: 'I believe that God is not body and cannot be represented to us in any visible way.' The struggle against the anthropomorphism which is still evident in the Pentateuch began as early as the time of the prophets. The Talmudists were not satisfied even with this. In the Talmud we read: 'The prophets manifested great audacity in likening the creator to his creatures.'

Jewish philosophical thought went even further. Let us begin with Ibn Gabirol (1021-1070)—known to the Christian schoolmen as Avicebron. In his *Mekor Hain* (*The Fountain of Life*) we find such thoughts as this: 'The first active cause is absolutely one, without any plurality.' The epithets 'all-powerful' and 'all-wise' are not applied to Deity, since any definition or enumeration merely diminishes his perfection. (We find this motif in the Talmud.) We can gain an idea of God only on the basis of observation and inference from his influence in all that exists. Deity is the primary substance. One and the same matter forms the basis of everything that exists in the world, penetrating the whole hierarchy of existence like the steps of a ladder, from the heights of pure intellect to the depths of the purely material. Creation is necessarily contained in God because both creation and God are eternal and infinite.

At this point, it would seem, pantheism first appears in Jewish philosophy. Ibn Gabirol, attempting to express in figurative language the thought that creator and created are one and the same, says: 'The primordial being draws all things from the source of light without a vessel, and creates all things without an instrument.' *Keter Malhut* (*The Crown of the Kingdom*). No less interesting is the fact that Ibn Gabirol was the first to write a popular treatise on ethics in which ethical problems are treated independently of the propositions of religion or dogma and without quotations from the Bible or the Talmud. More than that, he established a close connection between the propositions of ethics and the physical and psychological facts of human nature. The title of the work in question is *Tikkun Middot ha-Nefesh* (*The Improvement of the Moral Qualities of the Soul*).

In the twelfth century we encounter another outstanding Jewish thinker, Maimonides (1135–1204). In his works we find the following propositions:

(1) Of God we may say only *that* he is but not *what* he is.

(2) 'To doubt the presence of God is to doubt the presence of everything that exists.'

(3) 'God is one, but not as an ordinary unit composed of fractions, nor a single object composed of dimensions. God is a unity of a kind which we do not encounter in the world of things.'

(4) God's knowledge is not analogous to human knowledge, for 'he is at the same time the knower, the known, and the process of knowing.'

(5) Only in God is there no distinction between essence and existence, for 'his being comprises his essence and his essence is being.'

(6) God cannot have new ideas, for all things are contained in him.

(7) God is not defined in time, just as 'a voice is not defined as either salt or fresh.'

(8) Concerning God it cannot be said that he possesses a will, for 'conditions of power and of will apply to God's creatures, not to God himself.'

(9) Everything that exists, except God, exists only contingently. God alone exists necessarily.

(10) Man's task is to acquire true knowledge, which is the same as the love of God.

(11) Man can overcome evil by trying through knowledge and the mastering of moral precepts to conquer his passions.

(12) We should be guided in all things by reason, not faith. Thus Maimonides asserts that 'philosophers, who study physics and meta-

physics, stand much higher than those men who study only the Torah.'

Before proceeding to an examination of the views of other Jewish thinkers, I should like to pause for a moment with an Arabian philosopher of the twelfth century, Averroes (1126-1198), who exercised great influence on the development of philosophic thought among the Jews. Many of his works were translated into Hebrew. The Jewish thinker Gersonides who, according to many scholars, served as a source for Spinoza, borrowed much from him. Averroes asserts that religion is for the unreasoning masses, who are incapable of philosophic thought, and that its aim is not to clarify man's consciousness but simply to raise the level of his morality. No less bold is his rejection of the Holy of Holies of that period, the immortality of the soul. He maintains that the soul does not continue to exist after death as a separate substance but only as a component of the universal reason which is embodied in the whole human race. He insists on the eternity of matter and the eternity of the world.

It is evident that it is not far from this to Spinoza's determinism. Indeed, if only a single universal soul exists, and if the human soul is only a part of this universal whole, we cannot speak of freedom of the will.

As has already been mentioned, the outstanding disciple of Averroes among Jewish thinkers was Gersonides (1288-1344). We note in his works a number of heresies. First of all, he denies the act of creation, which was the alpha and omega of traditional Judaism. Further, he asserts that 'the Torah cannot forbid us to consider as true whatever our reason demands that we recognize.' There is no supernatural. Miracles are the natural action of primary law. It was not without reason that Gersonides' contemporaries paraphrased the title of his book *The Wars of the Lord* to read *The Wars against the Lord*.

It is also worth recalling Gersonides' assertion that the act of thinking cannot be separated from the object of thought. No less interesting for us are the following words of his: 'No one has concerned himself to make the angles of a triangle equal to two right angles, therefore no one can connect teleology with such a phenomenon.'

We shall now turn to Hasdai Crescas (1340-1410). His most important assertions for us are the following: (1) Philosophy and theology are separate realms, apprehended through different kinds of knowledge. (2) All existence—the cosmic in nature as well as the ethical in man—is not free event but necessary consequence. Here are his words: 'God alone is self-caused and necessarily existing. All things else proceed from him.'

It is interesting to note that Crescas very often employs the categories 'necessity,' 'chance,' and 'possibility,' which bulk so large in Spinoza's system. (In general, Chapters XIII, XIV, and XV of the *Theologico-Political Treatise* are surprisingly reminiscent of certain chapters in the works of Crescas.) It may not be superfluous to call attention to the following passage in Crescas. He says: 'As space enters into the interstices of a body, so God fills all the parts of the universe; he is the locus (*Makom*) of the universe, which sustains and supports it.'

I shall pause briefly to consider the terminology of the period in question, which is in itself very typical. Thus, in all medieval Jewish philosophy God is characterized as '*mehuyav hametsiut*'—'necessarily existing'—as distinguished from everything else, the existence of which is merely possible. Furthermore, beginning with Talmudic times and ending with the latest Jewish schoolmen, the part of philosophy which we call ontology was called '*ma'ase merkava*'—'the affair of the chariot.' Of the driver, *natura naturans*, we cannot have an adequate conception. (I use the terms '*natura naturans*' and '*natura naturata*' here in the scholastic sense.) The high regard in which this branch of philosophy was held is evident from the following statement which we find in the Talmud: 'It is much more important to study "the affair of the chariot" than questions of a ritualistic nature.' At the same time, it is pointed out that this matter should not be discussed in public, for it can only result in confusion and will do more harm than good.

Let us now proceed to a brief examination of another branch of Jewish thought, Jewish mysticism and cabala. The latter originated in the thirteenth century. Its cornerstone is '*En Sof*,' 'the infinite.' Some of the favourite sayings of the cabalists are: 'All things are in God; God is in all things.' All things are one, like the 'burning coal and its flame.' 'There is no place free from God.' God is not positively defined, since this would limit him. Neither will nor intention nor thought nor word nor deed can be ascribed to God. Without God no event whatsoever can be understood. The connection between the infinite and the finite world proceeds through the sephiroth, which are unique 'potencies.' God is immanent in the sephiroth; yet taken together they do not make up the sum of his being. The cabalists enumerated ten such sephiroth or, in Spinoza's terminology, attributes.

Since it is not possible to go into the details of the doctrines of cabala, I shall confine myself to one typical quotation from the well-known cabalist book *Zohar*: 'Woe unto him who likens God to his attributes, and especially to men, who proceed out of the earth and are subject to decay.' God is without qualities, like the sea. 'Just as water does not have its own form, but takes on the form of the vessel in which it is contained, even so does the Infinite Light of God take on the character of the sephira in which it is contained.'

Finally, we shall pause with one of the Jewish thinkers of the sixteenth century, Moses Cordovero (1522–1570). In his *Pardes Rimmonim* (*The Garden of Pomegranates*) we read: 'All things which exist have their being exclusively in his essence. God is, as it were, the form of all essences, for they are all in him.' Further on we find such words as these: 'If we examine into things more closely we shall be convinced that we all proceed from him and are contained in him. Our life is an extension of his life and everything with which we nourish ourselves—the whole world of animals and plants—can exist only in him. All this is like a wheel which rolls on without end. ... He is all, all is in him, there is nothing beside him. ... Single things may withdraw from him, but in fact all things are contained and preserved only in him. ... Yet one should not speak of all this in public. More than that: the heart should not even reveal it to the lips. ...'

II

Another characteristic feature of Spinoza's doctrine is his calm, objective view of life and the absence of pessimism. We find this temper of mind in Judaism also. It is quite typical that in the Pentateuch good is identified with life and evil with death. And the admonition is frequently repeated: 'Choose thou life.' In the parables of Solomon we read: 'Take no care for the morrow, for ye know not what it will bring.' In the Talmud we find much that is directed against pessimism and asceticism. 'Whoever refrains from pleasure is a sinner.' 'Man is accountable (in this world) for all that has come before his sight which he has failed to make use of.'

In the Talmud there are also passages in which optimism is clearly evident: 'Everything created by God is for the good.' 'My son, if aught thou hast, refuse not thyself, for there is no pleasure in the grave and death gives no respite.' We find an equally severe attitude toward asceticism in many Jewish thinkers of the Middle

Ages. Saadia (892–942) says: 'Abstinence is an excellent trait if it be practised in moderation, but it becomes evil if carried to extremes.' Maimonides says: 'It will be wrong and even harmful if a man entirely refuses to eat meat, drink wine, marry, live in good lodgings, and dress well, for this path is full of sin.' We should point out that for Maimonides everything which furthers the perfection of the individual is considered good; everything which hinders such perfection is evil and sinful.

Cabala, on the other hand, was inclined to asceticism. The aphorism of the *Zohar*, 'In a strong body a weak soul, in a weak body a healthy soul,' is well known. No less well known are the predilections of the cabalists for fasting and self-torture. It is evidently no accident that Spinoza so frequently speaks disdainfully of cabala. Yet this latter tendency is an absolute deviation from Judaism. For one of the leitmotifs of Judaism is the struggle against asceticism and melancholy.

III

Further basic elements in Spinoza's teaching are love to man and love to God. And Judaism is permeated with these motifs. 'Love thy neighbour as thyself' is a fundamental proposition of Judaism, which extends to non-Jews as well, as is clearly evident from the context. In the same passage we read: 'Remain not unmoved at the sight of thy neighbour's blood.' The prophet Hosea exclaims: 'I desire loving-kindness and not sacrifice.' In the Talmud we read: 'The hatred of mankind leads to death.' Judah Abrabanel—Leo Hebræus —(1460–1530) in his *Dialoghi d'Amore* says that 'love is the life-creating principle, both in the cosmos and in humankind. Through love the mind is clarified and made capable of contemplating God.'

The love of God also has a long-established place in Judaism. The religious Jew repeats several times each day: 'Thou shalt love the Lord thy God with all thy heart and with all thy soul and with all thy strength.' In Philo Judæus we find the thought that love is the basis not only of philosophical knowledge but of the highest virtue as well.

There are many of these motifs in the Jewish religious philosophy of the Middle Ages. They are strikingly expressed in the works of Maimonides and Ibn Ezra, as well as in those of Ibn Gabirol, who was as much a poet as a philosopher. In the latter's works we read: 'My heart longs for thee, oh Lord. I cannot hide my love for thee, I must express it in words.' In Crescas we read: 'The love of God, which comprises his blessedness, is the most essential part of him, his innermost essence.' Crescas frequently emphasizes that the true end of human life is the sincere love of God.

In *Sefer Hasidim*, a book that was widely read among Jews in the twelfth century, we read: 'Let everyone worship God not for the sake of heavenly bliss but from pure love for him.' (We also find this motif in the Talmud.) It is interesting that when the author of this book, Judah the Pious, reflects on man's highest happiness, his union with Deity, the author is so carried away that he likens this state to 'the sexual passion of a young man.'

Nor is this motif alien to cabala. The latter teaches that the chief basis of morality is love to God, which determines the higher and the lower levels of all being and raises everything to the level where all should be one.

It may be safely said that the 'love of God' is emphasized throughout the whole of Jewish religious and philosophical literature.

IV

I should like at this point to consider a few well-known sayings and stock aphorisms from the Talmud and cabala which were almost certainly current in the school of Saul Morteira, so that Spinoza would involuntarily have absorbed them. I shall quote a number of them from memory, and without any particular order or system:

(1) 'Who is to be called a hero?—He who is master of his passions.'

(2) 'No one taps himself with his finger here on earth except it be established in heaven.'

(3) 'The quantitative significance of the letters of the word *Elohim*, "God," and the word *Hateva*, "nature," is the same,'[1] and thus God and nature may be equated.

(4) 'If a thing is as clear to you as morning, say it, but if not, it is better not to say it.'

(5) 'Only that may you declare to be true knowledge which is known to you as surely as you know that you must not marry your sister.'

(6) 'Whoever is subject to the passion of anger is an idolater.'

(7) 'The reward of a good deed is the deed itself.' 'The punishment of sin is the sin itself.'

[1] That is, the sum of the numerical values associated with the various Hebrew letters in these two words is the same.—*Trans*.

I think that these quotations will suffice. However, I consider it necessary to repeat here what I pointed out at the beginning, namely, that it would be a profound mistake for anyone to conclude on the basis of the material which I have presented that Spinoza borrowed his doctrines from one or more of these Jewish thinkers. Spinoza's teaching as a whole has no predecessor in Judaism. The thoughts cited above are widely-scattered, disconnected, and isolated. My purpose is to show that Judaism included many varied thoughts and dissimilar motifs, which in themselves did not make up a whole, just as a heap of stones is not a house. Yet they could provide excellent material for a skilful architect.

To speak here of direct influence or the continuation of a particular system within Judaism would be more than absurd. Indeed, Spinoza has as many points of divergence from preceding Jewish thinkers as points of contact with them. Let us mention merely that Maimonides was a most zealous partisan of teleology, that Crescas distinguished between God as spiritual and the visible world as material, and clearly asserted the preëminence of religion over philosophy; and finally, that on such fundamental problems as the creation of the world, the relation between body and soul, the origin of good and evil, Spinozism and cabala are as far apart as heaven and earth.

Here I wish only to show that there was a whole series of concepts and ideas deeply rooted in Jewish religious and philosophical thought, and that their influence on every critically-thinking Jew of the seventeenth century was certainly large.

Spinoza's greatness consists in the following: Whereas all of his predecessors were slaves of tradition, attempting to reconcile philosophy and religion, Spinoza as a great revolutionist of thought, conclusively and decisively broke the chains of tradition, destroyed the old idols, and in so doing came out upon a broad highway. If we recall that in Spinoza's time not only philosophizing rabbis but such great men as Descartes and Leibniz were conciliators of this kind, Spinoza's greatness shines all the more brightly.

However, let us return to the point. I should like to show that the greater part of the material cited above comes from works considered illegal or semi-legal in the traditional Jewish environment. These authors were the most radical thinkers in Judaism; they served as a bridge between Judaism and the universal doctrine of Spinoza. I should like to indicate that in Judaism itself there were sufficient materials, sufficient shades of thought, and a sufficient development of problems for the creation of Spinoza's system.

I shall take one stream of Jewish thought which appeared among our own Jews in the Ukraine and in Poland early in the eighteenth century and which doubtless drew exclusively from Jewish sources. And I shall show that this stream reminds us in many respects of Spinozism. In my discussion of Hasidism I shall confine myself to indicating the views most widespread in this movement, together with a few sayings of its founder, Rabbi Baal-Shem:

(1) 'Just as the fold of a garment is made up of the garment itself and remains in it, so the world is of God and in God.'

(2) 'God is in all things: in minerals, plants, animals, and man, in good and in evil. For there is no absolute good or absolute evil. In certain cases good may become evil, and vice versa.'

(3) 'God is not only the first cause of all that exists, but also its inner essence.'

(4) 'Man should strive to know himself as a manifestation of Deity.'

(5) 'Melancholy is of Satan. Holiness is to be found only where there is strength and joy.'

(6) 'Melancholy is not a good trait. Man should always be in a joyful mood.'

(7) 'The aim of human life is union with Deity.'

I believe that this list of propositions of Hasidism will remind the reader of passages in Spinoza's *Ethics*.

From all accounts it is evident that during the seventeenth century traditional Judaism began to break up and Jewish thought sought new paths for itself. At the beginning of the eighteenth century this search was expressed in Hasidism; in Spinoza's time there was the strong movement of Shabbetai Zevi (1626–1676). Even at the end of the sixteenth century we find a number of Jewish reformers who, under the influence of the new movement which was gathering momentum in Europe, wished to renew Judaism as well, to cleanse it of certain of its traditions. Among them the best known in Jewish literature are Joseph de Medigo, Judah Demodines, and Uriel da Costa. (The latter was perhaps more of a rebel than a theoretician.)

In Demodines' work *Sha'agat Arie* (*The Lion's Roar*), which was written in 1624, we find the following passage: 'There are those who affirm that God and the world are one and the same, that the soul does not live forever, that there is neither a Last Judgment nor a life beyond the grave.' Further on he says that, according to some, all the Jewish rites are inventions of the rabbis.

It is necessary, however, to point out that the influence of these reformers was not large. They expressed themselves very obscurely and contradictorily, their arguments were weak, and a great confusion and indecision was evident in the minds of the authors themselves. Yet it is very probable that they may have stimulated Spinoza's thought in certain directions. Their books were very widely read in Amsterdam.

It is interesting to note that the works of these authors, thanks to their ambiguity and allegorical language, were not subjected to persecution of any kind. Yet, as a matter of fact, they had already begun to undermine traditional Judaism. All this, however, was only the beginning of the end, a preparation for the mighty blow which Spinoza was to deal traditional, aristocratic, official Judaism. For Spinoza removed God from his throne and showed that God is everywhere, that there is no personal God anywhere, that all talk of a personal God and a divine will leads to the '*asylum ignorantiæ*.' Denying that the highest perfection can reside in one single thing, and proving mathematically that God does not exist outside the world or above it, Spinoza removed the foundation on which official Judaism, as well as all religion in general, rests. Spinoza's contemporaries understood this very well; Spinoza earned his persecution fairly.

On the question, 'What did Descartes give Spinoza?', I would say that Descartes taught Spinoza that for true knowledge it is necessary to deduce everything exclusively from principles that are clear and trustworthy in themselves; that one should assert only what is entirely clear and distinct; and finally, that no tradition whatsoever, no authority whatsoever, should stand in the way of philosophical inquiry. If Spinoza learned only this from Descartes, that in itself is sufficient to justify the well-known words in the preface to Spinoza's posthumous works, to the effect that 'Spinoza found a powerful support in the works of the most eminent René Descartes.' (Cf. Kuno Fischer, *Spinoza*, pp. 121, 273–9.) Precisely, a support. For Spinoza regarded Descartes as a contemporary whose opinion one should consider, and whose method one should adopt. Descartes doubtless influenced Spinoza in this sense. (Probably Spinoza's acquaintance with the physician Francis van den Enden and his other Christian friends was not without influence. But we cannot go into this problem here.)

I should like to conclude with the following remarks: Spinoza's *Ethics*, if we consider its content, is the most perfect and polished work that Judaism has produced; but it is expounded according to the method of Descartes. This does not in the least mean that any Jewish thinker before Spinoza had a clear and adequate conception of the problems which are treated in the *Ethics*. By no means. Here Spinoza is completely original and more profound than anyone who preceded him. But the reason why Spinoza constructed his system precisely as he did and not otherwise is to be sought in his close contact with Judaism during the best years of his life. Behind Spinoza was a rich past. It was necessary and it was possible for him to make use of it. Yet, for him, using the whole rich heritage of the past meant distinguishing, in all the ancient lumber, between what accorded with the modern spirit and those excrescences against which one should struggle. Expressed in another way: it was necessary to reject many old truths relentlessly, to have no fear of the new, and to throw out of one's mind everything that was not in harmony with 'natural light.' And it was necessary to develop those fruitful truths which were already available. In order to make such a selection, a definite criterion was needed. Spinoza found this criterion himself after long searching and reflection; in Descartes he found 'support' for his conclusions.

After all that has been said, may we regard Spinoza as a specifically Jewish philosopher? By no means. Jewish philosophy is basically idealistic, whereas in Spinoza's system materialism predominates. The basic points of view are different. The ethics of previous Jewish thinkers had been an ethics of obligation; in Spinoza we have the grandiose development of a naturalistic ethics, supplemented by elements of Stoicism. Furthermore, one of the pillars of Judaism is freedom of the will, whereas the heart of Spinoza's teaching is a consistent and sustained determinism. And finally, according to Judaism, man is the crown of creation, the final goal of all existence; and the history of mankind is explained in a purely teleological way. Spinozism has nothing in common with such a conception. (We may note here the intellectual connection of Judaism with another philosopher—who was not a Jew—with Leibniz.)

This is why we cannot agree with those who would see in Spinoza a specifically Jewish philosopher. Spinoza belongs not to any single people but to all mankind.

L. I. Akselrod (Ortodoks)

SPINOZA AND MATERIALISM[1]

THIS article is an amplification of a preface written for the new edition of G. V. Plekhanov's *Fundamental Problems of Marxism*. Its theme is the problem of the relation of Spinozism to materialism or, more precisely, an elucidation and interpretation of the theological elements—what Plekhanov called the 'theological trappings'—in Spinoza's system. This limitation is made in the realization that a study of the materialistic elements in Spinoza's philosophy would form a substantial and comprehensive work. A complete analysis of the theological elements alone would require much space. I shall therefore limit myself to indicating the path which an investigator of this problem should follow in order to elucidate the subject adequately.

I

In *The Fundamental Problems of Marxism*, G. V. Plekhanov defines materialism—with respect to its historical continuity—as a variety of Spinozism. However, he qualifies this definition of the relation of Spinoza's system to materialism by serious and important reservations. These reservations, if they are thoughtfully and attentively considered, clearly indicate that from Plekhanov's point of view Spinoza's philosophy as a whole is not to be regarded as a consistent and sustained materialism, that is, a materialism free from all contradictions.

Yet at the present time the view of Spinoza's system as a rigorously consistent materialism, sustained from beginning to end, is becoming more and more widespread and influential.[2] In support

[1] A translation of 'Spinoza i materializm,' *Krasnaya nov*, No. 7 (1925), pp. 144–68.
[2] The reference is to the views of A. M. Deborin and his followers.—*Trans.*

of this erroneous view, reference is usually made to Plekhanov's attitude toward Spinozism—but the essential reservations made by Plekhanov are entirely lost sight of. Such obscurity and misunderstanding should be removed as far as possible, for a correct appraisal of the predecessors of dialectical materialism determines to a significant extent the correctness of our understanding of dialectical materialism itself.

Let us begin our investigation by quoting a passage from *The Fundamental Problems of Marxism*, in which Feuerbach's attitude toward the philosophy of Spinoza is under discussion. It reads as follows:

'In 1843 in his *Grundsätze* [*der Philosophie der Zukunft*] Feuerbach remarked with much acuteness that pantheism is a theological materialism, is a negation of theology, but a negation which still professes a theological standpoint. Spinoza's inconsistency is manifested by the way in which he mixes up materialism with theology; but, this inconsistency notwithstanding, Spinoza was able to give "a sound expression, subject to the limitations of his day, of the materialistic conceptions of the modern age." Thus Feuerbach calls Spinoza "the Moses of the modern free-thinkers and materialists" (*Werke*, II, p. 291). In 1847, Feuerbach asks: "What does Spinoza mean when he speaks (logically or metaphysically) of substance and (theologically) of God?" To this question he answers categorically: "Nothing else but nature." According to Feuerbach, the main fault of Spinozism is that "in this philosophy the sensible anti-theological essence of nature assumes the aspect of an abstract, metaphysical being." Spinoza has suppressed the dualism of God and nature, for he regards natural phenomena as the actions of God. But, for the very reason that in his view natural phenomena are the actions of God, God becomes for him a kind of being distinct from nature and one on which nature rests. God is for him subject, and nature is predicate. Philosophy, now that it has at length definitely emancipated itself from theological traditions, must rid itself of this grave defect in the Spinozist doctrine, sound though that doctrine is at bottom. "Away with this contradiction!" exclaims Feuerbach. "Not *Deus sive natura*, but *aut Deus aut natura*. That is where the truth lies" (*Werke*, II, p. 350).'

Feuerbach's appraisal of Spinoza's system is expressed here, in general, with a clarity which leaves no room for doubt. From Feuerbach's point of view, certain traces of theology persist in Spinoza's system. Plekhanov's attitude toward this question is also perfectly clear, since Plekhanov quotes Feuerbach, in complete agreement with the noted German materialist's appraisal of Spinoza's system.

Let us examine this appraisal more closely. Feuerbach, and Plekhanov after him, saw in Spinoza's teaching an important and serious contradiction. The root of this contradiction lay in his theologizing of nature. 'The sensible, anti-theological essence of nature assumes for Spinoza the aspect of an abstract, metaphysical being.' Feuerbach overcame this contradiction quite simply, by rejecting all metaphysical essences and making natural phenomena, freed from theological colouring and metaphysical shrouds, the foundation of his philosophy. What precisely was it that Feuerbach found unacceptable in Spinoza's philosophy? Expressed in another way, what was it that represented to him its theological element? Surely not simply the word 'God.' The passages from Feuerbach cited above make it perfectly clear that he was convinced that the term 'God' has a relevant and definite content in Spinoza's system. As Plekhanov points out in his explication of Feuerbach's meaning: 'For the very reason that in Spinoza's view natural phenomena are the actions of God, God becomes for him a kind of being distinct from nature, and one on which nature rests.' Consequently it is clear that, according to Feuerbach and Plekhanov, the 'God' of Spinoza's system is not simply a term borrowed from the theologians, but a term which has its own definite content. And what is this content?

In the remarkable seventh chapter of the *Theologico-Political Treatise*, Spinoza, in setting forth the historical and philological method of investigating the Bible, remarks: 'Moreover it becomes easier to explain a man's writings in proportion as we have more intimate knowledge of his genius and temperament (*genium et ingenium*).'[1] And just before this, Spinoza speaks of the necessity, if we would understand a literary work, of studying the 'life, the conduct, and the pursuits of the author (*vitam, mores ac studia autoris*).'

This methodological rule, which is part of the general method of historical materialism, should be applied to the investigation of the term 'God' in Spinoza's system.

Spinoza's life and spiritual development differs sharply from the life and spiritual development of the thinkers of Christian nations. Thinkers who came from a Christian environment did not

[1] Spinoza, *Opera*, ed. Bruder, III, p. 108.

experience the soul-shaking inner dramas that were experienced by those who came from orthodox Judaism.

The Christian peoples possessed their own territory, their own states, their own national cultures. As a result, the Christian religion, in spite of itself, was forced to compromise with the scientific tendencies which opposed its very nature. However strong may have been the religious traditions, the religious education, and the religious feeling which grew up on this foundation, in the Christian world these elements were nonetheless tempered and dissolved in the general stream of historical culture: in science, art, politics, etc. As a result, in Christian thinkers religious tradition existed more or less peacefully side by side with the opposing scientific tendencies and cultural problems of a given period. This individual psychological compromise was at the same time a reflection of a larger compromise, prompted by the demands of those progressive classes which dominated economic life—a preservation of religious beliefs, on the one hand, and a furthering of the movement of scientific thought, on the other. Of course, the great philosophers of the Christian faith, the founders and moving forces of scientific critical thought, were often subjected to cruel persecutions. The 'Holy' Inquisition, for example, with its touching solicitude for the salvation of Christian souls, actively and energetically stifled creative thought. But external persecution, however harsh, does not evoke in strong natures tragic inner conflicts, that is, conflicts in the realm of world-view.

It was far different with the innovators who came from a Jewish environment. The Jewish people had for thousands of years been deprived of their own territory, their own state, and, consequently, of their own national culture, in the broad meaning of that term. Being strangers, 'foreign' competitors in the socio-economic arena of the various nations, they were systematically subjected to persecution and isolation, as a result of which they isolated themselves more and more, setting their own way of life and spiritual heritage in opposition to the way of life and the culture of their persecutors. Placed by all nations in the position of a renegade sect, the Jewish people, being highly cultured in things spiritual, zealously preserved and cultivated the remnants of their intellectual and moral heritage. One such historical remnant was religion. The Hebrew religion, which in itself and in its dogmas is one of the most realistic of religions, capable of compromise with the demands of reality—froze and ossified more and more as a result of the isolation of the Jewish people. This religious world-view was in fact the only remaining principle of unification of the national spiritual consciousness—that is, the sole form of national ideology.[1] And since science, art, politics, and literature represented the cultural riches of the Christian world, the world hostile to Judaism, orthodox Judaism bred in itself a religious hatred of all these cultural values. Cultural values of a secular nature were declared to be forbidden fruit, capable only of distracting men from the faith of their fathers and obstructing the true worship of God. And the worship of God was the only, the chief and highest, end of earthly existence. Earthly goods— wealth, the pleasures of the senses, fame, etc.—are not rejected by the Hebrew religion; asceticism is essentially foreign to it. But all these goods retain meaning and importance and receive religious sanction only when they are used in moderation and viewed as means to the worship of God rather than ends in themselves.

In the bosom of this ideology Spinoza received his first spiritual education. He was intended to be a rabbi, and it is quite clear that great hopes were placed in the gifted youth. This early religious training struck deep roots in the receptive, sensitive, and poetic spirit of our thinker. All of Spinoza's works are imbued with religious feeling, despite his rigorously rationalistic and geometrical method of argumentation. One feels clearly that the cult of Jehovah in which Spinoza was reared remained in firm possession of the sensitive poetic soul of the great philosopher. The central thought of Judaism, that the end of life and the supreme good are to be found in the worship and love of God, never left our atheistic thinker. This thought, in another form and with an essentially different content, became the final chord in his rationalistic system, under the aspect of *amor Dei intellectualis*, the intellectual love of God.

Despite his gentle, profoundly lyrical nature, Spinoza was, as Feuerbach aptly put it, a 'strong character.' He was a rigorous, merciless analyst, and at the same time a philosopher of Olympian calm who did not halt halfway on the path of criticism or the search for truth.

Because of the comparatively favourable social and political conditions in Holland during the period of the Renaissance, Spinoza

---

[1] Spinoza's remark in this connection is extremely interesting: 'Now the Hebrew nation,' he says, 'has lost all its grace and beauty (as one would expect after the defeats and persecutions it has gone through) and has only retained certain fragments of its language and of a few books.' *Theologico-Political Treatise*, VII, 3. (*Opera*, III, p. 113.)

came into intimate contact with the broad scientific problems which were springing up during that great historical period. The principal distinguishing features of Renaissance thought were a criticism of the religious world-view, and the origin of contemporary natural science. It was natural that mathematical reasoning should be opposed to mystical forms of thought, and in the seventeenth century mathematics attained a very high level in Descartes, Hobbes, Leibniz, Newton, *et al*. The rigour and precision of mathematical analysis was the model of the search for truth in all fields of knowledge, and the method of mathematics was the exemplary method. The significance of mathematics as the model of methodological thought is especially evident in the systems of Descartes, Hobbes, Leibniz, and Spinoza.

Spinoza's critical thought moves in two directions. On the one hand, he submits the entire historical religious world-view of his ancestors to thorough criticism. On the other, he attempts by analysis to establish a method for the investigation of truth. The results of the first undertaking are set forth in the *Theologico-Political Treatise*. *On the Improvement of the Understanding* is concerned with the problem of method. The principal goal which Spinoza sets himself in this treatise is the definition of the supreme good. But in order to attain to the supreme good it is necessary to cleanse the intellect of every kind of error. *On the Improvement of the Understanding* is concerned with investigating and establishing a criterion of truth, which for Spinoza is the highest good.

In defining the essence of method, Spinoza says: 'That will be a good method which shows us how the mind should be directed, according to the standard of the given true idea (*ad datæ veræ ideæ normam*).'[1] Method, consequently, begins with the very first assumption in conformity with which the investigation is carried out. Expressed in Hegelian language, the beginning, the point of departure, or (what amounts to the same thing) the initial assumption, must be included in the final result. We as dialectical materialists affirm that consciousness is determined by existence; the correct application of this methodological principle should lead us to the conclusion that in every manifestation of consciousness, however complex, existence is revealed. For Spinoza a clear and distinct, or, what amounts to the same thing, adequate idea is the initial idea with which correct method begins. The object of the clearest and most distinct idea is substance or God; and the mind of man possesses

[1] *On the Improvement of the Understanding*, Elwes' translation, p. 12.

this adequate idea. 'The human mind has an adequate knowledge of the eternal and infinite essence of God,' runs Proposition 47 of Part II of the *Ethics*. This knowledge of God is for Spinoza the fundamental source of truth. 'All ideas, in so far as they are referred to God, are true' (Prop. 32, Part II).

If the method of investigating truth begins with substance, and if the world as a whole represents the necessary modifications of substance, it is quite clear that from Spinoza's point of view a philosophical system may be developed and proved in a rigorously mathematical manner. From this conviction sprang the geometrical method of demonstration and the manner of proving fundamental axioms which we see in the *Ethics* and for which *On the Improvement of the Understanding* was a preparation.[1]

II

As has already been indicated, the other direction of Spinoza's thought found its expression in the *Theologico-Political Treatise*. This treatise is both the personal, intimate confession of a great man and a scientific, historical critique of the Bible and of religion in general. This scientific, historical critique of Scripture brought Spinoza to the important conclusion, which he was the first in history to express, that religion is an historical category, conditioned to a large extent by socio-historical factors. As an illustration of Spinoza's historical thinking in connection with religious ideologies, I cite the following passage from the *Theologico-Political Treatise*, in which the matter under discussion is the central moral commandment of the Sermon on the Mount: 'Whoever shall smite thee on thy right cheek, turn to him the other also.'

'We must consider,' says Spinoza, 'who was the speaker, what was the occasion, and to whom were the words addressed. Now Christ said that he did not ordain laws as a legislator, but inculcated precepts as a teacher: inasmuch as he did not aim at correcting outward actions so much as the frame of mind. Further, these words

[1] The mass of evidence which Polovtsova adduces so assiduously and pedantically to show that the *mos geometricus* is merely a form of exposition, will not stand up under the least criticism, in our opinion. The inner substance of Spinoza's whole system testifies to the contrary. The terminological and philological investigations which Polovtsova has undertaken have their importance, but what she attempts to prove remains unproven for the simple and natural reason that it is not possible to prove such a thesis.

were spoken to men who were oppressed, who lived in a corrupt commonwealth on the brink of ruin, where justice was utterly neglected. The very doctrine inculcated here by Christ just before the destruction of the city was also taught by Jeremiah before the first destruction of Jerusalem, that is in similar circumstances.'[1]

This moral precept, which comprises the essence of Christian non-resistance, is from Spinoza's point of view an expression and reflection of the decadent condition of the state. It arises in definite historical conditions and is determined by them. On the other hand, when civil life is normal, such a precept, according to Spinoza, is in direct opposition to morality, that is, it becomes immoral. Thus we read further on:

'Now as such teaching [the precept of non-resistance] was only set forth by the prophets in times of oppression, and was even then never laid down as a law; and as, on the other hand, Moses (who did not write in times of oppression, but—mark this—strove to found a well-ordered commonwealth), while condemning envy and hatred of one's neighbour, yet ordained that an eye should be given for an eye, it follows most clearly from these purely Scriptural grounds that this precept of Christ and Jeremiah concerning submission to injuries was only valid in places where justice is neglected, and in a time of oppression, but does not hold good in a well-ordered state. In a well-ordered state where justice is administered everyone is bound, if he would be accounted just, to demand penalties before the judge (see Lev. v. 1) not for the sake of vengeance (Lev. xix. 17, 18), but in order to defend justice and his country's laws, and to prevent the wicked rejoicing in their wickedness.'[2]

We thus see clearly that two systems of morality, both consecrated by religion, are viewed by Spinoza as ideologies growing out of socio-historical soil.

A systematic and consistent critique of religion leads Spinoza, in the first place, to the important and fruitful conclusion that religious views are *historical categories*. Further, in the process of criticizing religion, the fiction of transcendental teleology is gradually but inevitably exposed. The basic propositions and points of departure for a critique of transcendental teleology which are sketched in the *Improvement of the Understanding* and developed further in the *Theologico-Political Treatise* assume in the *Ethics* a complete and

---

[1] *Opera*, III, p. 110.   [2] *Loc. cit.*

finished form. The method of this critique is realistic and historical, though occasionally marked by rationalistic turns of thought. The pages of the *Ethics* which are devoted to the explanation of the origin of transcendental teleology are truly remarkable. We shall quote one of the most characteristic.

'As men find in themselves and outside themselves many means which assist them not a little in their search for what is useful, for instance, eyes for seeing, teeth for chewing, plants and animals for yielding food, the sun for giving light, the sea for breeding fish, etc., they come to look on the whole of nature as a means for obtaining such conveniences. Now as they are aware that they found such conveniences and did not make them, they think they have cause for believing that some other being has made them for their use. As they look upon things as means, they cannot believe them to be self-created; but, judging from the means which they are accustomed to prepare for themselves, they are bound to believe in some ruler or rulers of the universe endowed with human freedom, who have arranged and adapted everything for human use. They are bound to estimate the nature of such rulers (having no information on the subject) in accordance with their own nature, and therefore they assert that the gods ordained everything for the use of man, in order to bind man to themselves and obtain from him the highest honours.'[1]

From this and from further analysis of the purely material reasons for the rise of teleology, Spinoza draws the indubitable conclusion that the highest supernatural teleology, which results from causes being taken as means and effects as ends established in advance, is the principal content of religion as such. It thus follows that God is the establisher of ends who created the universe from a previously determined plan, and that the universe is operated by Deity in a fashion similar to that in which a mill is operated by a miller (Novalis' figure).

Spinoza's analysis and criticism of religion led him step by step to the systematic rejection and exposure of all teleological mythology. The God of the theologians is only an aggregate of human qualities, each raised to the level of an absolute. All the characteristics which the theologians ascribe to God are natural characteristics and, in particular, *human* characteristics. This anthropomorphic conception of the universe is to be repudiated once and for all. God as creator

[1] *Ethics*, I, Appendix.

and Establisher of ends is a contradiction that is thoroughly revolting and discreditable to human reason. There is no God beyond the universe.

Feuerbach, in summing up the conclusions of Spinoza's system, says: 'If we accept the fact that beyond God there are neither objects nor a world, then we must also accept the fact that there is no God beyond the world.'[1] In this correct formulation Feuerbach necessarily emphasizes the point that in Spinoza objects and the world are still in God. This turn of Spinoza's thought is not mentioned in passing; it represents the general view of the German materialist concerning the pantheism of the Jewish thinker. For the sake of clarity I shall quote another passage from Feuerbach which treats the same problem: 'Pantheism is theological atheism, theological materialism, a negation of theology, but a negation which still professes a theological standpoint, for it converts matter, the negation of God, into a predicate or attribute of the divine substance. But whoever makes matter an attribute of God declares it by the same token to be a divine substance.'[2] This characterization of Spinoza's pantheism is extremely acute and profound, and, what is more important, completely corresponds to the facts. By defining matter as an attribute of God, Spinoza gave it the character of Deity. This is as clear as day. Nevertheless, we must not stop at this conclusion; rather, we must proceed from it by the same path of analysis to discover the essence of the deification of nature in Spinoza's system. Thus we return to the question raised earlier: What is God, or the substance that is identical with God?

From the preceding discussion we know that Spinoza's investigation of the problem of method resulted in a criterion of truth which was essentially clarity and distinctness of perception. Mathematical thought, which dominated his age, provided Spinoza with a model of clarity and distinctness. On the other hand, his critique of religion led our philosopher to a complete and decisive rejection of supernatural teleology and an Establisher of ends, that is, to the unconditional denial of God as a creator standing outside the universe. These two streams of thought converged in a common centre whose essence was that all things in the universe should be regarded from the point of view of necessary conformity to law, in so far as we aspire to true and adequate knowledge. Once transcendental teleology had been critically examined and rejected, and with it the Establisher of ends, the universe appeared as *causa sui*—

[1] Ludwig Feuerbach, *Werke*, 1904, II, p. 263.   [2] *Ibid.*, II, pp. 264-5.

SPINOZA AND MATERIALISM 71

self-caused—an absolute, self-sufficient necessity, an independent and single entity, conditioned by nothing and created by no one.

In the world of events, regarded from the viewpoint of their universal and necessary connection, there are no ends; everywhere and in all things strict and inexorable causality reigns. There is nothing teleological, for example, in the fact that the shortest distance between two points is a straight line, or that the sum of the angles of a triangle is equal to two right angles. Yet both of these facts represent unalterable necessity. Every event in the order of the universe, taken in isolation, may either exist or not exist, but if it exists then it is necessarily the result of a preceding series of events and the cause of a subsequent series. And these series of events continue to infinity, since what is a cause in one connection is an effect in another, and vice versa. Consequently, from the point of view of the universe as a whole, each event and each series of events is conditioned by the universal, unalterable, and necessary connection of the world's conformity to law. What men call an 'end' is the idea of a desired value (whether in the material or the intellectual realm) toward the attainment of which an individual, or a group of individuals united by common interests, strives. In social and historical as well as in individual life, ends and teleologies exist, operate, and retain their full significance. Yet on a closer, objectively scientific inspection all ends, whatever their nature or content, are seen to be evoked and conditioned in the most rigorous manner according to the law of mechanical causality; hence it follows that *teleology itself is only a variety of mechanical causality*. Thus it is evident that the law of absolute necessity, that is, the rigorous conformity to law which characterizes all events, is in Spinoza's system the supreme sovereign law which governs the entire universe. *And this absolute, sovereign law is Spinoza's substance, or what amounts to the same thing, Spinoza's God.*[1]

[1] Among historians of philosophy the conviction has become widespread that Spinoza's system and its point of departure—the doctrine of substance—is a critical continuation of Descartes's philosophy. Such an explanation of the origin of Spinoza's philosophy does not correspond to the facts. On this question I fully share the opinion of Höffding, who writes: 'He was never a Cartesian, although he learned much from Descartes' (as well as from Hebrew theology, scholastic philosophy, and the works of Giordano Bruno). He read, and used some ideas of, Bacon and Hobbes. (Höffding, *History of Modern Philosophy*, Russian edition, p. 64.) And on the following page, Höffding defines Spinoza's substance as 'the principle of conformity to law of everything that exists.' This definition, which is substantially correct, is reached by Höffding through a series of arguments which is not entirely clear and which somewhat obscures the objective character of conformity to law in Spinoza's system.

That this is actually the case may be seen from the whole structure of Spinoza's system, as well as from individual passages in the *Ethics*. But, in an article whose limits are necessarily narrow in relation to its subject-matter, it is impossible to go into all the details of the argument. (A detailed examination of this problem, as was pointed out above, would require a comprehensive work.) Therefore I shall confine myself to quoting one passage from the *Ethics* which bears directly on the conclusion we have reached. In the scholium to the well-known seventh proposition of Part II we read:

'Substance thinking and substance extended[1] are one and the same substance, comprehended now through one attribute, now through the other. So also, a mode of extension and the idea of that mode are one and the same thing, though expressed in two ways.... For instance, a circle existing in nature, and the idea of a circle existing, which is also in God, are one and the same thing displayed through different attributes. Thus, whether we conceive nature under the attribute of extension, or under the attribute of thought, or under any other attribute, we shall find the same order, or one and the same chain of causes—that is, the same things following in either case. I said that God is the cause of an idea—for instance, of the idea of a circle—in so far as he is a thinking thing, and of a circle, in so far as he is an extended thing, simply because the formal being of the idea of a circle can only be perceived through another mode of thought as its proximate cause, and that again through another, and so on to infinity; so that, so long as we consider things as modes of thought, we must explain the order of the whole of nature, or the whole chain of causes, through the attribute of thought only. And, in so far as we consider things as modes of extension, we must explain the order of the whole of nature through the attribute of extension only, and so on, in the case of other attributes. Wherefore *God is really the cause of things* as they are in themselves inasmuch as he consists of infinite attributes.'[2]

We thus see that the two known attributes which Spinoza took from empirical reality—extension and thought—as well as the unknown attributes which he assumed, display the same connection and the same order. *Conformity to law* is the principle common to the unknown as well as the known attributes.

Imbued to the depths of his being with a deeply-rooted religious

---

[1] 'Substance' is used here instead of the term 'attribute.'
[2] *Ethics*, II, 7, scholium. [The italics are Akselrod's.]

feeling, Spinoza transferred this religious feeling to the supreme sovereign law of the universal order. Directing both an open and a veiled polemic against transcendental teleology and theology, our philosopher set up in opposition to the religious, anthropomorphic world-view his own world-view, which was permeated through and through with reverence for the infinite strength and power of the universal order. The God of theology is only an aggregate of contradictory, mutually exclusive human qualities, the more contradictory in that each of them is raised to an absolute degree. Such a God is a self-contradictory and absurd being; even if it actually existed it would not command the least respect of any thoughtful man. However, true religious feeling and genuine reverence are evoked by the universal bond of steel, the unconditional necessity and inexorable order which rules over all things and in all things, permeating the entire universe and all phenomena without exception. There lies strength, majesty, and infinite power. There is the true God of Spinoza.

Spinoza's philosophy was interpreted in this way by his great follower, the poet Goethe. Faust, in the dialogue with Gretchen—where he expounds Goethe's own philosophy—characterizes Spinoza's pantheism in poetic form. To Gretchen's question of whether he believes in God Faust answers:

> Mein Liebchen, wer darf sagen,
> Ich glaub' an Gott?
> Magst Priester oder Weise fragen,
> Und ihre Antwort scheint nur Spott
> Ueber den Frager zu sein.[1]

Here Spinoza's critique of theology and idealistic metaphysics is clearly in evidence. But what is God? He is:

---

[1] Dear, who can say
'I do believe'? Ask a philosopher,
Question a priest, and you will find that all
Their answers are but throwing words away,
And ring like mockery to the questioner's ear.
(*Trans.* G. M. Cookson.)

Der Allumfasser,
Der Allerhalter,
Fasst und erhält er nicht
Dich, mich, sich selbst?
Wölbt sich der Himmel nicht dadroben?
Liegt die Erde nicht hierunten fest?
Und steigen freundlich blickend
Ewige Sterne nicht herauf?
Schau' ich nicht Aug' in Auge dir,
Und drängt nicht alles
Nach Haupt und Herzen dir
Und webt in ewigem Geheimniss
Unsichtbar sichtbar neben dir?
Erfüll' davon dein Herz, so gross es ist,
Und wenn du ganz in dem Gefühle selig bist,
Nenn' es dann wie du willst,
Nenn's Glück! Herz! Liebe! Gott![1]

And Faust concludes:

Ich habe keinen Namen dafür![2]

The supreme principle for which Goethe has no name is here defined as the eternal order of nature, in accordance with which all of its parts and manifestations have their place and co-exist in

---

[1] The All-Enfolder,
The All-Upholder,
Does not He fold, uphold
Himself,—you,—me?
Is not the dome of heaven there?
Is not the stable earth beneath?
Do not the everlasting stars uprise
With lovingkindness in their eyes?
Do I not look in yours?
Do you not feel the sacred Whole
Throb through your soul?
Does it not weave its mystery,
Visibly, invisibly
About you everlastingly?
Open your heart until
That vastness fill
Your breast; then call it what you will,
Joy, Love, Felicity, God.
(*Trans.* G. M. Cookson.)

[2] There is no name that I dare give.
(*Trans.* G. M. Cookson.)

SPINOZA AND MATERIALISM 75

mutual harmony. The subjective aspect—the mutual love of Faust and Gretchen—is here a manifestation of this same objective universal order. Just as the heavens, the earth, and the stars exist in a rigorously defined relationship, so are the lovers' glances and the emotion that engulfs them permeated with this same order.

Goethe was more cautious than Spinoza: he did not venture to call this universal order 'God.' As a great scientist, an objective investigator, Goethe was captivated by Spinoza's calm, objective method of explaining nature. But as a poet and an artist, he perceived the eternal cosmic order æsthetically, artistically. Spinoza's religiously contemplative feeling assumes in Goethe the form of æsthetically contemplative feeling.

III

Let us return to Spinoza. Does this mean that in Spinoza's mind God still existed, that God was reflected in his system as a whole? —No, not the slightest trace of the God of theology remained in the doctrine of our thinker. That fantastic creature was demolished at its very foundation. *Causa sui* was put in the place of an act of creation. Spinoza was a *deeply convinced atheist*, but, because of the deeply-rooted religious temper of mind which remained from his earlier reverence and worship of God as creator, he *transferred this feeling of religious worship to the universal order. An isolation and separation of the universal order, that is, of the conformity to law of the universe, from the universe itself was the result of this religious reverence.* Spinoza's religious feeling hypostatized conformity to law—which by its very nature cannot be separated from the universe—into an independent entity. *It thus created from an anti-religious beginning an abstract entity, dyed with the hues of religion.* Consequently, Feuerbach was perfectly right when he said that in Spinoza we have a 'negation of theology, but a negation which still professes a theological standpoint.'

This 'theological standpoint,' which was a legacy from the religious past, this religious feeling which led to the separation of nature's conformity to law from nature itself, had a serious and decisive effect on the fundamental premises of his system. This fateful separation, which overflowed into a hypostatization and conversion of conformity to law into substance or 'God,' *separated matter and thought, turning them into independent and isolated attributes and thus depriving them of their vital internal causal connection.*[1] Therefore, in an

[1] Although the attributes—matter and thought—represent two aspects of a single substance, they nevertheless remain mutually independent, since 'body

ontological sense, and also, inevitably, in an epistemological sense as well, the basic assumptions of Spinoza's doctrine involve a static parallelism from which there is no escape.

Yet, despite the static character of his basic ontological assumptions, Spinoza's complete and decisive break with theology, with God as creator, and with extra-empirical teleology, exercised an incomparably greater influence on the course of thought of his system as a whole. As a result of his consistent critical rejection of extra-empirical teleology and his no less consistent establishing of mechanical conformity to law, Spinoza's system is thoroughly permeated with *genuine materialism*. His theory of knowledge is rigorously materialistic in those points where he proceeds from mechanistic principles. The whole basis of his theory of the origin of morality, toward which the majority of idealistic thinkers take a supercilious attitude—contemptuously calling it the 'physics of morals'—is rigorously materialistic to an even greater extent.

The famous seventh proposition of Part II of the *Ethics*, referred to above—'The order and connection of ideas is the same as the order and connection of things'—is developed in this very important section of the *Ethics* in a purely materialistic sense. The parallelism which is implied in this proposition gradually evaporates to the degree that the necessary dependence of mind and body, indicated by mechanistic principles, is developed. The body assumes a place of primary importance, that of the mind being secondary; the mind is wholly conditioned by the body.

Proposition 13 of Part II reads as follows: 'The object of the idea constituting the human mind is the body, in other words a certain mode of extension which actually exists, and nothing else.' And further on, in the scholium to this proposition, Spinoza asserts decisively that 'no one will be able to understand adequately or distinctly the union between mind and body, unless he first has adequate knowledge of the nature of our body.' It is quite evident that Spinoza abandons in essence the viewpoint of parallelism, taking his stand unambiguously on materialistic ground. For the unity of mind and body is known clearly only when as a preliminary, or as Spinoza says 'first' [*prius*], the body is 'adequately' known. But why, one might ask, should the body be known 'first'? For, from the point of view of parallelism, the unity of mind and body can be known only on the condition of the *simultaneous givenness* of the

cannot determine mind to think, neither can mind determine body to motion or rest or any state different from these, if such there be.' (*Ethics*, III, Prop. 2.)

processes of mind and body. (Here I leave aside the complex problem of whether, in general, simultaneous knowledge of the connection and order of two attributes is possible, that is, whether parallelism as such is possible. In my opinion, parallelism generally does not stand up under criticism, since by its essence it eliminates time. But this is in passing only.) It is perfectly evident that Spinoza's requirement of *preliminary* knowledge of the body is here completely materialistic, since knowledge of the indicated unity is dependent on *preliminary, adequate* knowledge of the body. In the first place, the process of knowing does not proceed *simultaneously*; in the second place, *knowledge of the body* is primary. Here is another striking passage with the same materialistic significance:

'In proportion as any given body is more fitted than others for doing many actions or receiving many impressions at once, so also is the mind more fitted than others for forming many simultaneous perceptions; and the more the actions of one body depend on itself alone, and the fewer other bodies concur with it in action, the more fitted is the mind for distinct comprehension.'[1]

The same thing is said in Proposition 14 of Part II: 'The human mind is capable of perceiving a great number of things, and is so in proportion as its body is capable of receiving a great number of impressions.' These lines need, I think, no further explanation. Their materialistic content is evident. However, it will do no harm to emphasize once more that the passages adduced are not accidental and that in all parts of the *Ethics* where theory of knowledge, psychology, and the origin of morality are under consideration, i.e. in its principal parts, parallelism evaporates and the materialistic principle emerges in clear predominance. Consequently, Feuerbach was right once more when, after defining Spinoza's philosophy as 'theological materialism,' he exclaimed: 'Away with this contradiction! Not *Deus sive natura*,[2] but *aut Deus aut natura*.[3] That is where the truth lies.'

IV

A century before Feuerbach, La Mettrie, the great and daring founder of eighteenth-century materialism, expressed his attitude

[1] *Ibid.*, II, 13, scholium.
[2] 'God or nature' (the identification of God and Nature).
[3] 'Either God or nature.'

toward Spinoza briefly but very clearly. This attitude is marked by great respect and sincere gratitude, but at the same time it is thoroughly critical. In the first place, La Mettrie criticizes Spinoza's view of thought as an attribute of the universe.

'It has been proven,' says La Mettrie, '(1) that thought is only an accidental modification of our sensitive principle and that consequently it is not a thinking aspect of the universe (*partie pensante du monde*); (2) that external things are not represented in the mind, but only certain of their properties, distinct from the things themselves, wholly relative and arbitrary; and that, finally, the greatest part of our sensations or of our ideas depend on our organs to such a degree that they change at once when the latter do.'[1]

Thus it is clear that from La Mettrie's point of view thought is a product of the interaction of man and nature and, consequently, is conditioned to a certain extent by the human organism. This means, further, that thought arises at a definite stage of biological development and represents, in Engels' words, the highest product of organized matter. It is clear, therefore, that from La Mettrie's point of view, as from that of materialism generally, thought is not an eternal and immutable attribute of the universe.

Furthermore, although La Mettrie considers Spinoza an *atheist* in the full sense of the word, he nevertheless compares his atheism to the labyrinth of Dædalus, 'so many are its tortuous paths and turns.' Concerning Spinoza's ontology, La Mettrie notes its similarity to the doctrines of the Eleatics and points out the metaphysical immobility of his system. But, after making all of these critical comments, La Mettrie strongly emphasizes that 'according to Spinoza, man is a veritable automaton—a machine subject to the strictest necessity, drawn by impetuous fatalism, as a ship is drawn by a current of water.'[2] And the famous materialist concludes his characterization by agreeing completely with Spinoza on what is for him the *most important* point: 'The author of the work *Man a Machine*,' says La Mettrie, 'wrote his book as though on purpose to defend this melancholy truth.'[3]

We see thus that in the first place La Mettrie, while disagreeing with one of Spinoza's basic propositions—that thought is an attribute of the universe—that is, while rejecting parallelism, at the same time

[1] La Mettrie, *Histoire naturelle de l'âme*, The Hague, 1745, p. 253.
[2] *Ibid.*, p. 250.
[3] *Œuvres philosophiques de la Mettrie*, Berlin-Paris, 1796, Vol. I, pp. 261–2.

finds Spinoza's doctrine of man consistently materialistic, for he identifies Spinoza's point of view on this subject with his own materialistic point of view. In the second place, La Mettrie lays chief emphasis on Spinoza's determinism—a doctrine which found precise expression in the title of his best known work (*Man a Machine*). It is also clear that La Mettrie was right in regarding determinism as one of the principal foundations of materialism.

Spinoza exercised a very important and decisive influence on Holbach's *System of Nature*. This remarkable and noble book, permeated through and through with a deep love of mankind—despite the absurd charges of immorality which have been levelled against it by idealistic historians—is the true manifesto of the revolutionary bourgeoisie. Its content is directed mainly against the ruling clergy and all forms of religious thinking, which Holbach regarded as the ideology of every kind of oppressor. The *System of Nature* has a social character; it carries on an energetic revolutionary struggle against the mythical heaven of religion and its fantastic inhabitants, in the name of the welfare, happiness, and enlightenment of mankind. Unlike Spinoza, Holbach was a rigorously consistent materialist. *Substance is matter and thought is a property of matter.* But leaving aside this difference, we see clearly his kinship to Spinoza *in the whole method of criticism of teleology and in the consistent defence of the law of mechanical causality*. Transcendental teleology, and the idea of God and creation associated with it, are the chief object of Holbach's attack and of the careful and subtle analysis which distinguishes the *System of Nature*. This critical analysis is carried out, as in the case of Spinoza, on the basis of a rigorously consistent and sustained determinism. The chief conclusions of this undertaking are gathered together in a truly remarkable passage, which deserves to be quoted in its entirety:

'From what has been said, it may be concluded that the names by which men have designated the concealed causes acting in nature, and their various effects, are never more than necessity considered under different points of view. We have found that *order* is a necessary sequence of causes and effects of which we see, or think we see, the entire connection and course, and which pleases us when it is conformable to our existence. We have seen in like manner that what we call *confusion* is a sequence of necessary causes and effects which we consider unfavourable to ourselves or irrelevant to our existence. *Intelligence* is the name given to the necessary cause that brings about in a necessary fashion the sequence of events which we designate by the word *order*. *Divinity* is the name given to the necessary and invisible cause which sets in motion a nature wherein everything acts according to immutable and necessary laws. *Destiny* or *fate* is the name given to the necessary connection of the unknown causes and effects which we observe in the world. The word *chance* has been used to designate those effects which we are not able to foresee, or of whose necessary connection to their causes we are ignorant. Finally, *intellectual* and *moral faculties* are the names given to those actions and modifications necessary to an organized being which, it was supposed, is moved by an incomprehensible agent, distinguished from the body and of a nature totally different from it, designated by the word *mind* or *soul* [*âme*].'[1]

In this profound and lucid formulation Holbach sets forth nature's conformity to law and the various aspects and manifestations of it which *prevent man from understanding it*. This lack of understanding itself occurs in conformity to law and depends upon whether given events or laws do or do not correspond to man's inherent striving for self-preservation. From this point of view human errors conform to law as much as anything else. Nevertheless, they can and should be dispelled when man grasps the principle of conformity to law which embraces all events without exception, including man himself and his entire 'inner world.' According to both Holbach and Spinoza, the religious world-view, as well as various metaphysical systems, have cultivated an anthropomorphic view of the universe, which consists chiefly in man's ascribing to himself free will and free intelligence, that is, *failing to consider himself from the point of view of necessary conformity to law*. This false view of man and his allegedly free actions was transferred to the universe as a whole, which was then regarded as the result of the free acts of beings similar to man but more powerful. A clear and distinct understanding of this error will remove the blindfold from man's eyes, and he will understand at last the laws of the world about him, the laws of his own being, and their reciprocal, indissoluble connection.

La Mettrie as a physician and naturalist strove chiefly to pave the way for biology, psychology, and medicine, at the same time understanding very well that these branches of knowledge could be set on the right scientific path only within a general materialistic world-view. But Holbach, being a follower of La Mettrie, broadened his task and attempted to create a general materialistic ideology

---

[1] Holbach, *Système de la Nature*, Paris, 1821, pp. 433-4.

which would embrace all forms of life. As a result, Spinoza's system was reflected with more variety and completeness in the *System of Nature* than in the works of La Mettrie.

Holbach, who reflected the rationalism and revolutionary tendencies of his age, was convinced that a correct understanding of the world's conformity to law in general, and of the laws of human nature in particular, must lead to a just social order and to human happiness. A hundred years before, Spinoza had reached these same conclusions from his own consistent determinism. For example, in the conclusion of Part II of the *Ethics*, we read:

'This doctrine raises social life, inasmuch as it teaches us to hate no man, neither to despise, to deride, to envy, nor to be angry with any. Further, as it tells us that each should be content with his own, and helpful to his neighbour, not from any womanish pity, favour, or superstition, but solely by the guidance of reason, according as the time and occasion demand, as I will show in Part III. Lastly, this doctrine confers no small advantage on the commonwealth; for it teaches us how citizens should be governed and led, not so as to become slaves, but so that they may freely do whatsoever things are best.'

In this summary of his position Spinoza, like his follower Holbach, directs his polemic against the representatives of theology and idealistic metaphysics who, from Plato on, have never ceased to criticize materialism for its alleged elimination of ethical ideals which, in their opinion, flow from the recognition of free moral will and transcendental moral values. From the point of view of materialism and objective conformity to law, they affirm, it is impossible to establish a distinction between virtue and vice, between crime and heroic action, in short, between good and evil. In a word, morality is impossible without the recognition of free moral will and, by the same token, social life is likewise impossible. Spinoza turns these propositions upside down. Recognizing, as the idealists do, the fact of the existence of ideals, the distinction between good and evil, and the absolute social function of ideals and moral values, he regards these necessary categories as a result of that same conformity to law. Conversely, Spinoza's objective view of man and of human conduct leads to a just and tolerant appraisal of all human actions; and from the whole doctrine it follows that the improvement of society as well as of individual men can be brought about not through impotent moral indignation but through active measures, through action and counteraction based on a knowledge of the causes of anti-moral and anti-social conduct.

These propositions, which follow from the principle of determinism and apply to social life as a whole, passed from Spinoza to the French materialists. The central revolutionary idea of the French materialists—which found its most radical social expression in Helvetius—the idea which was noted, emphasized, and elaborated by Marx, that man is the product of circumstances and that consequently the modification and improvement of man's moral nature depends on the modification of his circumstances, represents on the one hand the result of the critique of innate ideas carried out by Locke and on the other a further development of Spinoza's consistent determinism.

But to avoid distortion it should be mentioned that in the above-cited passages from the *Ethics,* which contain a correct appraisal of determinism as a truly social and humane principle, we note at the same time a passive, fatalistic tendency, expressed in the very important comment that determinism 'tells us that each should be content with his own.' In other words, an adequate understanding of the causal necessity of events should suppress the tendency to alter one's position. The resulting mental tranquillity, attained through an adequate knowledge of necessity, is inner freedom. This view of the relation of freedom to necessity is expressed with even greater definiteness in Proposition 6, Part V, of the *Ethics,* where we read: 'The mind has greater power over the emotions and is less subject thereto, in so far as it understands all things as necessary.' And then the explanation follows:

'The more this knowledge that things are necessary is applied to particular things which we conceive more distinctly and vividly, the greater is the power of the mind over the emotions, as experience also testifies. For we see that the pain arising from the loss of any good is mitigated as soon as the man who has lost it perceives that it could not by any means have been preserved. So also we see that no one pities an infant because it cannot speak, walk, or reason, or lastly, because it passes so many years, as it were, in unconsciousness. Whereas, if most people were born full-grown and only one here and there as an infant, everyone would pity the infants, because infancy would not then be looked on as a state natural and necessary, but as a fault or delinquency in nature; and we may note several other instances of the same sort.'

SPINOZA AND MATERIALISM

Spinoza attempts to prove by these extremely acute examples that freedom is conditioned by the complete and absolute recognition of necessity. In general this thesis is not open to question. But in Spinoza it assumes a fatalistic colouring. Concentrating most of his attention on inner freedom, Spinoza came to the conclusion that the recognition of absolute conformity to law should lead to complete mental tranquillity, even in cases of the most terrible blows, whether of a personal or social character. From his point of view, a knowledge of the causes of suffering eliminates suffering and leads to happiness. Thus, in the scholium to Proposition 18, Part V, of the *Ethics*, we read:

'It may be objected that, as we understand God as the cause of all things, we by that very fact regard God as the cause of pain. But I make answer that, in so far as we understand the causes of pain, it to that extent ceases to be a passive condition, that is, it ceases to be pain; therefore, in so far as we understand God to be the cause of pain, we to that extent feel pleasure.'

The knowledge of the causes of suffering, according to Spinoza, is an active principle and as an active principle it: (1) eliminates passivity, which is caused by imaginative, i.e. confused and inadequate, knowledge; and (2) as true knowledge, it affords pleasure, since the activity of infinite intellect is manifested in it. Freedom and happiness are thus attained through the adequate comprehension of necessity and conscious subordination to it. Confirmation of this important idea is supposed to be provided by the facts adduced, such as, for example, our complete unconcern for the fact that infants first appear in the world in a helpless condition.

From the premises, chains of reasoning, and examples which Spinoza offers, it follows with full logical necessity that for our freedom, happiness, and mental tranquillity we should assume an attitude of stoic indifference toward all the negative events of our life, since they are strictly conditioned by causality and from this standpoint are in no way different from the helplessness of infants. Thus the question arises: Is not determinism identical with fatalism? Are not the indeterminists right in affirming that the doctrine of determinism undermines will and activity? And if this is not true, if the indeterminists are mistaken, then in what does Spinoza's error lie?—Spinoza's error consists principally in his conceiving human freedom in the sense of the Stoic doctrine of 'inner freedom.' The whole struggle for the attainment of freedom and happiness is carried on exclusively within the subject. Activity, as opposed to the principle of passivity, is declared to be a manifestation of infinite intellect, revealing itself in the adequate knowledge of necessity and finding tranquillity in this knowledge. This inner mental activity leads in the final analysis to a passive contemplation of the universe.

The question of the relation of freedom and necessity is quite different in dialectical materialism, according to which the relation of freedom to necessity consists in the knowledge of necessity, i.e. the knowledge of the laws of nature and of history, and the influencing of nature and history on the basis of this knowledge. The recognition and knowledge of these laws, that is, the *realization of necessity*, guarantees the positive results of human action and influence and at the same time strengthens and reinforces the striving and active will. The attainment of the goal—the acquisition and increase of power over the external world, i.e. over the forces of nature and over social relations—is itself freedom. *Spinoza's freedom leads in the final analysis to the dominion of the intellect over the emotions, over what is called man's sensuous world; freedom according to dialectical materialism consists in the achieved results of creative activity, changing and subjugating the environment, since the environment determines the inner life and freedom of the individual.* In the first case, the knowledge of necessity leads the individual to passive inner contemplation; in the second, the knowledge of necessity is the prerequisite for activity directed toward the changing of the external world, which is the determinant of individual freedom.

Concentrating all of his philosophical attention on inner 'stoical freedom,' identified with the knowledge of universal necessity, Spinoza came naturally to the culminating point of his system—the intellectual love of God. True—that is, adequate—knowledge, freedom, and supreme happiness coincide. The ultimate attainment of this ideal leads in the final analysis to the complete dissolution of individuality. Beginning with freedom and the perfection of individuality, Spinoza ends by seeking the dissolution and annihilation of the latter in Deity.

Against this final conclusion of Spinoza's system, Schelling raised an acute and forceful objection:

'No visionary could ever have taken pleasure in the thought of being swallowed up in the abyss of Deity if he had not in every case replaced Deity by his own ego. No mystic could ever have conceived of himself as annihilated if he had not always conceived his own ego as the substratum of this annihilation. The necessity of continuing to conceive *oneself* everywhere, which came to the aid of all the visionaries and mystics, came to Spinoza's aid also. While he contemplated himself as *submerged* in the absolute object, he yet contemplated *himself*; he could not conceive himself as *annihilated* without at the same time conceiving himself as existing.'[1]

In this penetrating passage Schelling shows with profundity, acuteness, and classic simplicity that the ideal of mysticism—the absolute overcoming of the concrete personality—is unattainable, and that even if the mystic could attain it he would not find in it the freedom or the happiness which he seeks. For surely complete absorption in the 'abyss of Deity' is slavery.

The final ethical result of the system as a whole is strictly conditioned by its point of departure, i.e. the identification of Deity with universal conformity to law. Religious feeling, reverence, and worship were transferred to this universal conformity to law. From this it followed that instead of knowing the laws of nature in order to subject nature to man, and thus attain all possible freedom, Spinoza would have us know the laws of nature in order to attain a conscious, tranquil, and reconciled subjection to them. The intervention of religious feeling led inevitably to a religious, mystical culmination; Spinoza's determinism in this very important problem of the relation of freedom to necessity assumed the fatalistic character natural to religious thinking.

Yet even here we must make a reservation, namely, that the consistent and logical culmination of the *Ethics* in a spirit of passive stoicism and rationalistic mysticism is significant only in relation to the wise man. Only exceptional natures, individuals endowed with inner intellectual strength, are able to rise to the highest level of adequate knowledge and attain to true freedom and happiness. The attainment of this height is as 'difficult' as it is 'rare,' runs the conclusion of the *Ethics*. The ordinary morality of the majority of mankind has its origin in egoism and is entirely conditioned by material, earthly interests. And our philosopher, remaining true to his objective scientific method of investigation, to determinism, inspects and investigates the fundamental human emotions disinterestedly and dispassionately, exactly as though they were geometrical figures. Involvement, in the analysis of human mores,

[1] Schelling, 'Philosophische Briefe über Dogmatismus und Kriticismus,' Letter VIII, *Sämmtliche Werke*, Stuttgart, 1856, I, pp. 319-20.

indignation and sentimental moralizing about a given form of human conduct, are subjected to quiet yet biting irony. The subjective method or, what amounts to the same thing, the method of evaluation, is capable only of obscuring the true causes of moral conduct and thus of hiding from us the nature of events which are of great importance to us. Every Marxist knows that this scientific, objective method permeates the whole world-view of Marx and Engels, beginning with their general philosophical assumptions and ending with their socio-political conclusions and principles of tactics in the realm of political activity.

V

We have seen how its religious foundation gave Spinoza's determinism a fatalistic colouring and led in the final analysis to the mystical culmination of his system. But, on the other hand, its rigorously developed determinism made the system materialistic in many of its most important points. Certain important elements of materialism have been indicated above. It will not be superfluous at this point to turn our attention to an important element of Spinoza's materialistic thinking—to his theory of the state.

Spinoza's *Political Treatise* is on the whole a rationalistic work. Like all of his contemporaries who wrote about the state, he was unfamiliar with the idea of the development of societies and governments. He was not aware of the objective material conditions which lie at the basis of the social group. The class structure, the content of class contradictions, and the class struggle remained entirely hidden from his view. For this reason, Spinoza's picture of the state did not embrace all the varieties of existing correlations of power. For him the point of departure is not concrete social man but the abstract metaphysical 'nature of man,' not social classes, but the individual. As a result, his construction is on the whole abstract and rationalistically oversimplified. Yet, despite his general rationalistic approach, Spinoza established the legislative system of his state on a foundation of *material interest*. Thus, for example, whenever it is a question of the creation of some important and responsible governmental institution, our philosopher recommends placing at its base the *economic* interests of its members. In the selection of the supreme council of the state it is necessary, according to Spinoza, to be guided by the following considerations:

'As human nature is so constituted that everyone seeks with the utmost passion his own advantage, and judges those laws to be most equitable which he thinks necessary to preserve and increase his substance, and defends another's cause so far only as he thinks he is thereby establishing his own, it follows hence that the counsellors chosen must be such that their private affairs and their own interests depend on the general welfare and peace of all.'[1]

And here is another characteristic passage in which Spinoza sets forth his conception of the way in which it is possible to avoid unnecessary wars (Spinoza did not, however, reject war in principle):

'The emoluments of the senators should be of such a kind that their profit is greater from peace than from war. And therefore let there be awarded to them a hundredth or a fiftieth part of the merchandise exported abroad from the dominion or imported into it from abroad. For we cannot doubt that by this means they will, as far as they can, preserve peace and never desire war.'[2]

The whole *Political Treatise* is permeated with this materialistic thought, and many similar passages could be adduced. But those that have been cited are, I think, sufficient. From these passages it is clearly evident that Spinoza sees the guarantee of just actions in affairs of state not in the moral qualities of the statesman, but in his property interests, for 'everyone ... judges those laws to be most equitable which he thinks necessary to preserve and increase his substance.' If we translate this into Marxist language, it would state that the legal consciousness of the individual is conditioned by his property interests. This same thought is also developed in the second passage, where the important problem of maintaining peace is under discussion: war may be prevented not by the preaching of brotherly love, but by having the representatives of the state materially interested in the preservation of peace. As has been mentioned, Spinoza's materialism takes a rationalistic turn at this point, as a result of his general individualistic rather than class point of view; but in principle the direction of his thought remains materialistic. And for this reason we may say without exaggeration that wherever Spinoza is an *investigator* he stands on firm materialistic ground, that is, he persistently seeks the material basis of events and he finds it, *to the extent permitted by the level of knowledge of his time.* Our philosopher follows this method with complete awareness of its correctness.

[1] *Political Treatise*, VII, 4.   [2] *Ibid.*, VIII, 31.

Because of his general deterministic view, matter—in the socio-historical sense as well as in the cosmic sense—does not represent to him something sinful, but is essentially an attribute which has equal status with thought. Hence his calm, objective, truly scientific attitude toward all the manifestations of reality, regardless of which of the attributes they are modes of. And hence his famous rule: not to bewail, not to deride, but to understand.

It will not be superfluous in this connection to recall the very eloquent lines—forgotten by the idealistic historians for quite understandable reasons—in which our philosopher expresses with great clarity his attitude toward both materialism and idealism. In a letter to Boxel, Spinoza wrote:

'The authority of Plato, Aristotle, and Socrates does not carry much weight with me. I should have been astonished if you had brought forward [to prove the existence of ghosts, which was the subject of Boxel's letter—L. A.] Epicurus, Democritus, Lucretius, or any of the atomists or upholders of the atomic theory. It is no wonder that persons who have invented occult qualities, intentional species, substantial forms, and a thousand other trifles, should have also devised spectres and ghosts, and given credence to old wives' tales, in order to take away the reputation of Democritus, whom they were so jealous of that they burned all the books which he had published amid so much eulogy. If you are inclined to believe such witnesses, what reason have you for denying the miracles of the Blessed Virgin and all the Saints? These have been described by so many famous philosophers, theologians, and historians that I could produce at least a hundred such authorities for every one of the former.'[1]

The appraisal here given of the founders of idealism and materialism does not require extensive commentary. The essence of classical idealism, the transcendental ideas of Plato and the transcendental forms of Aristotle, are scornfully likened to old wives' tales. The philosophical doctrines of the creator of idealism are compared to belief in 'the miracles of the Blessed Virgin and all the Saints.' On the other hand, our thinker regards the founders of materialism—Democritus, Epicurus, and Lucretius—as his authorities. It is from them that Spinoza traces his philosophical lineage.

The unity of the universe is the central doctrine of Spinoza's system. The basic propositions which follow from this universal

[1] Spinoza, Letter LX (LVI) to Hugo Boxel.

principle are, in essence: (1) the rejection of the act of creation, of creator, and of transcendental teleology; (2) the recognition of investigation of mechanical causality as the only and universal method. These basic propositions, which permeate Spinoza's whole system, testify to its kinship to the old materialism as well as to the new—to dialectical materialism.

A. M. Deborin

SPINOZA'S WORLD-VIEW[1]

THE 21st of February of this year [1927] was the two hundred and fiftieth anniversary of the death of Benedict Spinoza. On that day a solemn celebration in Spinoza's memory was held under the auspices of the Spinoza Society (*Societas Spinozana*) in The Hague—the city where Spinoza spent the last years of his life and where his ashes rest. At this grand meeting there were in attendance, besides official representatives of the universities and of science, an official representative of the League of Nations, who demonstrated in his speech that if Spinoza were alive today he would be an ardent admirer of the League of Nations, since it strives for the realization of universal peace. A representative of the church—no celebration, as is well known, can get along there without a representative of the church—for his part, demonstrated that Spinoza's teaching does not in the least contradict the Christian religion.

There were other speeches as well, but I shall not dwell on them. At all events, everyone was agreed that Spinoza was a great idealist, pantheist, and mystic, the founder of a new religion, etc. But at The Hague no voice was raised to cry out loudly to all these fine gentlemen: 'You are impudent liars.'

I

We have gathered within the walls of the Communist Academy and are devoting this evening to Spinoza's memory not from the considerations which guided the organizers of the Hague celebration, but from quite different considerations; for us Spinoza is *essentially a great atheist and materialist*. In this appraisal of Spinoza I am in com-

[1] A translation of 'Mirovozzreniye Spinozy,' *Vestnik kommunisticheskoi akademi*, Bk. 20 (1927), pp. 5–29.

plete agreement with Plekhanov. In all of Plekhanov's works, as you know, the fundamental thought is emphasized that Marxism, considered as a world-view, is nothing other than a 'variety of Spinozism.' But I shall set this question aside for the moment, in order to cite a passage from Plekhanov's preface to my *Introduction to Philosophy* (the preface was written in 1914) in which he sharply criticizes the historians of philosophy who have numbered Spinoza among the idealists.

'With the present universal prevalence of idealism,' he says, 'it is quite natural that the history of philosophy should now be interpreted from the idealistic point of view. As a consequence, Spinoza has long since been numbered among the idealists. Hence, certain readers will probably be very much surprised to learn that I understand Spinoza in the materialistic sense; yet this is the only correct understanding of Spinozism.

'As early as 1843 Feuerbach asserted his fundamental conviction that the teaching of Spinoza was "an expression of the materialistic conceptions of the modern age." Of course, even Spinoza did not escape the influence of his time. His materialism, as Feuerbach remarked, was clothed in a *theological costume*, but the important thing was that, in any case, he eliminated the dualism of mind and nature. Nature in Spinoza is called God, but *extension* is one of the attributes of this God. And this constitutes the radical difference between Spinozism and idealism.'[1]

With such a universal prevalence of idealism it is not surprising that Spinoza has long since been enlisted in the camp of the idealists. Unfortunately, there are even some Marxists who defend the tradition of the historians of philosophy, despite the fact that Feuerbach, to some extent Engels, and more recently Plekhanov have done a great deal in explaining Spinoza's materialistic views. We still have to struggle against this idealistic tradition, to prove to comrades from our own midst that Spinoza is not to be ranked among the idealists. In the last few years, two 'fronts' have been formed in connection with the treatment of Hegelian dialectics and Spinoza's world-conception: the Hegelian front and the Spinozistic front. The disagreements and disputes which are going on in our own midst focus on two basic points: the disputes about Hegel touch the foundations of our *method*; the differences of opinion with regard to Spinoza

[1] Deborin, *Vvedeniye v filosofiyu* (*Introduction to Philosophy*), G. V. Plekhanov's preface, pp. 34–5.

concern our *world-view* and involve the conception of materialism itself. But, since method and world-view are not separate from one another, the disputes and disagreements in the first area—those concerning method—are indissolubly connected with the disputes in the second area—those concerning world-view. I shall not dwell further on this point; I wished merely to indicate the extent to which these two fronts are connected.

Let us now proceed to a *general* characterization of Spinoza's world-view as a whole, to an examination of what Spinoza brought into philosophy, science, and the scientific view of the world that was new, and how Spinozism as a new, scientific, philosophical world-view differs from the world-view with which Spinoza had to contend.

The first proposition which links Spinoza to the materialists of our time, that is, to the Marxists, is his recognition of the existence of the objective world, the avowal of a principle for the enunciation of which Spinoza was subsequently branded a 'dogmatist' by the partisans of Kantian 'critical philosophy.' This appraisal of Spinoza by the critical philosophers is extremely important, for by 'dogmatism' such writers often mean materialism. According to Fichte, only two consistent and rigorously sustained philosophical systems are possible: dogmatism and critical philosophy, meaning by dogmatism Spinozism or materialism. By dogmatism is meant the 'uncritical' admission of the possibility of adequate knowledge of the world. A critical investigation of our cognitive faculties, it is held, leads to the establishing of the truth that the external world is unknowable. In this connection it should be pointed out that Spinoza devotes a good deal of space to the investigation of our cognitive faculties, but the conclusion which he reaches is the exact opposite of the conclusion reached by the critical philosophers. As is well known, empiriocriticism, Machism, empiriomonism, and other varieties of positivism also deny the external world. But the denial of the external world leads inevitably to idealism. In Spinoza we find a brief but extraordinarily apt critique of the point of view which assumes that sensations are all that exist and that we can know only our own sensations. Here is what Spinoza writes in this connection:

'They assert that the mind can be conscious of and perceive in a variety of ways, not itself nor things which exist, but only things which are neither in itself nor anywhere else, in other words, that the mind can, by its unaided power, create sensations or ideas unconnected with things. In fact, they regard the mind as a sort of god.'[1]

Thus those who deny that the mind feels and knows external things, who assert that the mind by its own unaided strength creates sensations and ideas, turn the mind into a god, i.e. into a substance which creates the whole world out of itself. This means that the mind, from their point of view, is entirely independent of the external world, being self-caused and creating the world of things. But such a point of view is entirely unacceptable to Spinoza, who considers that 'it is before all things necessary for us to deduce all our ideas from physical things.'[2]

Another characteristic feature of Spinoza's over-all world-view is his denial of teleology and his assertion of strict determinism. In studying reality—whether natural or social—it is necessary to use the *category of causality* exclusively. With unsurpassed power of thought and rare sarcasm he ridicules those philosophers who see final causes everywhere. For these final causes are only human inventions, the product of ignorance, prejudice, and superstition. In attempting to prove that nature does everything for the use of men, these philosophers 'seem only to have demonstrated that nature, the gods, and men are all gone mad together.'[3] Since men find in themselves and in nature many means which assist them in their search for what is useful, says Spinoza, they come to look on all natural means as means for obtaining what is useful, and they explain everything by ends, seeing everywhere the will of God.

'For, by way of example, if a stone has fallen from some roof on somebody's head and killed him, they will demonstrate in this manner that the stone has fallen in order to kill the man. For if it did not fall for that purpose by the will of God, how could so many circumstances concur through chance (and a number often simultaneously do concur)? You will answer, perhaps, that the event happened because the wind blew and the man was passing that way. But, they will urge, why did the wind blow at that time, and why did the man pass that way precisely at the same moment? If you again reply that the wind rose then because the sea on the preceding day began to be stormy, the weather hitherto having been calm, and that the man had been invited by a friend, they will urge again—because

[1] *On the Improvement of the Understanding*, Elwes' translation, p. 19.
[2] *Ibid.*, p. 34.
[3] *Ethics*, I, Appendix.

there is no end of questioning—But why was the sea agitated? why was the man invited at that time? And so they will not cease from asking the causes of causes, until at last you fly to the will of God, the *asylum ignorantiæ*.'[1]

Thus Spinoza declares the will of God to be a refuge of ignorance. Our philosopher sees everywhere only *natural* events, which are subject to investigation and explanation by means of the universal law of necessity. In contrast to many contemporary philosophers and scientists, who consider it possible to study social processes, if not natural phenomena, from the point of view of morality, Spinoza extends the law of necessity to man and society. He denies completely the validity of applying ethical or teleological principles to reality. The study of reality leads to a discovery of the causal connections and objective laws which operate therein. Spinoza is much closer to Marxism in this respect than are many contemporary trends in philosophy.

Spinoza entered into history with the honorary title 'prince of atheists.' Actually, what we have already said adequately characterizes the world-view of our philosopher as purely materialistic and atheistic. But Spinoza considered it necessary to wage direct warfare on religious prejudices—the special type of ignorance which supports the power of the clergy and every kind of authority. Today we consider it especially important to emphasize our philosopher's historic contributions in this field, and the enormous cultural and educational role which was played by his *Theologico-Political Treatise*. Spinoza was the true leader of the whole period of Enlightenment which followed.

Spinoza's name is indissolubly linked and historically has always been associated with freethinking, for he was one of the first to raise the banner of revolt against religious superstition in defence of free scientific thought. He was the first to subject the Scriptures to *scientific* criticism, not being satisfied with a simple, bare rejection of religion. And all subsequent scientific biblical criticism takes Spinoza's *Theologico-Political Treatise* as its point of departure. It is impossible for us now to imagine the liberating influence of this work. As a matter of fact, the period of the Enlightenment dates from its publication. All the leading, progressive elements, all the philosophers of the Enlightenment in whatever country, drew from Spinoza's writings, directly or indirectly, irrefutable arguments for

[1] *Loc. cit.*

their struggle against religious prejudices. For this reason we should in justice regard Spinoza as the *father of freethinking*. Although it is not possible for me to analyse the *Theologico-Political Treatise* here, I consider it necessary to point out that we find the basic motifs of this treatise later in the French and German philosophers of the Enlightenment.

Religion, as Spinoza makes clear, has no *theoretical* significance; it has always been significant only for *practical* life, i.e. those in power have used it in order to keep the people in check. Superstition arises, is sustained and supported by *fear*. Hence religious prejudices are essentially the vestiges of an *ancient bondage*, maintained in our time. Since religious prejudices are connected with ancient bondage, there can be no place for these superstitions in a free state, and here at least freedom of judgment regarding these prejudices should prevail. Spinoza shares the opinion of Curtius that 'the mob has no ruler more potent than superstition'. (*History*, Bk. IV, ch. 10). By this he wishes to emphasize the connection of *politics* and *religion*—a proposition that received its further development in the French *philosophes* and materialists. Among the Turks, men's minds are weighed down by such a mass of prejudices, says Spinoza, that there is no room left for sound reason, not even for doubt. But what is said about the Turks applies to all other nations in which monarchical government prevails. Monarchical government, according to Spinoza, rests largely on religious superstitions. The French *philosophes*, we repeat, shared this view.

If, in despotic statecraft, the supreme and essential mystery be to hoodwink the subjects, and to mask the fear which keeps them down with the specious garb of religion, so that men may fight as bravely for slavery as for safety, and count it not shame but highest honour to risk their blood and their lives for the vainglory of a tyrant; yet in a free state no more mischievous expedient could be planned or attempted. Wholly repugnant to the general freedom are such devices as enthralling men's minds with prejudices, forcing their judgment, or employing any of the weapons of quasi-religious sedition.[1]

'Faith has become a mere compound of credulity and prejudices,' Spinoza says in another place, 'aye, prejudices, too, which degrade man from rational being to beast, which completely stifle the power of judgment between true and false, which seem, in fact, carefully fostered for the purpose of extinguishing the last spark of reason.'[2]

[1] *Theologico-Political Treatise*, Elwes' translation, p. 5.   [2] *Ibid.*, p. 7.

Perhaps no thinker of modern times has used such biting and blasphemous language as Spinoza here does. The social order, and especially the monarchical form of government, is based on fear, and the people's fear is supported and cultivated by religious superstitions and ignorance. These basic motifs, put forward by Spinoza in his critique of religious superstitions, were taken up by all the later philosophers of the Enlightenment and in particular by the French Encyclopedists and materialists of the eighteenth century.

In a *free* state *reason*, that is, free judgment, should prevail and hence religious prejudices, being survivals of a regime of slavery, are incompatible with the new form of social organization. Religion should not be looked upon as theoretical knowledge of the world; it demands of its adherents a definite form of *practical* conduct—obedience and piety, which are the result of certain historical and political conditions. The church should be subordinated to the state, that is, to the civil interests of the people. Science and the state are based on natural knowledge and natural law and have nothing in common with theology.

Proceeding from these considerations, Spinoza contends for the separation of philosophy, that is, natural knowledge, from religion. He demands the broadest freedom of philosophizing, freedom of thought and scientific knowledge. We are leaving aside the question of how far Spinoza's biblical criticism may be considered scientific from the point of view of contemporary scholarship. This is not essential to our purpose. We are concerned here with an *historical* appraisal of Spinoza's activity, and from this point of view the significance of the *Theologico-Political Treatise* is enormous. It was this book which served as a basis for the accusation of atheism levelled at Spinoza, and as the pretext for new persecutions. Spinoza's expulsion from the Jewish community has, as it were, a local, national significance; the second catastrophe in his personal life was connected with the publication of the *Theologico-Political Treatise*. Spinoza now became a target of attack and an object of persecution on the part of clergymen of all sects, theologians and metaphysicians, professors of philosophy, and state authorities. Many of his personal friends, who as a result of their narrow-mindedness had not been able to foresee that Spinoza would take such an extreme anti-religious position, also turned away from him. But, on the other hand, the appearance of the *Treatise* made our philosopher world famous. Around his banner the radical, and revolutionary elements of all countries gradually gathered.

Having underlined a few basic principles of Spinoza's worldview, we can now consider the central problem which faced Spinoza. His chief work bears the title *Ethics*. But it would be erroneous to suppose that Spinoza, like Kant, set himself the goal of discovering some sort of supersensory, divine, ethical law on the order of the Kantian categorical imperative. In general, Spinoza denies the existence of two levels of reality: what *is* and what *ought to be*, the latter being opposed to the former and supposedly having its source in another, extra-empirical world. By 'ethics' Spinoza meant simply a certain *way of life*, which must result from a knowledge of the reality of nature, man, and human society. Ethics defines the place of man in nature and derives his mode of life in a completely realistic and materialistic way from a knowledge of his natural passions and strivings. In this quite definite and natural sense, ethics is also a doctrine of what *is*, unopposed by abstract ethical norms or laws of what *ought to be*. Man's power over nature, his cultural creativity, in the broadest sense of the word, is a basic factor in the right conduct of life, whether individual or social. For this reason, all the sciences and all human knowledge have a definite *practical goal*. But I shall return to this question later.

II

Having sketched the basic orientation of Spinoza's thought, of necessity schematically and very briefly, we can now turn to the question of what the elements were which went into the formation of our philosopher's world-view. A definite groove has been established in the literature of this subject. Some see in Judaism the source of Spinozism. Since Spinoza was a Jew and was trained to be a rabbi, since he studied the Talmud and its many commentators, and even cabala—the flat conclusion is drawn that Spinozism has its roots in Judaism. Without in the least denying that the great Jewish thinkers (such as Maimonides) had a certain influence on Spinoza, we nevertheless regard the assertion that our philosopher's teaching came from the womb of Judaism as entirely erroneous. In particular, as far as cabala is concerned, Spinoza's expressed opinion is extremely negative.

Others are inclined to see the source of Spinozism in scholastic philosophy. Still others regard Spinoza as a follower and pupil of Descartes. Of course, no one can deny Spinoza's indebtedness to scholasticism, or Descartes's enormous influence on our philosopher.

Nevertheless, we should say that all of these judgments concerning the sources of Spinozism touch only the surface of the problem; for the scholars concerned lose sight of the currents and philosophical tendencies of the period in which Spinoza lived and worked. Surely it is strange and quite naïve to imagine that the seventeenth century was some kind of vacuum in which no movement of thought was taking place. Furthermore, these conceptions are evidently based on the assumption that Spinoza was not a living human being, vitally interested in the problems which disturbed his contemporaries, but some kind of Egyptian mummy, immured within the four walls of his study, grubbing ceaselessly like a bookworm in the ancient folios of the scholastics or the mystical books of cabala. Yet surely such conceptions contradict all the known facts. We now know very well even the contents of Spinoza's library. For this reason I consider that it is necessary for the elucidation of the sources of Spinozism to turn first of all to an investigation of the fundamental trends and tendencies in philosophy and science during the seventeenth century; for Spinozism was a product of its time. It was one of the philosophical attempts to solve the problems which were of commanding interest in the seventeenth century. Moreover, in my opinion, Spinozism was above all a synthesis of the *materialistic tendencies* of this period.

Of the many investigators of Spinozism, only Dunin-Borkowski,[1] it seems, has interested himself in the problem of the connection of Spinozism with contemporary currents of philosophical and scientific thought. And it should be said that, despite the fact that the author himself is a Catholic, idealist, and mystic who would very much like to treat Spinoza in this same spirit, he has been forced to admit at least one thing: *Spinoza was actually a materialist at one time*—during his youth, to be sure, and briefly; but there is no doubt that he was a materialist, indeed a mechanistic materialist. Later, however, according to Dunin-Borkowski, Spinoza made a radical break with materialism. My opinion on this point is different, but, be that as it may, Dunin-Borkowski, having become more intimately acquainted with Spinoza's life and with the period in which he lived, was forced to admit that Spinoza passed through a materialistic stage during his development. This in itself represents a certain triumph.

In the seventeenth century a number of materialistic writings appeared, and it is natural that Spinoza should have studied them carefully. In Holland during Spinoza's lifetime stormy disputes and literary polemics raged over the propositions of Henry de Roy

[1] Dunin-Borkowski, *Der junge De Spinoza*, 1910.

(Regius). The works of materialists which were prohibited in other countries were printed in Holland. In addition to legal literature, all kinds of *illegal* extremist works circulated there. Spinoza was vitally interested in all of these tendencies. After his excommunication from the Jewish community he set out, as it were, to voyage widely, greedily seeking the truth. We see him among various religious sects which were recruited from the democratic elements of the population and which opposed the ruling church and, to some extent, the social order.

But, in addition to the religious ferment among the masses of the people, a lively conflict of ideas was going on in the heights of science and philosophy. Holland was at this time one of the most prosperous and progressive countries in Europe. It had already passed through its bourgeois revolution; and the new form of society had generated corresponding groupings and currents of ideas. Are we to admit even for a moment that Spinoza was not interested in the intellectual life of his country, that he confined himself to the study of scholastic wisdom? Surely not, and most especially since in his works he attempted to solve precisely those problems which were uppermost in the minds of his contemporaries.

There were two fundamental groupings of ideas in the field of philosophic thought: orthodox Cartesianism, which at this time had already concluded an alliance with the Church; and the materialistic tendencies of various shades. It should be particularly emphasized that Cartesianism both in Holland and in France generated one of these materialistic tendencies from its own womb. At the head of the materialistic trend in Holland was Henry de Roy. At first an orthodox follower of Descartes, he later drew materialistic conclusions from Descartes's teaching. A bitter struggle began between de Roy on the one hand and the theologians, idealists, and Cartesians on the other. Although de Roy expressed himself very cautiously for fear of persecution, the materialistic character of his position was difficult to conceal. He set himself the goal of overcoming Cartesian dualism. In one of his twenty-one theses, which were posted at Utrecht in 1647, at the very climax of a bitter struggle with his opponents, he said that *mind is a mode of body*. And in *Philosophia naturalis*, a work which he published in 1654, he developed the idea that, although extension and thought are different, they are not mutually exclusive opposites. From a purely philosophical point of view, the mind may be regarded as a mode of the body. 'According to some wise men,' the author continues, 'extension and thought are merely attributes belonging to one and the same subject, which unites in itself both of these properties.'[1]

Is it not evident that de Roy, whom Marx considered as definitely a materialist, is here analysing Spinoza's formulation of the interrelation of thought and extension—dual attributes of a single substance? If we recall that de Roy's book appeared in 1654 and that Spinoza published his first work (*The Principles of Descartes's Philosophy*) in 1663, no doubt remains that the materialist de Roy influenced Spinoza in the solution of one of the central problems of his system. Moreover, de Roy himself was influenced by still another materialist, Gassendi, who had advanced the thesis that *body and mind are so bound together that they form a single object*. That Gassendi, in turn, also came close to the point of view later accepted by Spinoza is known to everyone who is familiar with the doctrines of this thinker. Consequently there can be no doubt, as Dunin-Borkowski correctly emphasizes, that Gassendi, de Roy, and Sebastian Basso had a direct influence on Spinoza. But this supports our assertion that Spinoza studied his *materialistic* contemporaries with particular zeal and sought what he needed in their works; that he was directly linked to them, and that he developed, deepened, and elaborated their views. It would take us too far afield if we were to prove this extremely important proposition in detail.

Let us now turn to another thesis in Spinoza's doctrine—namely, the problem of the universal animation of matter. It appears that this problem too was at the centre of attention of the thinkers of the time, to a certain extent. The idea of the universal animation of the world was very popular in the Renaissance; it was defended by both Telesius and Campanella. But this same idea was the subject of lively discussion in the seventeenth century as well (especially during the 1650's and '60's). Scientists and philosophers in Holland and England split into two camps: one held to a purely mechanistic point of view; the other defended hylozoism. The leader of the 'biusists' in England was the well-known scientist Glisson. 'Glisson,' says Dunin-Borkowski, 'with good reason, is usually counted among the biusists, the hylozoists. They were so called in contrast to the materialists, who were designated as "mechanists" at the time. The hylozoists taught that life (*bios*, *zōē*) is inherent in matter (*hylē*) as such, that movement, desire, and thought are inherent in it. Without these characteristics substance in general could not be conceived.'[2]

[1] Regius, *Philosophia naturalis*, 1654; cf. also Dunin-Borkowski, *op. cit.*, p. 395.
[2] Dunin-Borkowski, *op. cit.*, p. 389.

Thus this problem too was considered important at the time and was an object of lively discussion among scholars. Spinoza provided *his own* solution for this problem.

In this connection I want to say a few more words about the most abused term in Spinoza's system—the concept 'God' (*Deus*). Of course, according to the whole sense of Spinoza's teaching, God is nothing other than substance or nature. This follows with sufficient clarity from Spinoza's doctrine. But I consider it necessary to draw attention to another aspect of this question. We shall clear up a great many things if, instead of reading the customary meaning into this concept, we attempt to find out how it was used during the period under consideration. For this purpose, let us turn to another seventeenth-century materialist, Thomas Hobbes. In *De Corpore*, the famous work which he completed in 1655, Hobbes wrote as follows:

'In saying that the *world is God*, they say *that it hath no cause*, that is as much as *there is no God*. In like manner, they who maintain the world not to be created, but eternal; because there can be no cause of an eternal thing, in denying *the world to have a cause*, they deny also that *there is a God*.'[1]

But Hobbes himself, as is well known, speaks in his works of an *extended, corporeal* God. In Spinoza nature is called 'God' and extension is one of its attributes. Thus Proposition 2, Part II, of the *Ethics* reads: 'Extension is an attribute of God, or God is an extended thing.'

According to Hobbes' authoritative explanation, whoever calls the world or nature 'God' implies that the world was *not created*, that it exists eternally; in other words, whoever calls the world 'God,' *wishes to say that there is no God*. This should be remembered by those Marxists who are not prepared to 'cope with' Spinoza's God. In explaining this point I once more permit myself to agree with Dunin-Borkowski. 'That which is usually called God,' he writes, 'is understood here [i.e. by Gassendi, Harris, and other contemporaries.— A. D.] as something infinitely extended, which fills all things and embraces all things, and besides which nothing else exists.'[2]

Drawing his support from Spinoza's biographer, Maximilian Lucas (who was an immediate pupil and friend of the philosopher), as well as from other data, Dunin-Borkowski comes to the conclusion that Spinoza was at one time under the influence of 'radical

[1] Hobbes, *English Works*, ed. Molesworth, 1841, Vol. II, p. 214.
[2] Dunin-Borkowski, *op. cit.*, pp. 280–1.

popular materialism.' At this stage of his development Spinoza considered God *matter*. But afterwards Spinoza renounced this viewpoint and endowed substance with thought as well. Dunin-Borkowski wishes to disqualify Lucas' report, based on Spinoza's oral statement, that his whole philosophy comes down to the following four propositions: God is corporeal; the soul (*âme*) is only the principle of life; spirits are products of the imagination; and immortality is a phantom. Dunin-Borkowski does not doubt the authenticity of Lucas' account, but he assumes that these words of Spinoza's refer to the early materialistic stage of his development. I think that this construction on Dunin-Borkowski's part is somewhat forced. I see no reason for disqualifying Lucas' valuable report. This same corporeal God can have thought as an attribute. In any case there is no doubt about the fact that Spinoza's 'God' is to be understood as matter (nature), which has the two fundamental properties, extension and thought. It is quite possible that Spinoza originally conceived of matter as having only the single attribute of extension and later raised thought to the status of an attribute of substance. This would indicate an evolution of views. But that does not in the least disprove Lucas' report,[1] that Spinoza spoke to him of a *corporeal God*, that is, of matter, as substance, and did not refer this to the first period of his development. I consider the *second* stage as merely a further development of the same materialistic views which Spinoza had held somewhat earlier. This is a natural evolution, not a shift to an opposite point of view. Lucas expounded Spinoza's world-view in the materialistic spirit. How could this happen? If Spinoza was really a pantheist, a mystic, an idealist, how could it happen that one of his immediate pupils and friends emphasizes the materialistic character of Spinoza's system, pointing out that God is body?

In this connection I consider it necessary to remind you of the legend which circulated in Holland during the first quarter of the eighteenth century. It goes without saying that I do not attach any special significance to this legend; but it is characteristic, nevertheless. In 1724 Le Clerc, the well-known publisher of the 'Library of Ancient and Modern Authors,' related in one of his little books that he knew from a reliable source that only the concept 'nature' figured in the original text of the *Ethics*, and that it was only upon the advice of friends that Spinoza included the word 'God' as well as 'nature.' I repeat that I do not attach serious significance to this legend. Nevertheless, the fact is interesting as an indication that Spinoza's

[1] M. Lucas, *La Vie et l'esprit de M. Benoit de Spinoza*, ed. Freudenthal, pp. 5–6.

close contemporaries understood and felt clearly that the 'God' in Spinoza's system was something external and that the *Ethics* could get along very well without it.

After what has been said, it seems to me that the question of what we are to *understand* by God in Spinoza has been made sufficiently clear. It is only a theological term used to designate a real, material thing. It may be asked: did Spinoza himself feel that his *terminology* was unsatisfactory? It seems to me that he was aware of this inadequacy, but considered it necessary to speak in a language that would be intelligible and accessible to his contemporaries. All of his philosophical contemporaries, as we have seen, used this terminology, although they injected new meaning into the old terms. Spinoza himself pointed out, as though it were a rule of life, the necessity of expressing oneself in accordance with the development of the masses. In this connection he wrote:

'We can gain from the multitude no small advantages, provided that we strive to accommodate ourselves to its understanding as far as possible: moreover, we shall in this way gain a friendly audience for the reception of the truth.'[1]

Thus Spinoza was able to use the theological terminology of his time consciously, knowing that through this terminology he could gain the ear of his contemporaries. This argument has a certain force. But besides this, the concept 'God,' as I have already said, was used in the sense of nature, matter, etc., beginning in the Renaissance and continuing through the seventeenth century. After all that has been said, it seems clear to me that the term '*Deus*' is to be understood purely in the sense of 'nature.' And we should not lose sight of the fact that those who struggled against the scholastic, ecclesiastical world-view attempted to transfer to nature all of the predicates which in general were applied to God. Spinoza proceeded on the assumption that at some time in the past the predicates which applied to nature (and to man) had been transferred to God. The problem of the day was to prove that God's properties were in essence only the properties of nature.

The end result of Spinoza's veiled conflict with the old world-view was that he transferred to nature the predicates which the old world-view had attributed to God, and applied the term 'God' to nature. In any case, it is necessary in studying Spinoza's system to remember that in the seventeenth century men thought in theological

[1] *On the Improvement of the Understanding*, Elwes' translation, p. 5.

terms and categories, and that this theological costume was forced upon Spinoza by the period; however, the essence of the matter, the inner meaning of Spinoza's system, is not in the least altered by this fact.

I have indicated above the basic materialistic trends of the seventeenth century which in a certain sense *paved the way* for Spinozism. Needless to say, these remarks have not in the least exhausted the sources of Spinozism. For example, one can scarcely doubt that Spinoza was acquainted with the works of Giordano Bruno, of Vanini, of the French humanist and materialist des Périers, *et al*. But what I particularly wish to emphasize in this connection is Spinoza's acquaintance with what was perhaps the most radical book of his time. I have in mind the work called *Theophrastus redivivus*. The author of this curious work develops a definitely materialistic point of view; he denies the existence of God, of spirits, and of the soul as an independent entity. In this book we find extraordinarily sharp attacks on religion and the clergy, as well as a critique of the existing political and social order. The 'new Theophrastus' is one of the first writers of the modern period to advance the famous slogan 'Back to nature.' In Spinoza we find a reaction to this slogan. Our philosopher condemns the idea of man's returning to the state of nature. He calls mankind forward—to cultural creativity and the strengthening of social ties.

The new Theophrastus' radicalism on all questions amounts to a unique anarchism. Man should make himself *absolutely free*; on this basis the author demands the elimination of marriage. Man's fundamental aim is *pleasure, the satisfaction of all his natural appetites and needs. Joy is the highest happiness.* It should be noted that, although Spinoza is far from the new Theophrastus' position, certain elements of the latter's teaching were evidently taken up by our philosopher and reworked in his own language. Rejecting the slogan of a return to the state of nature, Spinoza at the same time assigned an important place to pleasure and joy in human life.

Furthermore, Spinoza could not have been ignorant of the works of Kaspar Lyken, whose sharp critique of *capitalism* has caused certain scholars to see in this writer virtually a predecessor of Marx, in so far as criticism of the capitalistic system is concerned. But what is especially significant for our characterization of Spinoza's intellectual development is the fact that our thinker studied Thomas More's *Utopia*. I assert definitely that in Spinoza's *Ethics* there are certain echoes of More's ideas.

Such are the general features of the intellectual atmosphere in which Spinoza developed. The conclusion to which we are led is that our philosopher took up and reworked in his own way all of the problems which disturbed his contemporaries, synthesizing the basic trends of thought—and above all the materialistic trends—into a grandiose, new, materialistic system.

III

In the first part of my paper I pointed out the fundamental problem which Spinoza set himself in his chief work. The problem grew out of the necessity of establishing a *new way of life*. This *practical* aim is emphasized in all of Spinoza's writings. But the right way of life can be defined and established only after *man's place in nature* (we should add: *and in society*) has been clarified. However, the question of man's place or situation in nature leads us directly to the study of nature itself. Man's way of life must necessarily result from the place which he occupies in nature, for man's life should correspond, as it were, to the life of nature itself. The 'new Theophrastus' demanded man's return to the state of nature; Spinoza strove for the attainment of a form of human life in which man would not be nature's *slave* but its *master*. Spinoza likewise considered that man should live *in harmony with nature*, but in a higher sense. In opposition to Christian asceticism, which preached renunciation of the flesh and suppression of all the passions, Spinoza called man to the enjoyment of life, the satisfaction of all passions, and the creative development of all his powers and abilities. But all this is possible only on the basis of man's subordination to the laws of nature. His dominion over nature presupposes nature's dominion over him. It is possible to conquer nature only by obeying nature's laws. Spinoza develops this Baconian motif in his own special way.

The first task which faces us is the *study of nature*, an *adequate knowledge of it*. But in order to be able to acquire objective, adequate knowledge of nature we must first of all equip ourselves with an appropriate method, which in turn involves an investigation of our intellect, our cognitive powers.

Since it is not possible for me to develop Spinoza's whole train of thought here, I shall emphasize only that Spinoza saw in method a *tool of the intellect* which, like the *tools of labour*, makes it possible to master nature—in one case theoretically, in the other practically.

But it goes without saying that the theoretical and practical aspects are mutually interrelated in the most intimate way.

Let us hear what Spinoza says about method:

'Now that we know what kind of knowledge is necessary for us, we must indicate the way and the method whereby we may gain the said knowledge concerning the things needful to be known. In order to accomplish this, we must first take care not to commit ourselves to a search, going back to infinity—that is, in order to discover the best method for finding out the truth, there is no need of another method to discover such method; nor of a third method for discovering the second, and so on to infinity. By such proceedings, we should never arrive at the knowledge of the truth, or, indeed, at any knowledge at all.

'The matter stands,' he says, 'on the same footing as the making of material tools, which might be argued about in a similar way. For, in order to work iron, a hammer is needed, and the hammer cannot be forthcoming unless it has been made; but, in order to make it, there was need of another hammer and other tools, and so on to infinity. We might thus vainly endeavour to prove that men have no power of working iron. But as men at first made use of the instruments supplied by nature to accomplish very easy pieces of workmanship, laboriously and imperfectly, and then, when these were finished, wrought other things more difficult with less labour and greater perfection; and so gradually mounted from the simplest operations to the making of tools, and from the making of tools to the making of more complex tools, and fresh feats of workmanship, till they arrived at making, with small expenditure of labour, the vast number of complicated mechanisms which they now possess. So, in like manner, the intellect, by its native strength, makes for itself intellectual instruments, whereby it acquires strength for performing other intellectual operations, and from these operations gets again fresh instruments, or the power of pushing its investigations further, and thus gradually proceeds till it reaches the summit of wisdom.'[1]

An analysis of Spinoza's method as such is not part of my task. Needless to say, from our present-day point of view, this method suffers from substantial shortcomings. But this aspect of the question does not concern me in the present connection.

For adequate knowledge of nature, then, we need a suitable

[1] *On the Improvement of the Understanding*, Elwes' translation, pp. 9–10.

method. This general theoretical formulation of the problem is, of course, entirely correct, regardless of whether the particular *concrete method* is correct or incorrect.

Having equipped himself with his method, Spinoza set about the study of nature. His *Ethics* opens with eight famous definitions, which lay the foundation of the whole system. I shall not, of course, enter into an examination, analysis, or critique of these definitions. However, I consider it necessary to say a few words about the first two definitions, for from them alone it will be possible to draw certain conclusions as to the character of Spinoza's whole system and the course of his thought in general.

The first definition deals with what appears at first sight to be a purely scholastic concept—*causa sui*. But Spinoza's whole system is contained in this concept in embryonic form.

'By *that which is self-caused (causa sui)*,' he says, 'I mean that of which the essence involves existence, or that of which the nature is only conceivable as existent.'

Nature (or in Spinoza's terminology 'God'), the universe as a whole, is absolutely infinite and self-caused. Spinoza thus leads us at once, as it were, into the chasm of infinity. He does not begin, as one might expect, with an investigation of individual things. Such a method of studying nature can be shown to be incorrect in many respects, yet, in this approach of Spinoza's, we should recognize a certain advantage, even a merit of our thinker.

Indeed, the problem before Spinoza was primarily the establishment of a new principle of explanation of nature as a whole rather than an explanation of this or that separate, individual phenomenon. For this reason, Engels was quite right in emphasizing that Spinoza stated and established a new principle, that of the explanation of the world through itself.

'It is to the highest credit of the philosophy of the time,' says Engels, 'that it did not let itself be led astray by the restricted state of contemporary natural knowledge, and that—from Spinoza right to the great French materialists—it insisted on explaining the world from the world itself and left the justification in detail to the natural science of the future.'[1]

Spinoza's philosophical greatness consists in the fact that, *in spite of* the empirical natural science of the time, he freed nature—the universe—from its prime-mover, God, a principle of explanation

[1] Engels, *Dialectics of Nature*, New York, 1940, p. 7.

which even such an outstanding scientist as Newton later clung to with tenacity.

If nature is self-caused, it does not require any external cause, that is, God; it should be explained exclusively through itself, the internal powers inherent in it, the laws which act within it. But such a point of view is *purely materialistic*. And the importance of this point of view is deepened by the fact that it takes *nature as a whole* as its object. For many of those who do not consider it necessary to seek refuge in 'divine aid' with respect to particular phenomena, are unable to get along without God as soon as the discussion turns to nature as a whole.

Spinoza's greatness consisted in winning the independence, the autonomy of nature, so to speak, by dethroning its former monarch, God.

Nature, then, is self-caused. Its essence involves existence; it exists by virtue of its own essence, requiring for its existence no external cause, no other essence. As a result, nature is an absolutely infinite being.

To the *infinite* Spinoza opposes the *finite*: 'A thing is called *finite after its kind* when it can be limited by another thing of the same nature.'

In order to bring out here—although superficially and in broad strokes—Spinoza's remarkably profound *dialectical* formulation of the problem of finite and infinite, we must quote the seventh definition, which reads as follows: 'That thing is called free which exists solely by the necessity of its own nature, and of which the action is determined by itself alone. On the other hand, that thing is *necessary*, or rather *constrained*, which is determined by something external to itself to a fixed and definite manner of existence or action.'

Unfortunately, I am not able to analyse Spinoza's dialectics of finite and infinite, freedom and necessity, in this paper. The one thing that should be said is that Hegel in his *Logic* develops Spinoza's basic ideas with respect to finite and infinite, freedom and necessity. Hegel's dialectics, in so far as it is concerned with these opposites, represents only a further development and deepening of Spinoza's dialectical ideas.

The concept of *free necessity* is applied by Spinoza primarily to nature as a whole, which is *causa sui*, self-caused. The opposition between each individual thing, that is, the finite, and nature as a whole as infinite, consists in the fact that the finite has the cause of its existence in something else, whereas the infinite, the universe as

SPINOZA'S WORLD-VIEW

such, contains the cause of its existence (as well as its essence) within itself. To put it another way: the universe does not have an external cause, that is, it is *uncaused*, autonomous, independent of any external God-force whatever. But this is possible only if the universe is *without beginning* and *without limit*. If the universe had a *beginning*, then something else must have produced it. If it were finite, then something would have to exist which *limits* it, which is located *beyond* it. But that which is beyond it, in its turn, would be limited by something else, and so on *ad infinitum*. Consequently, we must conceive the universe as infinite, that is, not limited, not determined by anything else; and without beginning, that is, eternal. Thus Spinoza affirms that nature is *eternal*, that is, *uncreated*. The idea of the creation of the universe suffers a complete collapse. But it is impossible to arrive at such a purely *materialistic* result on the basis of formal logic, because formal logic requires the extension of the law of causality to the universe as a whole, whereas the dialectical meaning of Spinoza's doctrine is that the category applied to a *part* of nature cannot be extended to the *whole of nature*. Each individual phenomenon in nature is limited by another and has an external cause, but we cannot say this about nature as a whole. The same thing applies to the concepts of coming into being and passing away. These concepts are applicable, in one way or another, to individual phenomena, but not to the universe as such. The universe does not come into being or pass away.

Thus nature or God is, in Spinoza's words, *ens absolute indeterminatum*, that is, a being absolutely undetermined, unlimited. *Indeterminatum* is usually translated as 'undefined.' But this contradicts the whole sense of Spinoza's teaching, for nature (or God) is a being which contains in itself the whole fulness of being, the whole wealth of determinations. Consequently, *indeterminatum* means simply 'unlimited,' 'undetermined,' as opposed to what is limited and determined. Spinoza's well-known proposition, '*Omnis determinatio est negatio*' should also be understood in the sense that 'every limitation is a negation,' i.e. that every finite thing contains in itself its own negation. Usually this proposition is interpreted in the sense that every definition (*logical* determination) is a negation. But this does not correspond to the actual meaning which Spinoza put into this proposition.[1]

Nature as a whole, then, is not limited or determined; but every

[1] Cf. M. Friedrichs, *Der Substanzbegriff Spinozas*, 1896; A. Wenzel, *Die Weltanschauung Spinozas*, 1907; C. N. Starcke, *Baruch de Spinoza*, 1923.

finite thing is limited and determined by other things, that is, it is ephemeral and subject to change. But though nature in itself, as a whole, is determined by nothing and is uncaused, natural activities are determined through and through. And in this sense Spinoza speaks of *free necessity*. 'To say that necessary and free are two contrary terms, seems to me . . . absurd and repugnant to reason,' says Spinoza.[1] That which exists solely by the *necessity* of its own nature and is determined to action by itself alone is *free*. But only the world as a whole exists by the necessity of its own nature.[2] Consequently, from the *absolute necessity* of nature it follows that nature must be *uncaused*, and vice versa; being uncaused signifies absolute necessity, absolute existence.

Turning to the nature of finite things, I must draw your attention once more to the purely *dialectical* character of Spinoza's formulation of this problem. Every finite thing (in contrast to nature as a whole) has the cause of its existence not in itself, for in that case it would be an absolute *causa sui*, but in other things. Each finite thing is determined by the totality of things; it does not exist in isolation; *all things are reciprocally connected*, are *in reciprocal interaction*. Therefore every finite thing is limited, i.e. it contains in itself the *negation* of its own being, while nature as a whole represents absolutely *positive being* and excludes every negation. On the other hand, all the *negative* definitions of nature as a whole ('infinite,' 'unlimited,' 'indivisible,' 'uncaused,' etc.) express not negation, but, on the contrary, its *absolutely positive* determinations. Negation here passes dialectically into affirmation. But all the *positive* definitions of finite things express negation, revealing their ephemeral nature.

Referring to the reciprocal connection of finite things, Spinoza expressed himself in one of his letters as follows:

'Now, all the bodies of nature can and should be conceived in the same way as we have here conceived the blood: for all bodies are surrounded by others, and are mutually determined to exist and to act in a definite and determined manner, while there is preserved in all together, that is, in the whole universe, the same proportion of motion and rest. Hence it follows that every body, in so far as it exists modified in a certain way, must be considered to be a part of

---

[1] Letter LX to Hugo Boxel.

[2] Spinoza makes a very important distinction between what is infinite by virtue of its essence or its own nature and what is infinite by virtue of its cause. This distinction is the same as Hegel's doctrine of good and bad infinities.

the whole universe, to be in accord with the whole of it, and to be connected with the other parts. And since the nature of the universe is not limited, like the nature of the blood, but absolutely infinite, its parts are controlled by the nature of this infinite power in infinite ways, and are compelled to suffer infinite changes. But I conceive that with regard to substance each part has a closer union with its whole. For as I endeavoured to show in my first letter, which I wrote to you when I was still living at Rhynsburg, since it is of the nature of substance to be infinite, it follows that each part belongs to the nature of corporeal substance, and can neither exist nor be conceived without it.'[1]

Consequently, it would be incorrect to assume that from Spinoza's point of view nature represents some kind of frozen, dead, motionless, immutable being. Our thinker, as we see, definitely emphasizes that the parts of the universe can undergo *infinite modifications*. In nature generally there is nothing from which some effect does not follow (*Ethics*, I, 36). All natural things act upon each other, that is, they exist in reciprocal interaction. Every body is a part of the universe and is connected with all its other parts, as well as dependent upon the whole. All of nature, as Spinoza expresses it, 'comprises one individual, whose parts, that is, all bodies, vary in infinite ways without any change in the individual as a whole.'[2] The form or aspect of the whole universe (*'facies totius universi'*) remains unchanged through all the modifications of its parts. I shall not dwell here on the question of how the *changelessness of the form of the whole universe* is to be understood. For my purpose it will be sufficient to quote Engels' opinion on this question:

'*Reciprocal action* is the first thing that we encounter when we consider matter in motion as a whole from the standpoint of modern natural science,' writes Engels. 'We see a series of forms of motion, mechanical motion, heat, light, electricity, magnetism, chemical union and decomposition, transitions of states of aggregation, organic life, all of which, if *at present* we *still* make an exception of organic life, pass into one another, mutually determine one another, are in one place cause and in another effect, the sum-total of the motion in all its changing forms remaining the same (Spinoza: *substance is causa sui*—strikingly expresses the reciprocal action).'[3]

[1] Letter XV to Henry Oldenburg.
[2] *Ethics*, II, lemma 7.
[3] Engels, *op. cit.*, p. 173.

Thus we have an almost complete coincidence of the views of Spinoza and Engels (also of Hegel) on this point.

What is man's place in nature?—We can now give a definite answer to this question. Man is not some kind of special, privileged creature; he does not stand outside nature or above nature. Man is a *part of nature*, whether we regard him under the aspect of body or that of mind. As a part of nature, man is subject to the same influences from other bodies as are other parts of nature. Consequently, man's life is determined not by some supernatural power but by the universal laws of nature.

However, before pausing, even though briefly, with man, we must say a few words about the relation of substance to its attributes. It seems to me that Spinoza established an extraordinarily important materialistic proposition, which may be expressed briefly as: *matter is capable of thinking*. According to Spinoza's doctrine, there are not two substances in nature, but only one substance, which is at the same time both extended and thinking. What Spinoza calls *substance* in his language, when translated into everyday language is called *matter*. And matter comprises, so to speak, the secret of Spinoza's substance. Spinoza objected to the identification of thought and extension, but he definitely considered thought a property of matter. Therefore he could not accept the Cartesian identification of *matter and extension*. In one of his letters to Tschirnhaus, he wrote:

'You ask whether the variety of things can be proved *a priori* from the conception of extension alone. I believe I have already shown sufficiently clearly that this is impossible, and that therefore matter is badly defined by Descartes as extension, but that it must necessarily be defined by an attribute which expresses eternal and infinite essence.'[1]

If the nature of matter is exhausted by extension, if it is identical with the latter, then thought cannot be a property of matter, for thought and extension are entirely different qualities. For this reason, Spinoza wrote in a letter to Henry Oldenburg as follows: 'But you say: perhaps thought is a corporeal action; be it so, though I by no means grant it, you, at any rate, will not deny that extension, in so far as it is extension, is not thought. . . .'[2]

It seems to me that this quotation throws a flood of light on the question of the interrelation between substance and its attributes. On the one hand, Spinoza definitely emphasizes the *qualitative differ-*

[1] Letter LXXXII to Tschirnhaus.   [2] Letter IV to Oldenburg.

ence between extension and thought (even when thought is regarded as a purely corporeal action, as Spinoza apparently thought in the first, 'mechanistic,' phase of his development), but on the other hand, his efforts were directed toward establishing their *unity*. Accordingly, matter must not be thought of as identical with extension. But from this it follows clearly that by substance we are to understand matter, comprising the unity of two attributes: matter has the capacity of thinking, and there is no thought without matter.

I have already pointed out that G. V. Plekhanov included Spinoza's among the materialistic systems and that he regarded the materialism of Marx and Engels as a *variety of Spinozism*. In the preface to *Ludwig Feuerbach*, Plekhanov wrote:

'If the "critics of Marx" emitted a unanimous cry of amazement when I expressed the idea in my polemic with Bernstein that the materialism of Marx and Engels was a variety of Spinozism, this is to be explained solely by their own amazing ignorance. To make this thought more comprehensible it is necessary, in the first place, to remember that Marx and Engels studied Feuerbach's philosophy and, in the second place, to attempt to see clearly how this philosophy differs from Spinoza's. Anyone who can understand what he reads will soon see that, *in respect to his basic view of the relation of being and thought*, Feuerbach is a Spinozist who has ceased to magnify "nature with the name of God, and has studied at the school of Hegel."'[1]

Plekhanov, then, considers that Marxism is close to Spinozism in the basic problem of the relation of thought to being. That Plekhanov in fact correctly interpreted the point of view of the founders of Marxism we can now document by Engels' own words. In a fragment (in the *Dialectics of Nature*[2]) entitled 'Unity of Nature and Mind,' Engels wrote:

'To the Greeks it was self-evident that nature could not be unreasonable, but even today the stupidest empiricists prove by their reasoning (however wrong it may be) that they are convinced from the outset that nature cannot be unreasonable or reason contrary to nature.'[3]

In another place Engels formulated his viewpoint on the problem of the relation of thought to matter as follows:

[1] Engels, *Ludwig Feuerbach* (Russian edition), 1906, p. 11.
[2] This unfinished work was first published (in Russian translation) in 1925 by the Marx-Engels Institute in Moscow.—*Trans.*
[3] Engels, *Dialectics of Nature*, p. 178.

'The point is, however, that mechanism (and also the materialism of the eighteenth century) does not get away from abstract necessity, and hence not from chance either. That matter evolves out of itself the thinking human brain is for him a pure accident, although necessarily determined, step by step, where it happens. But the truth is that it is the nature of matter to advance to the evolution of thinking beings, hence, too, this always necessarily occurs wherever the conditions for it (not necessarily identical at all places and times) are present.'[1]

It is evident that Engels' viewpoint coincides substantially with that of Spinoza.

But let us return to man. We know that man forms a part of nature. 'Mind and body comprise one and the same individual, conceived in the one case under the attribute of thought, in the other under the attribute of extension.' Consequently, man represents only a modification of the attributes of nature or substance. But it is remarkable that in Spinoza the body is everywhere first: it has priority, so to speak, over the mind, which is only the idea of the body; the body is the actual object of the mind, in which are reflected all the modifications occurring in the body as a result of the action upon it of external bodies.

The materialistic character of Spinoza's psychology has even given one recent writer cause for misgivings about our philosopher's idealism. 'If the contents of the mind,' writes B. Kellermann, 'are only the stimuli of the body, what remains for the mind as its own content, independent of bodily stimuli?'[2] And Kellermann sensibly asks: on what grounds is Spinoza considered the founder of scientific *idealism*? In his opinion, there are no grounds for this—an opinion in which we entirely concur.

Unfortunately, I cannot dwell on Spinoza's theory of knowledge, nor on his theory of the emotions; and I shall proceed to the concluding portion of my paper, to the problem of ethics, that is, the *way of life* which follows from Spinoza's whole teaching.

Man is a natural creature who strives, like all natural creatures, for self-preservation, the satisfaction of his needs, and happiness, that is, for everything that is *useful* to him. The striving for self-preservation, says Spinoza, is the primary and only basis of *virtue*. To act virtuously means to act, to live, to preserve one's being in

[1] Engels, *Dialectics of Nature*, p. 228.
[2] B. Kellermann, *Die Ethik Spinozas*, 1922, p. 256.

accordance with the dictates of reason on the basis of seeking what is useful to one's self.[1] Thus virtue consists solely in acting according to the laws of one's own nature. And we *act* only in so far as we *know*. Being a part of nature, man follows its general order. He is subject to passive conditions, he obeys the general order of nature and *adapts himself* to it, in so far as the nature of things demands. The essence of a passive condition is determined by the ratio of the power of an external cause to our own power. If man were subject exclusively to his emotions he would be their slave, a completely passive creature. But reason makes man an *active* being through the *knowledge* of the laws of nature and as a result of his placing his emotions and passions at the service of reason, subordinating them to himself and using them for his good. Man is subject in every way to the actions of nature; but, as a being endowed with reason, he in his turn is able to act upon nature. In this sense reason makes man free. But since nature's power infinitely surpasses the power of individual men, man's struggle with nature cannot be successful in solitude, but only conjointly, through collective power.

'Therefore, to man there is nothing more useful than man—nothing, I repeat, more excellent for preserving their being can be wished for by men, than that all should so in all points agree, that the minds and bodies of all should form, as it were, one single mind and one single body, and that all should, with one consent, as far as they are able, endeavour to preserve their being, and all with one consent seek what is useful to them all. Hence, men who are governed by reason—that is, who seek what is useful to them in accordance with reason—desire for themselves nothing which they do not also desire for the rest of mankind, and, consequently, are just, faithful, and honourable in their conduct.'[2]

We see that Spinoza here overcomes the viewpoint of individualism, although the individual is for him the point of departure. Only in the collective can the individual develop all his powers and become capable of attaining the highest happiness and perfection. In another place Spinoza definitely emphasizes that the existing social order does not satisfy him, since hatred and mutual hostility prevail within it. Perhaps Spinoza did not understand the social roots and conditions of this order, but that did not prevent him from enunciating a demand for a community of men, a social organization, in which the interests of all would be in harmony, where the human collective

[1] Cf. *Ethics*, IV, 24.   [2] *Ibid.*, IV, 18, scholium.

would form, as it were, one mind and one body, where all men would be friends.[1] It is evident that we would have such an organization of society under *communism*. And in this sense, the contemporary proletariat is striving to realize the ideal advanced by Spinoza, regardless of what Spinoza understood *concretely* by a social organization in which all men should form one body and one mind.

'It is before all things useful to men,' Spinoza says in another place, 'to associate their ways of life, to bind themselves together with such bonds as they think most fitted to gather them all into unity, and generally to do whatsoever serves to strengthen friendship.'[2]

Precisely because human power is limited and the power of external things infinitely exceeds man's power, it is necessary that men in their struggle with nature should adapt external things to their use through collective strength. *But a part of nature* cannot become the *whole* and, consequently, mankind will never be able to adapt and subjugate external things *absolutely*, so to speak. However, there is nothing tragic in this, and we should reconcile ourselves in this sense to nature's necessity in so far as we acknowledge the limits of our possible dominion over nature, which follow from this necessity.

Thus our philosopher's gaze is not turned backward to a primitive and uncivilized life, but forward to cultural creativity, to the building of life.

'Let satirists then laugh their fill at human affairs,' Spinoza exclaims, 'let theologians rail, and let misanthropes praise to their utmost the life of untutored rusticity, let them heap contempt on men and praises on beasts; when all is said, they will find that men can provide for their wants much more easily by mutual help, and

---

[1] And among friends, Spinoza says, *all things should be held in common.* Thus, in a letter dated February 17, 1671, he sharply attacks the author of a pamphlet which had recently appeared under the title 'Homo Politicus,' in which the author developed the thought that rank and *riches* are the highest good. Spinoza intended to write a pamphlet against the author. In this letter he writes, among other things, the following: 'How much better and more excellent than the doctrines of the aforesaid writer are the reflections of Thales of Miletus, appears from the following: *All the goods of friends,* he says, *are in common.* . . .' (Letter XLVII to Jarig Jellis.)

[2] *Ibid.,* IV, appendix 12. Spinoza considers that society should look after its needy citizens and *provide them with the necessities* of life. 'Hence *providing for the poor* is a duty which falls on the state as a whole, and has regard only to the general advantage.' (*Ethics,* IV, appendix 17.)

that only by uniting their forces can they escape from the dangers that on every side beset them: not to say how much more excellent and worthy of our knowledge it is, to study the actions of men than the actions of beasts.'[1]

Spinoza's world-view as a whole corresponds to the basic tendencies which I have developed; it radiates optimism and the joy of living. To look upon Spinoza as a kind of hermit, preaching submissiveness and an ascetic Christian morality, is quite erroneous. On the contrary, the *right way of life* for man consists in the development of the fulness of strength and power inherent in the human collective, the striving for reasonable pleasures, and the attainment of the highest perfection and joy. On this subject Spinoza expresses himself clearly in the *Ethics*:

'Assuredly, nothing forbids man to enjoy himself, save grim and gloomy superstition. For why is it more lawful to satiate one's hunger and thirst than to drive away one's melancholy. I reason, and have convinced myself as follows: No deity, nor any one else, save the envious, takes pleasure in my infirmity and discomfort, nor sets down to my virtue the tears, sobs, fear, and the like, which are signs of infirmity of spirit; on the contrary, the greater the pleasure wherewith we are affected, the greater the perfection whereto we pass: in other words, the more must we necessarily partake of the divine nature. Therefore, to make use of what comes in our way, and to enjoy it as much as possible (not to the point of satiety, for that would not be enjoyment) is the part of a wise man. I say it is the part of a wise man to refresh and recreate himself with moderate and pleasant food and drink, and also with perfumes, with the soft beauty of growing plants, with dress, with music, with many sports, with theatres, and the like, such as every man may make use of without injury to his neighbour. For the human body is composed of very numerous parts, of diverse nature, which continually stand in need of fresh and varied nourishment, so that the whole body may be equally capable of performing all the actions, which follow from the necessity of its own nature; and consequently, so that the mind may also be equally capable of understanding many things simultaneously. This way of life, then, agrees best with our principles, and also with general practice; therefore, if there be any question of another plan, the plan we have mentioned is the best, and in every way to be commended. There is no need for me to set forth the matter more clearly or in more detail.'[2]

[1] *Ibid.*, IV, 35, scholium.   [2] *Ibid.*, IV, 45, scholium.

From all that I have said it follows that Spinoza's fundamental aspiration was for the attainment of the 'right way of life' for the individual and the collective, the attainment of a 'perfect' social organization in which it would be possible to achieve the highest happiness, the highest joy and fulness of life for all men, or, expressed in another way, the conscious unity of the mind with nature. Man's very essence is comprised in the knowledge of the unity which the mind has with nature as a whole.

'This then,' says Spinoza, 'is the end for which I strive, to attain such a character myself, and to endeavour that many should attain to it with me. In other words, it is part of my happiness to lend a helping hand, that many others may understand even as I do, so that their understanding and desire may entirely agree with my own. In order to bring this about, it is necessary to understand as much of nature as will enable us to attain to the aforesaid character, and also to form a social order such as is most conducive to the attainment of this character by the greatest number with the least difficulty and danger. We must seek the assistance of moral philosophy and the theory of education; further, as health is no insignificant means for attaining our end, we must also include the whole science of medicine, and, as many difficult things are by contrivance rendered easy, and we can in this way gain much time and convenience, the science of mechanics must in no way be despised. But, before all things, a means must be devised for improving the understanding and purifying it, as far as may be at the outset, so that it may apprehend things without error, and in the best possible way.

'Thus it is apparent to every one that I wish to direct all sciences to one end and aim, so that we may attain to the supreme human perfection which we have named; and, therefore, whatsoever in the sciences does not serve to promote our object will have to be rejected as useless. To sum up the matter in a word, all our actions and thoughts must be directed to this one end.'[1]

Thus for Spinoza the sciences have a purely *practical* value, since they serve our final ends. And the end of all the sciences and of all human knowledge is the attainment of the highest human perfection. Spinoza assigns an extremely important role to mechanics and technology, that is, in contemporary language, to the development of the forces of production; since this leads to an increase in our power over nature. Technology is bound up in the most intimate

[1] *On the Improvement of the Understanding*, Elwes' translation, pp. 4–5.

way with *natural science*, which is the most important of the sciences; it has as its subject-matter nature, that is, the essence of substance (and of man as a part of nature). On the foundation of natural science (and the science of man) an appropriate *social organization* must be built. Moral philosophy, which is based on the knowledge of nature, is the theory of the *right way of life*, in the sense which I have already developed. Medicine provides for human health, since health is the first condition of happiness. And the science of the intellect or the methodology of knowing has as its goal the attainment of objective, adequate knowledge of the world.

Such are the fundamental elements of Spinoza's philosophy.[1]

I shall not attempt to speculate as to what Spinoza might have been if he had lived in our time. For me, in any case, one thing is not open to doubt: Spinoza would never have been an agent of the League of Nations. The second point that I wish to emphasize is that we do not agree to yield Spinoza to our enemies in any case. There is no reason at all for this. Spinoza was a great materialistic thinker, and in this respect he should be considered a predecessor of dialectical materialism. The contemporary proletariat is Spinoza's only genuine heir.

[1] I have emphasized today only the strong points of Spinoza's doctrine, without undertaking an evaluation of these positive components from the standpoint of our contemporary views. I have considered it even less necessary to submit to criticism the elements of Spinoza's teaching which are unacceptable to us. I have considered it necessary today to emphasize especially that in general Spinoza's point of view was materialistic and that the basic motif of his philosophical activity was the dominion of the human collective over nature, with the end of attaining the greatest perfection and happiness of men and their greatest solidarity within society.

V. K. Brushlinski

SPINOZA'S SUBSTANCE AND FINITE THINGS[1]

Spinoza . . . ein glänzender Vertreter der Dialektik.—Engels.

THE following proposition will serve as the general thesis of the present paper: In Spinoza, with all his grandiose *monism* and his doctrine of the *immanence* of God or substance, there is nevertheless a certain visible *break* or, more precisely, a certain discrepancy, between substance and its modes; between infinite and finite; between the essence which is indissolubly connected with existence and the essence which does not involve necessary existence; between intuition, which comprehends eternal and immutable being, and imagination, which has as its object individual, ephemeral things. But, at the same time, we find in Spinoza a dialectical overcoming of this break or discrepancy, which has enormous theoretical significance and is of exceptional interest to us.

We shall attempt to show all this without entering into particulars, limiting ourselves to the general, fundamental principles and propositions of Spinoza's philosophy.

The very first definitions of substance and modes are concerned with the disparity of these categories and a certain break between them. Substance exists in itself and is conceived through itself; the conception of substance can be formed independently of any other conception.[2] On the other hand, the modes, which are essentially *conditions* of substance, exist in and are conceived through something other than themselves, that is, in and through substance.[3]

[1] A translation of 'Spinozovskaya substantsiya i konechnyie veshchi,' *Pod znamenem marksizma*, No. 2-3 (1927), pp. 56-64.
[2] *Ethics*, I, def. 3.   [3] *Ibid.*, I, def. 5.

From these two definitions Spinoza draws the direct conclusion that substance is by nature prior to its modifications, that is, to its modes.[1]

We thus see the priority in principle of substance, which does not exist exclusively in its modifications, but in itself, independent as it were of its modifications.

However, for us as dialectical materialists matter exists *only* in its concrete manifestations or modifications and is known *only through* the latter, not in itself or through itself.

The separation of substance from its modes is very clearly expressed in the proof of Proposition 5, Part I, of the *Ethics*. Assuming that two substances having the same attribute are distinguished from one another only by their modes, Spinoza demonstrates the impossibility of this assumption in the following words: 'As substance is naturally prior to its modifications, it follows that, setting the modifications aside, and considering substance in itself, that is truly, there cannot be conceived one substance different from another, that is, there cannot be granted several substances, but one substance only.'

And further on, after Spinoza has proved that there is only one substance, which is God, he emphasizes repeatedly that modes can exist only in God and can be conceived only through God (for example, in the proofs of Propositions 15 and 23 of Part I). But on the other hand, he nowhere says directly that God exists only in modes and cannot be conceived without the latter: on the contrary, Spinoza's God exists *in se* and is conceived *per se*.

Another fundamental characteristic which indicates a certain break between the Spinozistic absolute and finite things is to be found in Spinoza's conception of eternity (*æternitas*) as a fundamental predicate of substance. The fact is that in Spinoza eternity is understood as *timelessness* and decisively opposed to duration in time (*duratio*). Such qualifications as 'when,' 'before,' and 'after' are absolutely inapplicable to eternity, Spinoza says, for in eternity there is neither 'before' nor 'after.'[2]

The question arises as to how the temporal world of finite things is produced from timeless substance. In answering this question, Spinoza suddenly shifts from an ontological to an epistemological analysis and declares that time is only our subjective manner of imagining things. Such a shift, needless to say, does not solve the

[1] *Ibid.*, I, 1.   [2] *Ibid.*, I, 33, scholium 2.

problem, for the question immediately arises of how and why the finite human intellect, which is compelled to view things *sub specie durationis* and to measure this *duratio* by means of time, was produced from timeless substance.

Let us set this question aside as insoluble on the basis of Spinoza's assumptions, and proceed. It might be asked: Why did Spinoza need to postulate the timelessness of substance and by what was this conception evoked? It seems to us that *this* question is not difficult to answer. Like Descartes, Spinoza considered mathematics with its so-called 'eternal truths' as the model of science. Moreover, Spinoza gave particular preference to *geometry*, which *entirely disregards the concept of time, excluding it in principle from its reasonings*. Spinoza's goal was to understand the whole universe from the viewpoint of unalterable geometrical *necessity*. The dominant idea in Spinoza's thinking was the idea of *strict determinism and strict conformity to law*.

From this it followed that Spinoza made real causes, acting in time, equivalent to logical sequences or timeless 'conclusions' ('*causa* sive *ratio*,' for example, in the second proof of Proposition 2, Part I). Spinoza says:

'From God's supreme power, or infinite nature, an infinite number of things—that is, all things, have necessarily flowed forth in an infinite number of ways, or always follow from the same necessity; in the same way as from the nature of a triangle it follows from eternity and for eternity that its three interior angles are equal to two right angles.'[1]

Let us now proceed to those features or components of Spinoza's fundamental views which indicate a certain *dialectical* overcoming of the above-noted break or discrepancy between infinite substance and its finite modes.

Here it is necessary first of all to emphasize the thought which Spinoza formulates in Proposition 16, Part I, and which he himself stresses continually (referring repeatedly to this proposition), namely, the proposition that 'from the necessity of the divine nature must follow an infinite number of things in infinite ways—that is, all things which fall within the sphere of infinite intellect.' This proposition means that from substance all of its modes, finite as well as infinite (for finite modes too can be objects of infinite intellect, that is, intellect which embraces in thought an infinite number of things),

[1] *Ethics*, I, 17, scholium.

always and necessarily follow—and all of these modes follow from substance with such absolute necessity that it is impossible for them not to follow. This means that *substance is impossible without its modes*. Although, according to Spinoza's definition, which we emphasized at the beginning, substance exists *only in itself*, it is nevertheless manifested *only in its modes*, which necessarily flow from it and, as necessary effects of substance, are essentially *inseparable* from it. Proposition 33, Part I, proves that the modes of substance could not follow from it in any other way than they in fact do. If the nature and order of the modes were other than it actually is, the nature of *substance* would have to be different from what it is. Spinoza says this himself in the proof of this proposition. And in Proposition 24, Part V, he draws a further direct conclusion from the doctrine of individual things as modifications of a single substance—a conclusion which speaks again of the necessary unity and indissoluble connection between substance and its modes. This conclusion reads: 'The more we understand particular things, the more do we understand *God*.'

Furthermore, on the problem of the relation between infinite and finite, we find in Spinoza hints of a dialectical solution. And here I am in complete agreement with those colleagues who consider that the scholium to Proposition 15, Part I, contains profound dialectical thoughts on the problem of the relation between infinite and finite. True, in Spinoza, these thoughts are not carried to their conclusion, and they are obscured by such non-dialectical elements as the absolute distinction between intellect and imagination. But if we set aside the absolute character of this distinction and turn our attention to the meaning and significance of the parallel, adduced by Spinoza, with the problem of line and point, we find the following extremely interesting conception: just as a finite extended line is not a simple mechanical aggregate of non-extended points, but a particular quality or a relation of a particular kind between points arranged *continuously*, that is, such that between any two given points there is an infinite number of intermediate points, in the same way, infinite extended substance is not a mechanical aggregate of finite bodies, but a certain *continuous* and limitless unity, including in itself all finite things, which in essence are not *discrete* objects, absolutely isolated one from the other, but merely parts, *relatively* distinct from one another, of a *single continuum*, a universal and continuous whole. In the scholium to lemma 7, Part II, Spinoza calls the universe 'one individual, whose parts, that is, all bodies, vary in infinite ways without any change in the individual as a whole.' According to Spinoza, the 'form' of the world-individual always remains immutable, and it is the *reciprocal connection or union* of the bodies making up this individual which constitutes its form. The changelessness of the world-individual as a whole accords with Spinoza's views of the timelessness of substance. Dialectical materialism, needless to say, rejects both the timelessness of substance and the changelessness of the world-whole. But Spinoza's fundamental idea of the *continuity* of universal being and the *universal connection and union of all things* fully corresponds to our contemporary views, that is, to the views of dialectical materialism.

On the problem of the relation between a line-segment and the points which are contained in it, it would perhaps not be superfluous to cite the explanation given by another great rationalist, Spinoza's younger contemporary Leibniz, who may justly be called the philosopher of the continuum. In his eighty-second letter to the mathematician Johann Bernoulli (in 1698), Leibniz wrote:

'Just as there is no element of number, that is, no minimum part of a unity, or minimum among numbers, so there is no minimum line, or element of line. . . . And, in fact, I conceive points not as elements of line [for such elements, as has been said, do not in general exist] but as limits or negations of its further extension, that is, as terminals of the line.'[1]

We could say that a point is, as it were, the *lower limit* of a line; in that case the *upper limit* of a finite straight line would be an infinite straight line.

Developing Spinoza's and Leibniz' views on this question further, we might say that we are here dealing with the following remarkable dialectical proposition: A line-segment has a definite extension, a definite *length*. However, the points which lie on this segment—and there is nothing else on it except points, *plus* the relationship of continuity between them—have no extension, no magnitude; neither length nor width. Thus the segment and its *points differ in nature*; they are different in principle and *opposed as to quality*: the segment is something extended and has a definite length, while the points are non-extended and have no length at all. At the same time, however, the segment *presupposes* points as its boundaries or limits and as that which it contains or includes in itself, in infinite numbers. And conversely, the point *contains in itself the necessary*

[1] *Leibnizens Mathematische Schriften*, ed. by Gerhardt, Vol. III, p. 536.

SPINOZA'S SUBSTANCE AND FINITE THINGS

condition of the segment: for the path of a moving point is a line or segment. Thus the point and the line are *correlative polarities* which presuppose one another and condition one another.

According to Spinoza, such a relationship of correlative polarity obtains between infinite substance and its finite modes. A non-extended point (and a point must be conceived as non-extended) is, as it were, a spatial zero, for a point is the lower limit of a line, as zero is the lower limit of number. Consequently, no matter how many points we put together, we will never obtain a segment of even minimum length: a segment is something more than and qualitatively different from a simple mechanical aggregate of points. Thus, just as a line-segment is not merely the sum of the points which make it up, so Spinoza's substance is not a simple mechanical aggregate of finite things. Infinite substance and its finite modes differ in principle, by their nature or quality: substance is one, infinite, indivisible, indestructible; it embraces all things and is determined only from within; whereas finite things are many, limited, destructible, and determined in the final analysis by the whole aggregate of things, and not exclusively by their own inner nature or essence. But this difference in principle, this opposition between substance and its modes, does not prevent them from existing in such a close and indissoluble connection that they presuppose one another and condition one another. In a word, they are essentially *correlative polarities* like the line and the point.

The problem of the relationship between essence and existence is directly connected with the problem of the relationship between infinite and finite. Only in substance, according to Spinoza, do we have a unity of essence and existence. In the case of the modes there is a certain break between essence and existence. This is certainly true. But it is necessary to observe that this break occurs only when we consider some particular mode *in isolation*. If, however, we take the *order of the whole of nature* ('*ordo universæ naturæ*,' second proof, Proposition 11, Part I), or the *order of all causes* ('*ordo causarum*,' first scholium, Proposition 33, Part I), or the *concatenation of all things* ('*rerum concatenatio*,' appendix to Part I), then we obtain a *complete definition of each individual thing not only according to its essence but also according to its existence*; for the existence of each individual thing and the continuation of this existence follow just as *necessarily* from the universal world order as do the properties of a triangle from its essence. The only difference is that it is not difficult to comprehend the essence of a triangle; this is completely within our powers. But, as finite beings, we are not in a position to embrace cognitively the complete structure of things, the whole infinite order of causes and effects. Hence it follows that certain things seem to us only contingent, although in fact they are strictly necessary. And thus in our thoughts we separate the existence of things from their essence and are able to imagine individual finite things as non-existent. It is only the one substance, as the immanent cause and totality of all reality, that cannot be conceived by us as other than existing.

Thus, on this point too, the metaphysical discrepancy—in this case, the break between essence and existence—gives way, at least as a hint and an ideal for knowledge, to the *dialectical unity* of essence and existence as two distinct but interconnected *aspects of one and the same thing*. 'But indeed,' Spinoza says in the *Cogitata Metaphysica*, 'in their ignorance they invent distinctions in things [the distinction between possible and impossible, between that which follows directly from the essence of a thing and that which does not so follow, is under discussion.—V. B.]. For,' Spinoza continues, 'if men could understand clearly the *whole order of nature* (*totum ordinem naturæ*) they would find *everything just as necessary as that which is treated in mathematics*; but since this exceeds human knowledge, we judge some things to be merely possible, not necessary.'[1]

Bringing essence and existence together in a higher unity, Spinoza emphasizes—in order to avoid misunderstanding—that the mathematical objects, e.g. triangles, lines, etc., which he so frequently uses to illustrate his understanding of necessary sequence, do not embody in themselves a unity of essence and existence, for they are considered only under the aspect of their *essence*. Accordingly, mathematical knowledge does not represent for Spinoza the highest kind of knowledge; it is only rational, *abstract* knowledge. The truths of mathematics are eternal truths, but they are *abstract* and *incomplete* according to their essence. The highest knowledge—intuitive knowledge—deals with the concrete *unity* of essence and existence, with the absolute fulness of all reality, with substance or God as an absolute and necessarily existing being.

It is interesting to note that Leibniz solves the problem of essence and existence in the same general way. Distinguishing and opposing the 'truths of reason' (which are evident solely from the *essence* of the thing about which such truths are asserted) and 'truths of fact'

[1] *Cogitata Metaphysica*, Part II, ch. 9, par. 2; cf. *Ethics*, I, 33, scholium.

SPINOZA'S SUBSTANCE AND FINITE THINGS 127

(which are given in experience, simply as existing *facts*), Leibniz remarks:

'However, truths of fact also have their necessary grounds (*rationes*) and hence are by nature capable of being resolved [into their first principles.—*Trans*.], but they can be known by us *a priori* through their causes only if the whole order of things (*tota serie rerum*) is known, and since this exceeds the power of the human mind, they are known *a posteriori* through experience.'[1]

In this way the great seventeenth-century rationalists overcame the dualism of essence and existence, of logical ground and empirical fact, of reason and experience, of the *a priori* and the *a posteriori*.

Let us now return specifically to Spinoza and consider a very famous and very important passage from Part I of the *Ethics* which is often the occasion for accusing Spinoza of self-contradiction on the question of the relation of substance to individual finite things. We have in mind Propositions 21–3, on the one hand, and Proposition 28, on the other. In order to clarify the question of whether this latter proposition contradicts Propositions 21–3, we shall present the proof of Proposition 28 with all the necessary details (borrowing as necessary from the earlier propositions to which Spinoza himself refers in his argument).

This proposition, as is well known, is concerned with the principles of the existence of individual finite things.

Finite things, says Spinoza, are not essentially *causæ sui*, that is, their essence does not involve existence.

What then is the cause of their existence?

Nothing exists except God and the modes, and the latter are only God's conditions: this means that God alone can be the cause of the existence of finite things.

But in what sense and in what respect?

From the *absolute* nature of God, that is, from God insofar as he is considered *absolutely*, in other words, *directly* from his attributes, only infinite not finite things can follow.

Consequently, finite things flow from some *modification* of God.

But not from an infinite modification, for only infinite things can flow from an infinite modification.

Consequently, finite things flow from one of God's *finite* modifi-

[1] 'Præcognita ad Encyclopædiam sive Scientiam universalem,' *Die philosophischen Schriften von Gottfried Wilhelm Leibniz*, ed. by Gerhardt, Vol. VII, p. 44.

cations, that is, one finite thing from another and so on without end. In other words, every finite thing follows from the necessity of the divine nature, in so far as this divine nature is modified *in some finite and determinate way*.

Such is Spinoza's argument. But we do not see why Spinoza's substance could not be modified in finite as well as infinite modifications. On the contrary, we think that this substance not only can but *must* include *finite* modifications, for, according to Spinoza, it is the absolute fulness of all things, and from it all things, finite as well as infinite, flow in a necessary fashion. The very concept 'infinite' necessarily presupposes the correlative concept 'finite,' and Spinoza himself hints in the above-mentioned scholium (Proposition 15, Part I) at the concept of *correlative polarities* (cf. the parallel which he indicates with the problem of line and point).

In the light of all this, we see no contradiction between Proposition 28 and Propositions 21–3, in which it is said that from God, in so far as he is considered *absolutely* ('*quatenus* absolute *consideratur*,' proof, Proposition 23), and from his *infinite* modifications, only infinite, not finite things can flow.

Now we may ask ourselves: what then is Spinoza's God or substance? Is it in fact absolutely cut off from the world of finite things? Taking into consideration all that we have said, we may offer the following approximate definition of Spinoza's substance (having in mind, as throughout this paper, only the question of the relation of substance to its modes, and disregarding for the time being the question of the relation between the attributes—of that another time): *Spinoza's substance*, we suggest, *is the world-whole from the point of view of its unity, its conformity to law, and its absolute fulness*. And this is what Spinoza characterizes by the term *natura naturans*. As distinguished from this, *natura naturata* signifies in this case the *totality of individual things from the point of view of their multiplicity and separateness*. How then are *natura naturans* and *natura naturata* related to one another? It seems to us that the most reasonable answer would be that they are essentially *two aspects of one and the same thing*. It is true that Spinoza does not always and in every respect hold to the viewpoint of two aspects of one and the same thing, and at the beginning of this paper we cited certain of his propositions which to a considerable extent isolate *natura naturans* from *natura naturata*. And if we were to treat this question in more detail, if in particular we were to spend more time on Part V of the *Ethics*, it would be possible to cite a number of pieces of evidence from Spinoza himself which support a certain separation of substance from its modes. But despite all this, the *monistic tendency* is dominant in Spinoza, and in any case, the most valuable and interesting achievement of his philosophy is to be found precisely in *this* tendency. In support of the basic idea that substance and its modes are in a *certain sense* essentially one and the same thing, and to supplement all the considerations presented in the preceding pages, we may cite Spinoza's famous remarks concerning water, in the scholium to Proposition 15, Part I: 'Water,' says Spinoza, 'in so far as it is substance (*quatenus est substantia*) is indivisible, and is neither produced nor destroyed; but in so far as it is water, it is divisible, and is produced and destroyed.' Thus, one and the same finite thing is viewed by Spinoza now as an individual finite mode, now as a manifestation of a single, indivisible, and infinite substance.

From this point of view we may even agree, in a certain sense, with the characterizations '*in se*' and '*per se*,' with which Spinoza endows his substance (in the third definition of Part I) as distinguished from the modes, which exist '*in alio*' and are conceived '*per aliud*.' For, while each individual thing is determined in the final analysis by all other things and in this sense exists '*in alio*' (that is, in the entire aggregate of things) and accordingly is conceived '*per aliud*'; the totality of things, embracing all things absolutely and containing in itself the fulness of all reality, is determined exclusively from within by virtue of the immanent necessity inherent in it, and in this sense exists only '*in se*'—for outside it there is nothing—and, accordingly, is conceived only '*per se*.'

Be that as it may, someone may object; all the same there is no *transition* in Spinoza from infinite substance to finite things: the causal chain of finite things has neither beginning nor end, and at no point can it come to rest in the infinite substance from which, according to Spinoza, these things must flow. In answer to this objection, we should say that there is such a transition in Spinoza, but not in the sense of a *gradual transformation* of infinite into finite (such as our hypothetical critic evidently requires), but in the sense of a *dialectical correlation* between them. In fact, our hypothetical critic might require with equal justice that he be shown a 'transition' from line to point or from point to line. But it is evident that there is not and *cannot be* any gradual transformation of a line into a point, or vice versa. For no matter how much we may divide a line, we will never come to 'rest' at a point, and however many points we place together, we will never obtain a line, even of minimum length.

The unique peculiarity of the line consists precisely in this, that, however short it may be, it contains an infinite number of points. And the *dialectical nature of Spinoza's substance* consists precisely in this, that it *necessarily presupposes within itself an infinite series of finite modes, and in a certain sense is entirely exhausted by this series*—just as a line-segment is entirely exhausted by the aggregate of points lying upon it, not by their mechanical aggregation, but by their unification into a single whole of a particular kind through the relationship of continuity between them.

S. Ya. Volfson

SPINOZA'S ETHICAL WORLD-VIEW[1]

A paper read before the Scientific Society of the Belorussian National University in Minsk on the two hundred and fiftieth anniversary of Spinoza's death, February 21, 1927.

I SHOULD like to begin this paper, which is dedicated to the memory of Baruch Spinoza, and has as its object a characterization of one of the aspects of this great thinker's philosophic legacy, with a brief general explanation.

The question may occur to some of those present: 'Why do we, a university born and bred in revolution, celebrate today the two hundred and fiftieth anniversary of Spinoza's death? Why do we, dialectical materialists, carrying on scientific work under the banner of orthodox Marxism, consider Spinoza's jubilee our holiday as well?'

I answer this question as follows: We do this not only because *'homo sum et nihil humanum mihi alienum est'*—'we are men and therefore nothing human is alien to us.' No, we honour Spinoza not only as a titan of thought, not only as a brilliant example of human intelligence, a majestic manifestation of the power of the human mind, a *'homo sapientissimus.'* We celebrate his anniversary because Spinoza was one of the greatest revolutionists of thought known to human history, one of the noblest fighters for a science freed from the fetters of moribund tradition, inertia, and otherworldly aspiration.

The emancipating movement which broke away from the dominant world-view of the Middle Ages toward the thinking of the new epoch, the ideological revolution experienced by European man in the period of transition from the medieval to the modern world, found in Spinoza one of its greatest exponents.

[1] A translation of *Eticheskoye mirosozertsaniye Spinozy*, Minsk, 1927.

Spinoza destroyed the most important support of medieval ideology, the teleological conception of the world, and deposed the religious myth to which the scientific thought of his time had been subordinated. He took his stand as an enemy of all the transcendental tendencies which dominated the philosophy of his day. In opposition to these tendencies, Spinoza developed a naturalistic philosophy, imbued with the principle of the strictest mechanical conformity to law and the causal conditioning of phenomena. He included man in a single system of the world—of nature—and subjected him to an iron-clad, deterministic law. He overcame the dualism of Descartes, opposing to it a system of naturalistic monism. To the problems which confronted the philosophy of his age, Spinoza gave answers which were materialistic to the extent permitted by the social conditions and natural sciences of the period. And for this reason Ludwig Feuerbach, the immediate predecessor of contemporary materialism, felt justified—and we have no reason to dispute this—in calling Spinoza 'the Moses of the modern freethinkers and materialists.'

I do not, however, wish these introductory remarks to be understood to mean that I unreservedly include Spinoza among the consistent materialistic philosophers. I should consider such an attempt an over-simplification and vulgarization of Marxism. On the question of Spinoza's materialism, I think, there is no point in voting 'for' or 'against.' Here we need a close and careful dialectical analysis. It seems to me that Marxism can show, indeed, has already shown, that the inclusion of Spinoza among the idealistic philosophers, which has been perpetrated for centuries by the idealistic historians of philosophy, is a flagrant, unscientific contradiction of reality. However, in refuting the multitude of conscious or unconscious falsifiers of Spinoza's teachings, we should not resort to the unconditional inclusion of Spinoza among the consistent materialists. Our task is to take into account those elements of idealism which are contained in Spinoza's system and which are the cause of its few internal inconsistencies, but to make clear at the same time that, freed from its theological veneer, this system is *fundamentally* materialistic. The predominance of materialistic elements in it gives us the right to include Spinoza's among the systems which are essentially materialistic, the right to recognize Baruch Spinoza as one of our ideological predecessors—even though a remote one. We may proudly say that in the great materialistic chain which the best minds of humanity have forged through the ages, beginning with Democritus and Epicurus, through Bacon, Holbach, Feuerbach, down to Marx-Engels, Plekhanov-Lenin—that in this chain there is a link which belongs to Baruch Spinoza, a glorious and courageous revolutionist of thought.

This explains why we not only note, but also *celebrate* his anniversary.

After these introductory remarks, let me turn directly to the theme of this paper: Spinoza's ethical world-view.

What do we mean by the ethical world-view of any thinker?— The rules of conduct which that thinker offers society as a system of ethical norms intended to regulate human relations. The ethical world-view of a thinker, it is evident, always represents a part of his general philosophical world-view.

This applies to all philosophers, and Spinoza is no exception in this respect. With reference to Spinoza we may emphasize only that his ethical system is the basic and central part of his whole philosophy. It is no accident that the work which made his name immortal bears the title *Ethics*; nor is it an accident that Spinoza regarded the general philosophical sections of this work—the first two parts— as having a subsidiary and secondary character in relation to his ethical doctrines.

Likewise, his *Theologico-Political Treatise* and *On the Improvement of the Understanding* have the fundamental aim of helping mankind through the elaboration of a system for human conduct and happiness. The ultimate aim of all of Spinoza's philosophical reasoning is the mastery and comprehension of those things which 'may conduct us, as it were by the hand, to the knowledge of the human mind and its highest happiness.'[1]

The point of departure for Spinoza's ethical doctrines was his profound conviction that man is not something standing outside nature and exempt from its universal laws. He was a destroyer of the anthropocentric fiction, and he sharply criticized its adherents who 'conceive man to be situated in nature as a kingdom within a kingdom: for they believe that he disturbs rather than follows nature's order, that he has absolute control over his actions, and that he is determined solely by himself.'[2]

Spinoza knew that man is subject to the laws which are in force throughout the universe, that the world's conformity to law controls man's actions and fate, that to regard man as outside this law is to create illusions unworthy of a scientist. 'For man,' declares

[1] *Ethics*, preface to Part II.   [2] *Ibid.*, preface to Part III.

Spinoza in the *Political Treatise*, 'whether sage or fool, is a part of nature . . . whether he be subject to the rule of reason or of passion, he acts always in conformity with the laws and rules of nature, that is, according to natural right.'[1]

I have called Spinoza an intellectual revolutionist, and it is to one of the boldest flights of his revolutionary thought that we owe the destruction of the barrier which the traditional science of his day had erected between man and the rest of the animal world. Spinoza broke down this barrier: 'We do not recognize any difference between man and other natural beings.'[2]

In all his reflections on man Spinoza consistently subordinates the latter to the supreme law of nature: 'It is impossible that man should not be a part of nature, and that he should suffer no changes but those which can be understood through his own nature alone, and of which he is the adequate cause.'[3]

Man, a mode of eternal attributes, is a fragment of all-embracing nature, which he can comprehend only by investigating and mastering its principles and laws. And only through such investigation can we understand man, with all his actions and emotions. With the fearlessness of the true sage, Spinoza turned to man's inner world, which the philosophy of his time had wrapped in the multiple veils of mysticism, otherworldliness, and theology, and with the bold hand of a revolutionist tore away these veils. He declared that the soul is an *automatum spirituale*—'a spiritual mechanism'—and he set out to investigate this mechanism like any other natural object.

'The passions of hatred, anger, envy, and so on, considered in themselves, follow from this same necessity and efficacy of nature; they answer to certain definite causes, through which they are to be understood, and possess certain properties which are as worthy of being known as the properties of anything else, whereof the contemplation in itself affords us delight. I shall, therefore, treat of the nature and strength of the emotions according to the same method as I employed in the previous parts. . . . I shall consider human actions and desires in exactly the same manner as though I were concerned with lines, planes, and solids.'[4]

These famous words from the preface to Part III of the *Ethics* express the methodological creed which was the point of departure

---

[1] *Political Treatise*, II, 5. [2] *Theologico-Political Treatise*, XVI, 5.
[3] *Ethics*, IV, 4. [4] *Ibid.*, preface to Part III.

for the development of Spinoza's ethical system. Not to bewail, not to deride, but to understand!

This system should first of all be characterized from the point of view of the determinism which permeates it. Spinoza's recognition that 'the will cannot be called a free, but only a necessary, cause,' was the decisive factor in his whole ethical system. An endless chain of causal conditioning determines our desires and actions. The wise man cannot be likened to the infant which thinks that it freely desires milk, or the drunkard who thinks that by his own volition he talks of things which the sober man guards in silence. Spinoza made gigantic efforts to break down the prejudices of man's free will and spontaneous activity. Being conscious of his desires and cravings, and not being aware of the causes which condition these desires and cravings, man creates the illusion of a freely self-manifesting will. However, 'in the mind there is no absolute or free will; but the mind is determined to wish this or that by a cause which has also been determined by another cause, and this last by another cause, and so on to infinity.'[1]

Only after having asserted the principle of determinism could Spinoza proceed to the working out in practice of his methodological creed, approaching human conduct with the same scientific criteria he would have employed in dealing with lines and planes. He approached the solution of ethical problems with what he considered the one and only scientific method; that is, he investigated morality 'by means of the general laws and rules of nature.' But in nature, Spinoza knew, there is nothing *obligatory*; there is only the *necessary*. And he made the principle of natural *necessity* the cornerstone of his ethical system, conducting his investigations of morality in the light of the principle of universal inevitability. By drawing morality into the orbit of naturalistic investigation, Spinoza performed a tremendous service for the philosophic thought of succeeding epochs. Transcendental morality, originating with Plato, and appearing now in the guise of 'divine commandment,' now appealing to the 'inner voice' of man, was shaken by Spinoza to its very foundations. Kant made an attempt to resurrect this morality, surrounding it with the aura of a non-spatial and non-temporal maxim—the categorical imperative; and, if the followers of Kant during the past century have attempted to canonize this doctrine of morality, the scientific materialistic thought of the past two and a half centuries has repeatedly made use of weapons from Spinoza's

[1] *Ibid.*, II, 48.

arsenal in its struggle against a morality proceeding from divine creator, inner voice, or abstract obligation. The science of morality, if only it be genuine science and not pseudo-scientific priestcraft, is not supposed to teach, to exhort, to harp endlessly about obligations—but to investigate, to study, and comprehend. Its sphere is not what *ought* to be, but what *is*. And for this reason Spinoza is merciless toward the philosophizing preachers and sermonizing philosophers who never tire of plaguing mankind with their ethical homilies. Spinoza's favourite rule was not to ridicule, not to despise, but to understand; however, in connection with this breed of moralizing philosophers who do not study morality, Spinoza broke his own rule. He not only understood them, he ridiculed and despised them as well. In the *Political Treatise* he wrote of them as follows: 'They take men not as they are, but as they would like to have them. And for this reason it happens that for the most part they have written satire instead of ethics.' Spinoza felt that these moralizing philosophers presented to mankind a wretched and subtle chimera instead of the knowledge necessary for life. He himself wished to take mankind, and did take it, as it is. A philosophic monist who took the world as a single, all-embracing whole, Spinoza remained a monist in his treatment of ethical problems. As such, he did not create a gulf between what is and what should be, between the naturally necessary and the humanly desirable, between fact and norm, the actual and the moral, the real and the ideal. This gulf is present in the system of any philosopher who, creating 'satire instead of ethics,' offers mankind his speculative chimeras. And Spinoza's very great scientific contribution lies in what his idealistic critics regard as his philosophical sin, namely, that he did not recognize a 'categorical imperative,' that he refused to accept the idea of absolute good, and thus denied the possibility of constructing that 'realm of ends' which these critics regard as the object of philosophical ethics.[1]

For Plato virtue was a 'comeliness of the soul'; morality was for him a raising up of the soul to pure contemplation. Aristotle affirmed that man's highest good consists in the development of virtue. Spinoza declared that 'virtue is nothing else than activity in accordance with the laws of our own nature,' that 'in so far as a thing is in harmony with our nature, it is necessarily good.'[2]

[1] Cf. S. F. Kechekyan, *Eticheskoye mirosozertsaniye Spinozy* (*Spinoza's Ethical World-View*), 1914, p. 102.
[2] *Ethics*, IV, 31.

Spinoza 'defetishized' morality, transforming it from a fetish, wrapped in the haze of mysticism and theological fiction, into an object of scientific investigation. In so doing, he emerged as the founder of scientific ethics. 'Spinoza saw in morality only a science, more elevated than other sciences, to be sure, but the same in nature and method as the rest,' says one of the interpreters of Spinoza's ethical doctrines. 'Science is valuable in his eyes only in so far as it provides a basis for morality, and morality, in turn, is valuable only as it makes use of the procedures and results of the other sciences. ... Science is only for morality, morality only for science.'[1]

These words are completely just. The more so, in that Spinoza not only *proclaimed* the rapprochement of ethics and science, but also undertook to *investigate* the origin of morality on the basis of the scientific data with which he was provided and which the science of his time could place at his disposal. The fruitful result of these investigations is already apparent in the answer which Spinoza gave to the question of the genesis of morality. Following Hobbes, who was close to him in this respect, Spinoza set out to derive morality from the impulse toward self-preservation. But, whereas Hobbes was not able to develop an ethical system around this principle, Spinoza constructed his sytem precisely on this foundation.

The premise of Spinoza's ethical system is the assertion that 'everything in so far as it is in itself, endeavours to persist in its own being,'[2] that anything whatever 'is opposed to all that could take away its existence.'[3] Man, like every other thing, is subject to the tendency *suum esse conservandi*. The tendency to persist in his own being follows from man's very nature; it is a consequence of a universal natural law.

'Since reason demands nothing which is opposed to nature,' Spinoza argues, 'it demands that every man should love himself, should seek that which is useful to him—that which is truly useful to him—should desire everything which really brings man to greater perfection, and absolutely that everyone should endeavour, as far as in him lies, to preserve his own being.'[4]

From this, Spinoza also arrived at the conclusion that 'the foundation of virtue is the endeavour to preserve one's own being, and that happiness consists in man's power of preserving his own being.'[5] On the basis of this conclusion he also developed his theory of moral

[1] René Worms, *La Morale de Spinoza*, 1894, p. 31.   [2] *Ethics*, III, 6.
[3] *Ibid.*, III, 6, proof.   [4] *Ibid.*, IV, 18, scholium.   [5] *Loc. cit.*

strength—*virtus*—as human power which is defined solely by man's essence, that is, 'which is defined solely by the endeavour made by man to persist in his own being.'[1]

This tendency to persist in his own being, the struggle for his own existence, is in Spinoza's eyes a peremptory human right, resting on the supreme and universal law of nature—*suum esse conservare*. And proceeding from this law alone it is possible to investigate human morality, reason about it, and establish ethical principles. 'Everything that man does for the preservation of his being,' we read in the *Political Treatise*, 'he does according to the highest natural right.' This certainty made it possible for Spinoza to say in the *Ethics* that 'the more every man endeavours, and is able to seek what is useful to him—in other words, to preserve his own being—the more is he endowed with virtue,'[2] and to equate the concepts 'to act absolutely in obedience to virtue' and 'to preserve one's being . . . on the basis of seeking what is useful to one's self.'[3]

Spinoza proclaimed that 'everything exists according to the highest natural right' and this recognition provided him with a sufficient basis for the sanctioning of all human actions, which follow from the necessity of human nature; to recognize that all our judgments of good and evil are made in accordance with this supreme natural right, and finally, that this right allows everyone to look to his own advantage according to his own understanding, to defend himself, to preserve what he loves, and to destroy what he hates.

Self-preservation is the controlling stimulus of all human actions and determines all our ideas of happiness and unhappiness, of good and evil. Therefore, 'no virtue can be conceived as prior to this endeavour to preserve one's own being.'[4] 'By good I understand that which we certainly know to be useful to us.'[5]

It is easy to see that Spinoza's derivation of virtue from the impulse of self-preservation should arouse, and has aroused, the indignation of all those for whom virtue is an abstract category of some transcendental order. And, indeed, how much noble pathos has been manifested, how much righteous indignation expended, how much denunciatory ink spilled on this subject! The historians of philosophy and the philosophical critics, Spinoza's countless interpreters—all those about whom Spinoza himself remarked that in their opinion utilitarian striving is the foundation of dishonour—have hurled words of wrath and shed tears of regret over the fact

---

[1] *Ethics*, IV, 20, proof.   [2] *Ibid.*, IV, 20.   [3] *Ibid.*, IV, 24.
[4] *Ibid.*, IV, 22.   [5] *Ibid.*, IV, def. I.

that Spinoza gave a philosophical sanction to man's animal egoism and cloaked amoralism with the name of morality. 'Complete ethical emptiness,' 'moral indifference,' 'a justification of man on immoral grounds,' 'a doctrine of immorality'—such is Spinoza's ethics in the opinion of a not unknown German scholar, Friedrich Dittes. And Dittes is not alone—there are many Ditteses. We are not speaking now of the time when, in Lessing's well-known phrase, Spinoza was treated like a dead dog. Down to the most recent times the high priests of idealism have spoken of him as does, for example, our Russian Spinoza scholar, Kechekyan, who calls Spinoza's morality 'miserable' and brands as 'immoralism' his 'grossly materialistic, cruelly egotistical' system. Only those among them more favourably inclined toward Spinoza have attempted to save his reputation, consoling themselves and others after the manner of René Worms that 'the striving for personal interest of which Spinoza speaks is not the gross animal interest of Hobbes and La Mettrie, but a purely metaphysical interest.'[1]

In thus attempting, for purposes of 'rehabilitation,' to oppose Spinoza's 'metaphysical' interest to the 'animal' interest of Hobbes and La Mettrie, Worms did both science and Spinoza a disservice. The connection between the ethical views of the seventeenth-century English materialists and Spinoza's system, on the one hand, and between Spinoza's ethical world-view and that of the pre-Revolutionary French materialists, on the other, is clear and may be easily detected by any careful investigator. They are 'berries from the same field' [i.e. 'birds of a feather'—*Trans.*]—'berries' which matured in the social atmosphere of the most economically advanced countries of Western Europe during the period of transition from feudalism to capitalism, appearing in response to the same social needs. All of these systems were and will remain equally amoral and egotistical—'grossly materialistic'—in the eyes of those who, like Kechekyan, think that 'ethics carries us out of our world into another world, so that we may return fortified with the steel weapons of principles, of established ends.'[2] But in reality these 'steel weapons' are only rusty trash, borne by the pensioned-off soldiers of idealistic philosophy. Ethics does not carry us out of our world into another, non-existent one; it investigates human conduct and regulates human relations in this one and only world.

For the disciples of idealism, defetishized ethics ceases to be ethics; it becomes amoralism, revealing itself as an embodiment of

[1] Worms, *op. cit.*, p. 170.   [2] Kechekyan, *op. cit.*, p. 91.

animal egoism. For us, defetishized ethics is the only scientific, and hence, the only possible, ethics. Indeed, Spinoza's defetishization of ethics has great and unquestionable merits. In defetishizing ethics he did not fall into the vulgar identification of egoistic advantage with the good. This problem he solved dialectically. Not abstract categories, but concrete truth! Neither absolute good nor absolute evil exists for Spinoza. 'Every action,' he wrote in a letter to Blyenbergh, 'is good in so far as it possesses reality.' And in the preface to Part IV of the *Ethics* he says, 'As for the terms *good* and *bad*, they indicate no positive quality in things regarded in themselves . . . one and the same thing can be at the same time good, bad, and indifferent. For instance, music is good for him that is melancholy, bad for him that mourns; for him that is deaf, it is neither good nor bad.'

These words testify to Spinoza's dialectical treatment of fundamental moral categories (for which he has often been branded an 'ethical relativist').

The dialectical approach to the problem of morality revealed all of its fruitfulness in the extremely difficult problem which faced Spinoza. Deriving morality from man's striving for self-preservation, he had at the same time to explain the conduct of man as a social animal whose morality is based on the limitation of this same striving. In his solution of this problem Spinoza anticipated in part our contemporary views as to the source of morality. We know that the instinct of self-preservation, which is inherent in every animal, generates a social instinct in the process of the animal's intercourse with others of his kind. We affirm that, inasmuch as the individual cannot exist in isolation, but is forced in the name of self-preservation to join with others of his kind, every animal learns to limit its egoistic impulses for the sake of collective advantage. Conventional ties are created through the exchange of services and through cooperation with other members of the community. In this way the instinct of self-preservation leads dialectically to the formation of the social instinct.

As I have already said, we find in Spinoza an anticipation of contemporary science's formulation of this problem. Indeed, in deriving morality from the striving for advantage, Spinoza realized that man gains the greatest advantage from association with others of his kind. *Homini nihil homine utilius.* 'Man is a god to man,' Spinoza says in one place [*Ethics*, Part IV, Prop. 35, scholium]. But the mutual association of men becomes impossible if each manifests his own egoistic impulses without restriction. Thus, in the interest of the most advantageous association among themselves, men are forced to limit and restrain their ego, with its impulse toward self-preservation. Every man has an *egoistical* interest in association with his kind, but the process of this association leads to a point where the component of *egoistic* advantage begins to yield to the component of *social* advantage; *individual* good is subordinated to *social* good, *communicabile sui*.

'To man there is nothing more useful than man,' says Spinoza, 'nothing, I repeat, more excellent for preserving their being can be wished for by men than that all should so in all points agree that the minds and bodies of all should form, as it were, one single mind and one single body, and that all should with one consent, as far as they are able, endeavour to preserve their being, and all with one consent seek what is useful to them all.'[1]

As a social animal, man realizes his striving for advantage on a *social* basis, for 'men derive from social life far more advantages than disadvantages.'[2]

Man's natural right is to act in furtherance of his greatest advantage, but, since men need mutual assistance, this right must be subject to certain restrictions. 'In order that men may live together in harmony and may aid one another, it is necessary that they should forgo their natural right, and, for the sake of security, refrain from all actions which can injure their fellow men.'[3] Subject to passions which often place them in hostile relations to one another, men can, nevertheless, overcome these emotions of mutual hostility by means of stronger and contrary emotions. Thus 'men avoid inflicting injury through fear of incurring a greater injury themselves.'[4] On this basis, according to Spinoza, society itself is strengthened, 'if only it claims for itself the right which every individual possesses of avenging himself and deciding what is good and what is evil.'[5] Thus there arises the conception of good and evil as determined by a given society.

And here we may note in Spinoza a certain similarity to our conception of morality, that is, a system of rules of conduct established on the basis of the valuations of 'good' and 'evil' of a given social collective. Spinoza's ethical system is a social system, imbued with the principle of sociality. And to this day, after a lapse of two and a

[1] *Ethics*, IV, 18, scholium.   [2] *Ibid.*, IV, 35, scholium.
[3] *Ibid.*, IV, 37, scholium II.   [4] *Loc. cit.*   [5] *Loc. cit.*

half centuries, his splendid words, directed against those who would flee from mankind—ascetics, misanthropes, mystics—have lost none of their profound meaning.

'Let satirists therefore scoff at human affairs as much as they please, let theologians denounce them, and let the melancholy praise as much as they can a life rude and without refinement, despising men and admiring the brutes; men will nevertheless find out that by mutual help they can much more easily procure the things they need, and that it is only by their united strength they can avoid the dangers which everywhere threaten them. . . .'[1]

Spinoza's ethics is an earthly, human, social ethics, and this gives it an immense advantage over all of the speculative metaphysical systems, from the predecessors of Plato to the followers of Kant.

I cannot agree with the remark of Friedrich Jodl—which reflects a very widespread opinion—that in constructing his ethics Spinoza ignored man's social inclinations and gave a place of secondary importance to the influence of sociality on our morals. One may say only that Spinoza had an inadequate conception of sociality as a factor which shapes morality, that, appealing to individual reason, he did not reach a clear conception of the process of transformation of egoistic into social instincts. And there is nothing surprising in this. It is true, as Kropotkin reminds us, that Spinoza's *Ethics* appeared at a time when Europe had already experienced two revolutions of a broad social character: the Reformation and the English Revolution. But it must not be forgotten that in Spinoza's day the science of society did not exist even in embryo, the natural sciences were extremely limited, and the course of the class struggle was hidden from the eyes of the investigator. Under such conditions, it is difficult to demand of a philosopher a correct appraisal of the social factor in the formation of such an ideology as morality.

Having noted that Spinoza's ethics is essentially social, we may admit only that its sociality is impaired by the fact that the activity which he demands of men is directed into individualistic rather than social channels.

In taking up the subject of activity, we must first of all show that this element is *contained* in Spinoza's ethical system, and then point out what character Spinoza assigns to it. This procedure is necessary because current opinion ascribes to Spinoza's ethics the preaching of passivity, quietism, and inaction—saying over and over

[1] *Ethics*, IV, 35, scholium.

SPINOZA'S ETHICAL WORLD-VIEW

again that Spinoza is 'the great voice calling men to acquiescence, to peace,' as A. V. Lunacharski expresses it.[1]

Spinoza's numerous idealistic critics find in the law of all-embracing necessity which he established a fatalism which they regard as inherent in his system. But actually Spinoza's determinism has nothing in common with fatalism. Spinoza happily joined the concepts of necessity and freedom, showing that these concepts must be combined dialectically with each other and not regarded as metaphysical [i.e., static or non-dialectical] contradictions. The solution which he gave to the problem of 'freedom and necessity' is one of his outstanding philosophical contributions.

Does Spinoza then require activity of men, or does he preach passivity? 'No one can desire to be happy, to act well and live well, who does not at the same time desire to be, to act, and to live, that is to say, actually to exist,' says Spinoza.[2] He identifies the concepts 'to be happy,' 'to act,' and 'to exist.' Only he who acts actually exists; happiness consists in activity. Everything that interferes with activity is evil. 'We call that thing evil which is the cause of sorrow, that is to say, which lessens or restrains our power of action.'[3]

Is it necessary from Spinoza's point of view to reconcile oneself to evil, to humble oneself before it and capitulate to it? By no means. 'Whatever in nature we judge to be evil or capable of hindering us from existing and enjoying a rational life, we may remove in whatever way seems safest to us.'[4] However, in order to have a correct conception of the character of the activity called for by Spinoza, we must remember that *the primary objective of this activity is the overcoming of our bondage*, by which Spinoza understood 'human inability to moderate or restrain the emotions.' Man is free to the extent that his passions do not rule him, and therefore he should resist the passions and desires which enslave him. Our activity should be directed toward this end. Through reason man should check and moderate his emotions. In so doing he approaches the model of human nature; and man is perfect or imperfect depending upon the extent to which he succeeds in bringing this about.

As we see, the activity which Spinoza calls for is directed into individualistic channels. What is the reason for this? Why did a philosopher whose ethical system is essentially a social system

---

[1] A. V. Lunacharski, *Ot Spinozy do Marksa (From Spinoza to Marx)*, 1925, p. 20.
[2] *Ethics*, IV, 21.   [3] *Ibid.*, IV, 30, proof.
[4] *Ibid.*, IV, Appendix VIII.

proceed in this way? It seems to me that the suggestion put forward in this connection by P. A. Kropotkin is not without foundation. Kropotkin suggests that

'this deficiency may be explained by the fact that in the seventeenth century, when mass slaughters were taking place in the name of the "true faith," the first urgent problem of ethics was to separate morality from every tinge of Christian virtue, and having done this, Spinoza may have decided not to invite even greater thunderings upon himself by defending *social* justice, that is, by defending the communistic ideas promulgated at that time by certain religious movements. It was necessary first of all to re-establish the right of *individual, independent, autonomous reason* . . .'[1]

This right Spinoza attempted to sanction ethically, in opposition to the theological ethics which had destroyed it.

In speaking of Spinoza's ethics, we should emphasize especially that it is a *eudæmonic* system, sanctifying man's striving for happiness and erecting on this foundation a series of moral principles. Theological ethics promised man otherworldly happiness as a reward for abstinence in this world, heavenly bliss for earthly suffering. It paid for *present* morality with *future* bliss. Spinoza gave human happiness a naturalistic sanction; he identified perfect morality and complete felicity. This is made clear by reference to a few of his basic definitions. 'By *joy* . . . I shall understand the passion by which the mind passes to a greater perfection; by *sorrow*, on the other hand, the passion by which it passes to a lesser perfection.'[2] 'By *good* I understand here every kind of joy and everything that conduces to it; chiefly, however, anything that satisfies longing, whatever that thing may be. By *evil*, I understand every kind of sorrow, and chiefly whatever thwarts longing.'[3] '*Joy* is man's passage from a less to a greater perfection. *Sorrow* is man's passage from a greater to a less perfection.'[4] Sorrow is for Spinoza a principle which counteracts man's striving to preserve his being and paralyses human activity. Thus sorrow comes into conflict with the supreme law of nature, while joy is in full accordance with this law. The conclusion to which Spinoza came, and which he sanctioned by the unalterable authority of nature, is that 'we endeavour to bring into existence everything which we imagine conduces to joy, and to remove or destroy every-

---

[1] P. A. Kropotkin, *Etika (Ethics)*, 1922, Vol. I, p. 122.
[2] *Ethics*, III, 11, scholium.   [3] *Ibid.*, III, 39, scholium.
[4] *Ibid.*, III, def. II and III.

thing opposed to it, or which we imagine conduces to sorrow.'[1] Spinoza's ethics is diametrically opposed to the ascetic ideal of Christian ethics; it is a healthy reaction against the cult of martyrdom, deformity, self-torment, mortification of the flesh, flight from worldly corruption, destruction of joy. And what a vivid contrast to the dominant ethical conceptions of an age which regarded all human joy, every healthy manifestation of human nature, as proceeding from the realm of Satan—the *civitas diaboli*—how proudly and splendidly, I say, did the words of the great lens-grinder, the thin, bent little Jew, fighting for the highest right of nature—man's right to joy—ring out against this background! 'Cheerfulness can never be excessive, but is always good; melancholy, on the contrary, is always evil.'[2] 'Assuredly, nothing forbids man to enjoy himself save grim and gloomy superstition,' says Spinoza. 'For why,' he asks, 'is it more seemly to satiate one's hunger and thirst than to drive away one's melancholy?' He declares that 'no deity, nor anyone else . . . regards our tears and sighs as a virtue.'[3] With what healthy reproach do these words sound to this day in the ears of those who, like the Russian poet of anarchy, keep repeating:

> Banish joy,
> Suppress laughter!
> All that brings joy
> Is vanity and sin!

Spinoza was indignant at the fact that dark superstition had humbled men. He considered humility, which was one of the foundations of the ethics of his time, an affront to human nature. 'Humility,' he says, 'is sorrow arising from man's contemplation of his own infirmities.' 'Humility is not a virtue, that is, it does not arise from reason.'[4]

In characterizing Spinoza's ethical world-view, we have one more feature to mention, which supports what we have said above: that Spinoza's ethics is human and earthly; and therefore it protests against the striving toward the transcendental, against the tendency of human thought to be carried away to a world beyond the grave, and of death's mystery to hold the human brain captive. On this subject, Spinoza uttered the following remarkable words:

'A free man is one who lives under the guidance of reason, who

---

[1] *Ibid.*, III, 28.   [2] *Ibid.*, IV, 42.   [3] *Ibid.*, IV, 45, scholium.
[4] *Ibid.*, IV, 53.

is not led by the fear of death, but who directly desires that which is good, in other words, who strives to act, to live, and to preserve his being on the basis of seeking his own true advantage; wherefore such an one thinks of nothing less than of death, but his wisdom is a meditation of life.'[1]

And to those who spoke of the vanity of the world, he pointed out that they most of all were covetous of earthly glory.[2] It is curious that even these unequivocal words have become an object of misrepresentation on the part of Spinoza's idealistic interpreters. Thus, for instance, René Worms—as we have already mentioned—attempts to assist Spinoza out of the suspicious company of Hobbes and La Mettrie; in another place he tries to group Spinoza with Plato and Christ. Concerning Spinoza's attitude toward life and death, Worms argues that 'Spinoza's conception is the conception of Plato and of Christianity, expressed in different words. . . . If Plato exalts meditation of death, and Spinoza meditation of life, it is because each of them sees behind these differing names the same thing: meditation of eternity.'[3] Such a statement represents the grossest distortion of Spinoza's thought and militates against the whole sense of his ethical teaching. Its worthlessness becomes evident when we recall the fact that Plato's world is dualistic, whereas for Spinoza the world is one. Plato's ethics is of heaven; Spinoza's ethics is of earth.

We have tried to show the groundlessness of a few of the assertions put forward by Spinoza's idealistic interpreters concerning his ethical world-view. But there are among these assertions some that are completely acceptable to us. When Friedrich Dittes says of Spinoza that 'no moral norm has for him an absolute and constant value,' that 'he has neither conception nor category for the moral norm which soars above humanity, or for the eternal obligations to which men are subject, or for the moral order of the world';[4] when Kechekyan points out that 'he consistently and boldly destroys all the conventional premises of morality,'[5] we willingly endorse these words. We repeat them, but with the difference that what was

---

[1] *Ethics*, IV, 67. [2] Cf. *Ethics*, V, 10, scholium.
[3] Worms, *op. cit.*, pp. 67–8.
[4] Friedrich Dittes, *op. cit.*, pp. 47, 49. [This work, not named in the original, is apparently: *Ueber die sittliche Freiheit, mit besonderer Berücksichtigung der Systeme von Spinoza, Leibniz und Kant*, 1860. Russian translation, 1900.—*Trans.*]
[5] Kechekyan, *op. cit.*, p. 152.

SPINOZA'S ETHICAL WORLD-VIEW 147

pronounced as censure and reproach we pronounce as an acknowledgment of the profound scientific quality and great historical significance of Spinoza's ethical views. Repeating them, we are saying that Spinoza transformed ethics from a fetish into an object of scientific investigation.

Spinoza provided a splendid commentary to his *Ethics*. This commentary was his life. Above all else he valued the freedom of human reason and the independence of scientific investigation.

Spinoza lived in a time of transition between two epochs. The dark, ascetic medieval period, which had crushed individuality, was beginning to retreat into the past, and a new era of human history was beginning, which was to release productive forces, enter into single combat with nature, reveal new intellectual horizons, and raise up new social strata. In the ethics of these two epochs, Spinoza showed what it means to be a revolutionist of thought and an independent scientific investigator.

The forces of the old world have more than once attempted to capture Spinoza. But none of them has succeeded in subduing his thought to its ideological yoke.

When the Jewish community excommunicated Spinoza for heresy and atheism, forbidding anyone to approach nearer than four ells to the accursed heretic, and the Christian magistracy banished him from Amsterdam, Spinoza remained as firm and imperturbable as at the moment when a wild fanatic sent secretly by the synagogue rushed at him with a dagger, or when his pupil Albert Burg, repudiating his teacher, declared Spinoza a despicable man, puffed up with diabolical glory, and in the name of Christ demanded from him a recantation of his 'arrogant and blind philosophy.'

When Prince Condé offered Spinoza a pension if he would agree to dedicate a work to Louis XIV, he refused this offer just as resolutely as, a year later, he refused the Chair of Philosophy at the University of Heidelberg; he did not wish to fetter his thoughts. Thus Spinoza remained unalterable, confirming with every step of his life the ethical ideal which he had created.

In concluding this characterization of that ideal, I should like to say that Spinoza struggled for the freedom of human reason and the independence of scientific thought. He rested his hopes in this struggle on the wisdom of the individual. We know now that these two ideals are attainable only under definite social conditions. A society based on class struggle, a society of exploitation and profit, cannot create these conditions. They will be created by a society based on emancipated labour and social harmony. Only in this society will the passions which lead to human bondage be humbled, and reason, which gives birth to human freedom, be victorious.

I. P. Razumovski

SPINOZA AND THE STATE[1]

... So wie er früher die Religion mit ihren Dolchen begriffen, so begriff er such jetzt die Politik mit ihren Stricken.—Heine on Spinoza.

IN the contemporary disputes about Spinoza, or, more precisely, in what reveal themselves as attempts to revise the basic Marxist conception of Spinozism, one is especially struck by a strange obliviousness to the fundamental condition of every genuine Marxist analysis: the obvious inattention of our innovators to the *concrete historical setting* in which the teaching of this great thinker was developed. The central point of departure for a correct appraisal of Spinoza's total system of ideas was and remains the *bourgeois revolution* which had occurred in the Netherlands and was impending in other European countries. To fail to understand this and to speak instead of 'Judaism' as 'being in firm possession' of Spinoza's spirit, is to fall into the point of view, so characteristic of bourgeois science, which appeals to the 'messianic ideas' of Marx or the 'Scythian' nature of Lenin!

From our point of view, all the discussions about the 'dualism' of Spinoza's philosophy, and about Spinoza's God as a purely rational 'world order,' 'a supreme law' separated from material being, are completely worthless. References to the well-known passage in Spinoza's correspondence with Oldenburg, where it is said that by 'nature' one should not understand merely 'mass or corporeal matter,'[2] are likewise completely inconclusive. Of course Spinoza—

---

[1] A translation of 'Spinoza i gosudarstvo,' *Pod znamenem marksizma*, No. 2-3 (1927), pp. 65-75.

[2] Letter XXI (LXXIII). An analogous reference may be found in the *Theologico-Political Treatise*. Having pointed out that 'the power and efficiency of nature are in themselves the divine power and efficiency, and that the divine

unlike certain contemporary mechanists—regards nature not simply as 'corporeal matter,' that is, not merely under the attribute of extension, but also under its other infinite attribute. He thinks of it dialectically, as the *concrete unity of being and consciousness, of matter and mind*, in which each aspect retains its unique character. In this unity the 'mind,' which is limited in its 'duration' only by its connection to the body, is at the same time endowed by Spinoza with 'infinity' and 'eternity' as 'a certain mode of thinking' through 'adequate ideas,' 'the power of conceiving things under the form of eternity.'[1]

In general, the notion that the concept 'God' dominates the whole system of Spinoza's thought is erroneous and superficial. Actually, Spinoza as a thinker of the new bourgeois epoch is far from being concerned with the entire essence of 'God'-nature, but 'only that which may conduct us as it were by the hand to a knowledge of the human mind and its highest happiness.'[2] Man is the centre of attention in Spinoza's *Ethics*, just as he had been earlier in the *Ethics* of Aristotle: *man in nature*, not as a 'kingdom within a kingdom,' but as a 'natural being'—man and the *rational organization of his social life*, through which alone he approaches the 'model of human nature.' Spinoza's whole theoretical construction is a skilful process of the 'secularization' of God, a process of dethroning the fetishistic and anthropomorphic ideas with which the human imagination had endowed nature. And at the same time it is a process of *exalting man*, of revealing in his soul the 'necessities and powers' of divine nature —that lofty conception of the human personality for which alone 'man is a god to man.'[3]

In this respect, Spinoza's theory of society and the state throws brilliant light on his whole philosophical system. It provides the most reliable criterion for exposing the mistakes and misunderstandings in the interpretation of Spinozism which may be provoked by its purely external 'theological costume.'

I

Contemporary pedantic scholarship, focusing all of its attention on the perishable *form* rather than the living *spirit* of Spinoza's philosophy, in the quite absurd fear of a possible identification of Spinozism and Marxism, repeatedly elaborates certain feudal and

power is the very essence of God,' Spinoza thereupon makes the reservation that he understands by nature not merely matter and its modifications, but infinite other things besides matter. (Ch. VI, 3.)

[1] *Ethics*, V, 23, 29, etc.　　[2] *Ibid.*, II, preface.　　[3] *Ibid.*, IV, 35, scholium.

medieval details of Spinoza's terminology. As a matter of fact, however, numerous indications scattered throughout the *Ethics* and the *Theologico-Political Treatise* give us a clear idea of the subordinate and pedagogical role which, according to our philosopher himself, his formal 'theologism' was intended to play.

We should proceed at this point from the distinction drawn by Spinoza between knowledge through 'adequate ideas' and 'inadequate,' 'mutilated knowledge' through 'inadequate and confused ideas.' The mind, receiving impressions from the surrounding world, usually 'conceives things imperfectly.' Men 'rather imagine things than understand them. . . . All those methods by which the common people are in the habit of explaining nature are only different sorts of imaginations, and do not reveal the nature of anything in itself, but only the constitution of the imagination.'[1] Despite the fact that the absence of a conception of motion and social development prevents Spinoza from formulating clearly the dialectical connection and succession of 'confused' and 'adequate' ideas, he nevertheless understands clearly that the 'form of falsehood' arises not from ideas themselves, but from 'a deficiency of knowledge.' The thinker's task is to produce changes in men's bodies and minds 'so that everything which refers to their memory and imagination will have almost no significance in comparison with the understanding.'[2] But, in order 'to be understood by all men in every particular,' 'he will seek to support his teaching with experience and will endeavour to suit his reasonings and the definitions of his doctrines as far as possible to the understanding of the common people, who form the majority of mankind.'[3]

In other words, Spinoza poses approximately the same problem with respect to feudal-religious ideology that later faced revolutionary Marxism in its relation to bourgeois culture: to what extent may the thinker of a new epoch make use of the old, habitual categories of religious thinking, *enclosing in these forms a new materialistic content*? Of course, such a utilization becomes possible only on the assumption—conscious or unconscious, but dialectical—that religious forms too are produced by a developing reality and constitute its reflection, however remote, 'confused,' or 'mutilated.' For this reason a differentiated approach to religious thinking is necessary: an historical critique of all that is a product of 'imagination and opinion,' and at the same time a correct philosophical interpretation of religious categories which can be regarded only as a specific,

[1] *Ibid.*, I, appendix.   [2] *Ibid.*, I, 39.   [3] *Theologico-Political Treatise*, ch. V, 35.

habitual expression of the natural order of things in the conception of the broad masses.

From this comes what seems at first glance the contradictory and ambiguous attitude toward religion which Spinoza assumes in his doctrine of *duty to the state*. The goal toward which he aspires is 'the separation of philosophy from theology':[1] the same goal, it would appear, toward which philosophers of the modern period both before and after Spinoza have aspired, now assigning to religion the sphere of 'innate ideas' (Descartes), now 'making a place for faith' in the realm of the 'unknowable' (Kant). But how differently this problem is solved by the Amsterdam thinker! On the other hand, we find in Spinoza a *destructive historical critique* of religious creeds, which in many respects anticipates Feuerbach. Spinoza wittily shows how men, reasoning by analogy from their own use of 'means,' 'came to the conclusion that some ruler or rulers of nature exist, endowed with human liberty,' that 'the gods direct everything for the use of man'; how they took refuge at last in 'the will of God, that is, the sanctuary of ignorance,' the notion that 'God himself takes pleasure in harmony,' etc.[2] In religious superstitions Spinoza sees 'the fantasy and delirium of a despondent and diffident mind'; in religious ceremonies and rites a special form of obedience, a fraud by which 'monarchical government' screens itself; in the religion of Moses he sees the historical 'laws of the Jewish state.' Conceptions of God as a ruler and lawgiver he regards as 'attributes only of human nature.' He indicates that both Christ and the apostles 'adapted his teaching to the spirit of the men of their time';[3] that 'miracles' should be understood only 'in relation to the opinion of men' who are ignorant of the natural causes of things.[4]

But if this is so, religion's right to exist is conditioned by *historical and social factors*. Religion, as a special form of 'obedience,' Spinoza accepts only in so far as the moral injunctions of Scripture do not contradict reason, since 'its meaning should be gathered from its own history,' since, finally, religion 'has proved such a comfort to those whose reason is comparatively weak, and such a benefit to the state.'[5] Accordingly, the *external* forms of religion—as distinguished from the 'inner worship of God'—are far from indifferent to the state:

[1] *Theologico-Political Treatise*, ch. II, 58; ch. XV, 43, etc.
[2] *Ethics*, I, appendix.
[3] *Theologico-Political Treatise*, ch. I, 5, 6, 8–10, 22; ch. IV, 30, 33; ch. XI, 23.
[4] *Ibid.*, ch. VI, 13.
[5] *Ibid.*, ch. XV, 26–43.

SPINOZA AND THE STATE

'the rites of religion and the outward observances of piety should be in accordance with the public peace and well-being.'[1]

This last does not refer only to religious rites and ceremonies. Spinoza extends the sovereign authority of state power to religious commandments, to the practical precepts of religion. In general, all observances of religious piety 'receive the force of laws and ordinances solely through the rights of dominion.' 'For instance, it is in the abstract my duty when my neighbour quarrels with me and wishes to take my cloak, to give him my coat also; but if it be thought that such conduct is hurtful to the maintenance of the state, I ought to bring him to trial. . . .' 'We are also bound not to help one man at another's loss, still less at a loss to the whole state. . . .' 'Public welfare is the sovereign law to which all others, divine and human, should be made to conform.'[2] Consequently, the sovereign power 'should have supreme authority for making any laws about religion which it thinks fit.'[3]

As distinguished from religious rules and precepts, from religious 'law,' Spinoza regards in quite a different light the question of inner religion, the freedom of the religious *conscience*, 'the freedom to judge and think,' which, according to our philosopher, should not be subject to legislative control. The character of 'natural, divine law' does not require belief in historical narratives; it excludes rites and is elucidated by an analysis of human nature. 'Inasmuch as it consists not so much in outward actions as in simplicity and truth of character, it stands outside the sphere of law and public authority.'[4] It is easy to see, however, that when it is emancipated from ritual and restricted to such general 'tenets' as 'the true knowledge of God,' 'the love of God,' or 'the just love of one's neighbour,' this 'inner religion' essentially ceases to be religion. As in Spinoza's own case, it easily passes into free philosophizing about man and nature. Not without reason does Spinoza say of this 'natural knowledge' that it 'has as much right as any other to be called divine, for God's nature, in so far as we share therein, and God's laws dictate it to us.'[5] Having purified religious thinking of everything connected with the practice of piety, with religious fetishism and anthropomorphism, he retains only such general and vague propositions of 'divine knowledge' as can easily be given a 'natural,' materialistic interpretation.

Spinoza is thus least of all inclined to make a 'place for faith.' He

[1] *Ibid.*, ch. XIX, 2–3.   [2] *Ibid.*, ch XIX, 23, 24, 26.
[3] *Ibid.*, ch. XVI, 63.   [4] *Ibid.*, ch. IV, 18–20; ch. VII, 90.
[5] *Ibid.*, ch. I, 3.

converts the very 'separation of philosophy and theology,' as we have seen, into an historical critique of religious ideas, an accommodation of the external aspects of religion to the interests of the state, and a philosophical conquest of its inner realm. Cruel irony of history! The same Spinoza who, according to certain contemporary commentators, was devoted to 'Judaism,' the Spinoza who was devoutly jealous of the freedom of religious conscience—this same Spinoza, in fact, did more than anyone else to bring about the *death of all religion*. As we have already convinced ourselves, here, in the struggle against the old feudal world-view, he was aided by his new *legal* ideology: it therefore deserves our more detailed consideration.

Marx once wittily remarked that in the period of trade capitalism man 'ceased to be a believer and became a creditor.' The conception of 'self-interest' as 'the strength and life of all human action,'[1] together with the conception of 'contract,' basic for all legal thinking —these two conceptions play an extremely important role in Spinoza's system of thought. *Money*, in his words, 'has furnished us with a token for everything.'[2] The possession of property seems to him an incontrovertible legal human institution;[3] the contrast between wealth and poverty must have appeared just as inevitable to him. Nevertheless, the characteristic seventeenth-century doctrine of 'natural right' [*jus naturale*] and the 'social contract' receives certain original features in Spinoza's treatment which distinguish it from the related views of Hobbes and Hugo Grotius, and later from those of Rousseau.

Like Hobbes, Spinoza proceeds from the presupposition that 'men are naturally prone to hatred and envy,'[4] that they are moved by the instinct of self-preservation, the striving for their own advantage. 'The natural right' of every individual leads to the natural law of his existence: the 'natural laws wherewith we conceive every individual to be conditioned by nature so as to live and act in a given way.'[5] 'The right of any person is limited by his virtue or power'; 'every individual has a sovereign right to everything which is within his power.'[6] Natural right knows no prohibitions, no values; it is moved only by 'desire and power.' But in order not to lead a 'miser-

---

[1] *Theologico-Political Treatise*, ch. XVII, 84.
[2] *Ethics*, IV, appendix, ch. XXVIII.
[3] *Theologico-Political Treatise*, ch. VII, 85.
[4] *Ethics*, III, 55, scholium.
[5] *Theologico-Political Treatise*, ch. XVI, 2.
[6] *Ethics*, IV, 37, scholium; *Theologico-Political Treatise*, ch. XVI, 4.

able and bestial life' men must come together to form mutual ties and furnish aid to one another. For this purpose 'it is necessary that they should forgo their natural right and, for the sake of security, refrain from all actions which can injure their fellowmen.' The state of nature is thus replaced by the state of society, the civil society (*civitas*), which preserves itself by 'laws and power.' The state of nature does not know sin, nor does it know private property, since 'all things are common to all.' It does not recognize the difference between good and evil, between justice and injustice. These are all 'extrinsic ideas,' and not natural attributes of the human mind; they are *social* rather than natural institutions. Society 'claims for itself the right which every individual possesses of avenging himself and deciding what is good and what is evil.'[1]

For Hobbes the state, like some threatening coercive force, restrains the inevitable conflict of men and at the same time guarantees the natural right of each. Spinoza, proceeding from the same principle of self-preservation and advantage, finds its clearest expression in *rational* human institutions. 'For man nothing can be more useful for the preservation of his being and the enjoyment of the rational life than his fellow-man who is led by reason.' 'Reason and experience show no more certain means of attaining this object than the formation of a society with fixed laws, the occupation of a strip of territory, and the concentration of all forces, as it were, into one body, that is, the social body.'[2] Law thus receives a significance distinct from the necessity of nature; it is a law 'which depends on human decree and which is more correctly called an *ordinance* [*jus*]'; 'it is a plan of living which men have for a certain object laid down for themselves or others.'[3]

Spinoza considers religious norms an early form of this new law, a form adapted to a people 'accustomed to the condition of slavery,' and in particular he regards from this viewpoint the religion of Moses and his 'covenant with God.' As may be gathered from certain indications of our philosopher, the state of nature 'is, both in nature and in time, prior to religion,' to the divine law.[4] However, the *democratic* state 'is the one most akin' to Spinoza's purpose; it is 'the most natural and the most consonant with individual liberty,' and represents that state in which 'the laws are founded on sound reason.'[5]

---

[1] *Ibid.*, IV, 37, scholium 2.
[2] *Ibid.*, IV, appendix, ch. IX; *Theologico-Political Treatise*, ch. III, 14.
[3] *Theologico-Political Treatise*, ch. IV, 1–5.
[4] *Ibid.*, ch. XVI, 53.   [5] *Ibid.*, ch. XVI, 34–7.

For a better understanding of Spinoza's political and legal ideas, however, it is also necessary to observe his dialectical opposition of the *human will* and the external *objects* which surround man. Spinoza defines the human will as 'the ability to affirm and deny,' a striving of the soul, a consciousness of its 'inclination.' He rejects the doctrine of free will: genuine freedom consists in the ability to restrain one's emotions, bondage in the inability to restrain them; man is thus freer in civil society than in solitude. If man were born completely free, he would have no conception of good and evil;[1] all of his actions would be good. However, man's lack of freedom results from external causes in so far as man is a part of universal nature, whose laws human nature is compelled to obey. Human strength is limited: we do not have absolute power to shape to our use those things which are outside ourselves.[2] At this point human weakness easily reveals itself: it consists in 'man's allowing himself to be led by things which are external to himself and to be determined by them to act in a manner demanded by the general disposition of things rather than by his own nature considered solely in itself.'[3] In such a man the strength of desires is determined not by human strength but by the strength of those things which are external to us. Social life increases our adaptability to things, moderates our passions, and enlarges our freedom.

Our valuations are also determined by the measure of our power over things and thus have a *relative* character. For this reason 'it is necessary to know both the strength and the weakness of our nature, so that we may determine what reason can do and what it cannot do in governing our emotions.'[4] Thus one should not be guided in his actions by the emotions and blind desires which arise as a result of our subjugation to things. It is necessary, for example, 'to regulate the measure of wealth according to one's needs' and not to seek money exclusively for the sake of the 'art of gain.' In the same way, the gratitude of men who are led by blind desires 'is generally a matter of business or a snare rather than gratitude.'[5] Love toward changeless and eternal nature (*amor Dei intellectualis*) should, in the opinion of our philosopher, displace 'the excessive love of things' which are subject to change and cause spiritual suffering.[6]

If we translate these ideas of Spinoza's into the language of historical materialism, we shall have in embryonic form the doctrine

[1] *Ethics*, IV, 68.   [2] *Ibid.*, IV, appendix, ch. VI, XXXII.
[3] *Ibid.*, IV, 37, scholium 1.   [4] *Ibid.*, IV, 17, scholium.
[5] *Ibid.*, IV, appendix, ch. XXIX; 71.   [6] *Ibid.*, V, 19.

of the accommodation of social man to external milieu and the tools of labour, the theory of material and commercial fetishism, and, finally, Marx's realistic doctrine of tasks' arising and being faced only when the material conditions for their realization are ripe. . . . And then much becomes understandable for us in Spinoza's moderate, drily realistic *Political Treatise*.

II

Numerous 'essays' on the interpretation of Spinoza's philosophy of law by professors and university lecturers have attempted to establish a 'continuity of his ideas' with contemporary trends in bourgeois legal theory. Here there are as many opinions as there are voices. But the main point is that all of these opinions are quite incapable of grasping Spinoza's doctrine of law and the state in its concrete, historical uniqueness.

The followers of Jhering try to find in Spinozism the historical roots of the famous German jurist's well-known assertions to the effect that 'law is *force* which is conscious of its own interest and at the same time of the necessity for moderation,' that 'law is the politics of force.'[1] Without doubt, isolated thoughts of Jhering's, characterizing law and the absolute authority of the state over the individual, subordinating private interests to social advantage, etc., could have had Spinoza's doctrine as one of their sources. However, it is easy to point out at once a very essential methodological difference between them: on the one hand, we have Jhering's *teleologism*, on the other, Spinoza's principle of *mechanical causality*, which excludes all teleology. For Jhering, law is a manifestation of state power, the product of a teleologically constructed state. For Spinoza, law is something primary, like the law of natural strength inherent in every individual. The process of creation of society and the state is a process of the further development—logical or historical—of natural law. In transferring his power to the state, man not only surrenders his merely imaginary right, but at the same time increases his genuine right. 'So long as the natural right of man is determined by the power of every individual, and belongs to everyone, so long it is a nonentity, existing in opinion rather than fact.' By uniting, men 'have jointly more power and consequently more right over nature than each of them separately.'[2]

[1] Rudolf von Jhering, *Geist des römischen Rechts*, ch. III.
[2] *Political Treatise*, ch. II, 13–15.

Even less felicitous are the attempts to connect Spinoza's conception of law and justice with contemporary legal *relativism* or legal *normativism*. Without doubt, Spinoza was one of the first—if we except the ancient Sophists—to establish the relativity of our moral and legal valuations. Good and evil, he says, 'indicate nothing positive in things considered in themselves. . . . For one and the same thing may at the same time be both good and evil or indifferent.'[1] But, on the other hand, Spinoza is not inclined to identify rights with moral valuations:

'We do not affirm that everything that is done by right is done in the best way. For it is one thing to till a field by right, and another to till it in the best way. One thing, I say, to defend or preserve oneself, and to pass judgment by right, and another to defend or preserve oneself in the best way, and to pass the best judgment; and, consequently, it is one thing to have dominion and care of affairs of state by right, and another to exercise dominion and direct affairs of state in the best way.'[2]

One gets the impression that Spinoza not only sets aside every criterion of value, but, as it were, places himself solidly on the ground of contemporary legal positivism and normativism, for which right coincides with the law of the state.

It is not difficult to see that these 'contradictions' in Spinoza's theory of natural law are only apparent. Our philosopher provides a somewhat abstract, but nevertheless profoundly materialistic criterion of good and evil. Good for him coincides with the *useful*: it is 'that which we certainly know to be a means of approaching more nearly to the type of human nature which we have set before ourselves.'[3] Thus, although from Spinoza's point of view 'every citizen depends not on himself, but on the commonwealth, all of whose commands he is bound to execute. . . . However iniquitous the subject may think the commonwealth's decision, he is none the less bound to execute them';[4] our philosopher is nevertheless very far from legal fetishism. 'A commonwealth,' he says, 'does wrong when it does, or suffers to be done, things which may be the cause of its own ruin. . . . A commonwealth is most independent when it acts according to the dictate of reason'; it 'is bound to preserve the

---

[1] *Ethics*, IV, preface. [2] *Political Treatise*, ch. V, 1.
[3] *Ethics*, IV, preface.
[4] *Political Treatise*, ch. III, 5.

causes of fear and reverence.' In a word, the state is also bound by a law independent of itself, a law which is not civil but natural.[1]

As Kuno Fischer quite correctly points out in his history of philosophy, on the question of the relation of individual rights and state coercion, right, and law, Spinoza constitutes a 'transition' between Hobbes and Rousseau. From the standpoint of social classes, his position was determined by the political temper of seventeenth-century bourgeois society. On the one hand, there was a tendency to consolidate the absolute power of the state in order to secure the foundations of 'civil society,' and the fear of a return to the feudal 'state of nature' of mutual conflict. On the other hand, apprehension was felt at such excessive strengthening of the state, which, in a majority of cases, still had a plainly feudal character; an apprehension for the freedom of the bourgeois individual, a tendency to set certain 'boundaries to the right and power of the government.'

'If,' says our thinker, 'it were really the case that men could be deprived of their natural rights so utterly as never to have any further influence on affairs, except with the permission of the holders of sovereign right, it would then be possible to maintain with impunity the most violent tyranny. . . . We must, therefore, grant that every man retains some part of his right, in dependence on his own decision, and no one else's.'[2]

Spinoza has in mind here freedom of speech and opinion, the 'freedom to philosophize' which cannot be suppressed. 'It is imperative that freedom of judgment should be granted, so that men may live together in harmony, however diverse or even openly contradictory their opinions may be.'[3]

In our appraisal of Spinoza's theoretical position we should not lose sight of the *methodological* basis of his theory, his proposal to take account of the weakness as well as the strength of our nature: to recognize what reason can do and what it cannot do as a result of the limitations and imperfections of human nature. The power of external things over man's will is still so great that it would be utopian for philosophers 'to bestow manifold praise on such human nature as is nowhere to be found,' 'to conceive of men, not as they are, but as they themselves would like them to be.' The ideal politics of such philosophers 'might be taken for a chimera, or might have been formed in utopia, or in that golden age of the poets when, to

[1] *Ibid.*, ch. IV, 4–5. Cf. *Theologico-Political Treatise*, ch. XVI, 4.
[2] *Theologico-Political Treatise*, ch. XVII, 4.   [3] *Ibid.*, ch. XX, 37.

be sure, there was least need of it.'[1] But here we need sober realism and an understanding of the fact that the norms of our society in the present condition of mankind cannot be the best; but that it is better to have some order, even though it is not ideal, than the subjugation to the emotions of the state of nature. 'The best we can do so long as we do not possess a perfect knowledge of our emotions is to frame a system of right conduct or fixed practical precepts, to commit it to memory, and to apply it forthwith to the particular circumstances which now and again meet us in life.'[2]

The entire structure of Spinoza's *Political Treatise* follows from the propositions which we have quoted. Those bourgeois investigators are profoundly mistaken who, like A. Menzel,[3] try to find in this last work of Spinoza's a retreat from democratic ideals, greater political 'moderation' as compared to the *Theologico-Political Treatise*; and who find the cause of this in the deposition of his friend Jan de Witt and other political events of which Spinoza was a witness. For in the *Political Treatise* the best sovereign power is determined for Spinoza by 'reason, the true excellence and life of the mind'; it is a power in whose presence 'peace does not depend on the sluggishness of its subjects,' a power 'established by a free multitude.'[4] But at this point our philosopher sets himself a quite different task: to point out the conditions, the *system of interrelations*, under which, without relying on the good conscience or reason of the sovereign power, every existing form of the state can nevertheless find maximum stability, that is, can guarantee peace and tranquillity and at the same time guarantee the 'natural rights' of the individual. In other words, while regarding as impossible the immediate and universal realization of the maximum programme of his democratic ideal, and clearly perceiving around him the 'bonds of politics' of which Heine speaks, Spinoza attempts to *concretize the minimal demands* which the individual of the bourgeois epoch can and should make upon every existing form of state power.

On this point our philosopher takes quite different positions in the cases of monarchy, aristocracy, and democracy. 'The transference of all power to one person,' in Spinoza's words, 'is in the interests not of peace but of slavery'; he points out how monarchical power easily degenerates into 'the worst kind of aristocracy.' For this reason he limits his projected monarchy by various means: by the

---

[1] *Political Treatise*, ch. I, 1.   [2] *Ethics*, V, 10.
[3] Cf. A. Menzel, *Wandlungen in der Staatslehre Spinozas*, etc.
[4] *Political Treatise*, ch. V, 4–6.

organization of the citizens into clans, by the election of 'counsellors' 'to defend the fundamental laws of the state,' and to make legislative proposals; by prohibiting the relatives of the king and court from holding state offices, etc. In a word, the monarchy should be ordered so 'that every law be an explicit will of the king, but not every will of the king a law.'[1] As further guarantees, Spinoza proposes the elimination of feudal landed property, and general levies made up exclusively of citizens rather than mercenary soldiers. While he does not regard the killing of tyrants as expedient, he nevertheless reserves for the citizens the right 'to take up arms against violence.'

Other conditions are set forth by Spinoza in the case of *aristocracy*, in which 'none are received into the number of the patricians save by express election.' Here the greatest increase in the number of electors is needed, in order to approximate more closely to the absolute power which in a democracy is held by the whole people.[2] On the other hand, power transferred to such a broad electoral college should not 'be exposed to danger at the hands of the people.' Spinoza's apprehension is explained by his theory of the historical development of the state, according to which the form of government customarily proceeds from primitive democracy to aristocracy and then to monarchy. But while attempting to secure the state from demagogic outbreaks on the part of the common people, which may be powerful enough to lead to monarchy, Spinoza at the same time sets up an ingenious system of 'checks and balances' (cf. Montesquieu) in the persons of the senators and syndics to whom the common people have the right to appeal against the patricians. Doubtless Spinoza here copies in many respects the governmental structure of the Netherlands and the Italian republics of his time.

Spinoza, as is well known, did not succeed in completing his picture of democracy. In the restriction of the rights of women, which he recommends on the basis of the 'weakness of their nature,' the man of the seventeenth century is still clearly in evidence. But Spinoza was also able to outstrip his age in many respects. And, of course, the universally human which he enunciated and raised to the foreground far outweighs the historically transient and class-bounded in his philosophy. Spinoza's lofty humanism, united with a consistent political realism, gains new living power. From an abstract thinker, Spinoza grows in our consciousness into a man of action, a political fighter—becoming in the process one of the most attractive figures in world history.

[1] *Ibid.*, ch. VII, 1.   [2] *Ibid.*, ch. VIII, 3.

I. K. Luppol

THE HISTORICAL SIGNIFICANCE OF SPINOZA'S PHILOSOPHY[1]

MUCH has been said and much written about the sources of Spinoza's philosophy. The two principal traditions in this connection are the Hegelian tradition, which derives Spinoza directly from Descartes, and the tradition which derives Spinoza from Judaism. I am not concerned here with the numerous traditions of minor significance which are less widely accepted by contemporary historians of philosophy. Taken alone, neither of these traditions is acceptable.

Spinoza as a representative of the leading bourgeois thought of the seventeenth century is often directly opposed to feudalism, medievalism, and scholasticism. This opposition is correct, but only in the sense that a skeleton gives the form of a living, full-blooded human being with muscles, a nervous system, and integument. It must not be forgotten that the seventeenth century was preceded by the fifteenth and sixteenth centuries. It must not be forgotten that Spinoza was separated from feudalism, as it were, both spatially and temporally. We should realize clearly that Spinoza stood on the shoulders of the Renaissance.

The disintegration of European feudalism did not begin in the Netherlands, where Spinoza was born and died, but in another place and under different conditions. Italy's convenient and fortunate position as the centre of the Mediterranean world, as a starting point for the armed trade-capitalist expeditions to the East which were called 'crusades,' resulted in the fact that the first but not yet irreparable breach in feudalism was made in the Italian cities. From the East a stream of new facts, new ideas, and new forms flowed in

[1] A translation of 'Istoricheskoye znacheniye filosofi Spinozy,' *Pod znamenem marksizma*, No. 11–12 (1932), pp. 180–9. (Slightly abridged.)

upon European feudalism, taking the form of a renaissance of antiquity.

On the crusaders' return journey the legend of the Three Impostors was born—one of the first catapults to begin breaking down the monopolistic ideology of the Catholic Church. Jesus, Moses, and Mohammed—the three founders of the historical religions of the period—had proved to be impostors. This was the meaning of the legendary book of the Three Impostors, of which men spoke from the twelfth and thirteenth to the eighteenth centuries, and which was attributed to forty-nine different authors, including Spinoza. The idea of the three impostors appeared as early as Boccaccio's *Decameron*, in the story of the three rings. But as late as the eighteenth century in backward Germany its liberating influence was still felt in the story of the three rings in Lessing's *Nathan the Wise*.

However, these armed trade-capitalist expeditions to the East were only the first of numerous conquistadorial expeditions to the rich countries of the Orient, and in particular to India. India, as early as the fourteenth century and especially in the fifteenth, provided a constant stimulus to the knights of this period of primitive accumulation of capital. The last decade of the fifteenth and the first decade of the sixteenth centuries furnish a constellation of names—Columbus, Vasco da Gama, Magellan, Cortez, Pizarro, *et al*. These were the men who discovered new lands and in so doing opened up new markets. In the course of some fifty years, two Indias presented themselves to the view of the growing bourgeoisie—one in the East, another in the West. (I have in mind the West Indies.) This brought about an incredible expansion of the geographical horizon, compared to that which had prevailed only a few decades before. And not only the geographical horizon, but the cosmographical horizon as well, expanded at a fantastic rate. Copernicus, Galileo, and Kepler did their great work in a period of about a century and a half.

There was not a single ideological realm in which a revolution did not take place. The ideal of the church was the saint, the hermit, the ascetic who, according to the teachings of the church, should concern himself more with the kingdom of heaven than with the earthly kingdom; the ideal of the young bourgeoisie was the bold hero, the fearless navigator, the man full of the joy of life and zest for living. Science began to seek the source of the world not in God but in the world itself. Art caused its madonnas to smile and liberated the human body from clothing. Literature began to call things by their real names, to scoff at the monks. We need only to think of Boccaccio, Bonaventure des Périers, and Rabelais to realize how the entire form and content of the ideological superstructure was changed in the course of a few decades.

Philosophy, of course, was not left behind. It quickly began to glow with sparks of materialism, which appeared first—for completely understandable reasons—in natural philosophy. Natural philosophy began to generalize, on a materialistic basis, the new facts and observations which had been arrived at through practical activity. Materialism forces its way through every page of Giordano Bruno. The bourgeoisie took a stand against the ecclesiastical and secular feudal lords, not only launching a critique with weapons, but employing the weapons of criticism. The class struggle became extremely sharp. Class conflict developed in the sphere of philosophy as well. Giordano Bruno was burned at the stake, and he was not alone in this fate; tens and hundreds of more ordinary and less important 'pagans' and 'heretics' shared his lot.

But this Renaissance which had begun in Southern Europe was nevertheless coming to an end. The ideological conflicts were rife with contradictions. The scholastic traditions which had been built up through the centuries and consecrated by the Catholic Church were still strong. The regenerated learning of antiquity struggled obdurately on behalf of secularism and against ecclesiasticism. Green shoots of genuinely new thought, new science, and new philosophy forced their way through. The struggle finally resulted in the retreat of the medieval schoolmen to the monasteries—from which they made quite effective sallies in the form of the Inquisition—and their ideological lapse into orthodox or heretical mysticism. Regenerated antiquity could not for long furnish an adequate, keen-edged weapon; about 1600 the weapon of antiquity became rusty and was no longer capable of breaking a path forward through the dense thicket. The green shoots of the new science and philosophy, which were not yet fortified by a theory of knowledge and were full of unverified facts not yet scientifically worked over, very often gave way to imagination and, although basically progressive and radical, turned toward magic, astrology, and alchemy.

The outcome of the Renaissance was scepticism—Montaigne. Montaigne asked, 'What do I know?'—Aristotle had lived and had written books; then came the Arabs who wrote commentaries on Aristotle; the scholastic interpreters put in their appearance and wrote commentaries on the commentaries. All we do, said Mon-

THE SIGNIFICANCE OF SPINOZA'S PHILOSOPHY 165

taigne, is write commentaries on each other, and meanwhile the truth is lost. Nevertheless Montaigne found the genuine object which demands man's attention. Not without reason do the French say that Montaigne taught them how to think. For *nature* is the object which was pointed out by the sceptic Montaigne. And if this period of transition from feudalism to capitalism, which may be conventionally limited to the fifteenth and sixteenth centuries, ended in scepticism, then, I repeat, nature as an object for the application of human powers was already found, and the new period, the period of the early stages of capitalist society, began with a firmly established object—nature. This conquest of the Renaissance is contained in a purified form in Spinoza.

The modern period in the history of philosophy has its origin in a different place. The discovery of America, the discovery of the sea route to India, the transformation of the Mediterranean routes into ocean routes, caused the displacement of economic centres, which brought with it a shifting of ideological centres as well. Spain and Portugal—especially Portugal, a country situated on the shores of the Atlantic Ocean—were carried for a time to leading positions. But only for a time. As early as the sixteenth century the Netherlands came into prominence. Spain, wallowing in the monopolies of its nobility and in the Catholic religion, cruelly exploited its unique European colony, the Netherlands. A bourgeois revolution broke out there, the first of numerous European bourgeois revolutions. This revolution ended in 1588 with the accession to power of the bourgeoisie. But the war with Spain dragged on much longer, ending in 1648 (which was already the period of Spinoza) with a declaration of independence by the seven Netherlands provinces, the chief of which was Holland.

Holland became the model capitalist country of the seventeenth century. In 1602 the East India Company was founded—a unique armed trading colonial organization of the capitalists of that time for the oppression and exploitation of native populations. In 1621 an analogous West India Company was formed. Somewhat earlier, in the last decade of the sixteenth century, the Dutch themselves had sought a sea route to India in another direction: not to the South around the Cape of Good Hope, but to the North through the Arctic Ocean. However, they were not able to get farther than Spitzbergen and had to return. . . .

Can we say that the Dutch bourgeoisie was opposed only from the right—only by the feudal lords and the Catholic Church?

Certainly not. The class struggle was already complicated in the highest degree, and we should not forget for a moment the exploiting colonial policy of the grasping Netherlands bourgeoisie or the oppression which they practised in respect to the masses, who were loosely united into communities of peasants, small artisans, apprentices, and even factory workers. But we should not lose our historical perspective, otherwise our view of Spinoza will be unhistorical and we shall not be able to understand Spinoza's greatness for us today, after three hundred years.

The Dutch bourgeoisie was a progressive class that had just come into power, and had already forged its ideology. Hence we find the liberation of the peasantry from bondage for the first time in Europe, hence religious toleration and free-thinking—'libertinism,' as the expression went in the sixteenth century—as distinguished from the Calvinism of the masses. Hence the comparative freedom of the press, the flowering of science, art, and philosophy.

I cannot speak of this in any detail in the present brief paper, but it will be sufficient to recall some of the names, the scientific discoveries and technical inventions, which distinguish the Netherlands provinces, and in particular Holland, during this period. We shall list only the best known. The compound microscope was invented by the Dutch lens-grinder Zacharias Zanser about 1590—approximately the generation of Benedict Spinoza's father; the telescope in its original pre-Galilean form was developed by the Dutch optical manufacturer Johann Lippershey [in 1608]. Stevin with his investigations of the mechanics of fluids lived about one generation before Spinoza. Van Helmont with his works in chemistry was an older contemporary of Spinoza. Huyghens, the well-known Huyghens, who studied optics and mechanics, revealed the mystery of Saturn's rings, and developed a theory of the pendulum clock, was an exact contemporary of Spinoza and did not die until after he did. Jan Swammerdam, Spinoza's contemporary, gave us a series of zootomical works and, incidentally, treated the problem of spontaneous generation correctly in principle. Finally, Leeuwenhoek, Spinoza's contemporary (they were born the same year), contributed a series of microscopic discoveries and the discovery of infusoria. Such is a brief and far from complete list of the contributions of Dutch science in the period of Spinoza.

In the realm of art the record is equally brilliant. If art in Italy, emancipated from the medieval conventionalities of pose, was already characterized by the full-blooded poses and actions of living men, its

THE SIGNIFICANCE OF SPINOZA'S PHILOSOPHY 167

religious subject-matter was nevertheless still quite strong. In the Netherlands this subject-matter was already significantly less frequent. It is true that in Rembrandt we find many religious and mythological subjects, but in Holland at the time of Spinoza bourgeois art was bursting into flower, with its own themes, its own subjects, its own form of presentation, and a realistic treatment of artistic problems. The scenes of ordinary bourgeois life, of ordinary bourgeois manners and customs—street scenes and domestic scenes —these were especially evident in Dutch painting in the late 1640's. There are countless scenes from the life of the well-to-do urban bourgeoisie; the impress of security, tranquillity, and confidence in the morrow lies in the faces here portrayed. Let us recall a few names: Gerard Terburg—simple compositions, without psychologism. His subject-matter: 'The Glass of Lemonade,' 'The Music Lesson,' 'The Letter.' Pieter de Hooch was especially outstanding in his representations of the character of the bourgeois way of life, of everyday life in the home. His works: 'The Mistress and the Servant,' 'The Concert.' Gabriel Metzu: 'The Family Luncheon,' 'The Prodigal Son,' and this 'Prodigal Son,' by the way, is not in the biblical tradition, but is treated in the most realistic manner, which was possible only in a seaport town with all its fascinations, down to the very sinks of iniquity.

And finally philosophy. Descartes came to Holland from feudal France in a unique philosophical emigration. Here Regius (Henry de Roy) drew the first materialistic conclusions from Descartes's system. Here the life of Spinoza's older contemporary, Uriel da Costa, was spent. The life of Uriel da Costa calls to mind in many respects the life of Benedict Spinoza, for he also was cursed and banished from the Jewish community. Here, finally, Spinoza, the crown of the philosophic structure of the seventeenth century, was born.

Uriel da Costa, of whom we know very little ..., belonged to Spinoza's older generation, to the generation of his father, Michael d'Espinosa. He fled from Portugal, as did Spinoza's father, between 1612 and 1615. The Jewish families which emigrated to Holland from the Iberian peninsula passed through the Renaissance of Southern Europe. They carried with them the western Sephardi tradition which had grown up on the shoulders of the Renaissance, and they found in Holland a Judaism moulded by two thousand years of the eastern traditions of Ashkenazim. The Dutch Jewish community of this period was split by these contradictions. On the one hand, a continuation and further development of the Renaissance was being carried out on a new foundation; these were the western forces, so to speak, which furthered the ideas of emancipation from the Middle Ages and radicalized and revolutionized philosophical thought; on the other hand, there were the very strong eastern traditions, the traditions of the Talmud and cabala. In this clash Uriel da Costa fell victim.

Uriel da Costa was the first to criticize the doctrine of the immortality of the soul. For this he was called a Sadducee; and he called his opponents Pharisees. But Uriel da Costa's doctrine of the mortality of the soul was directed not only against Judaism but also against Christianity. Uriel da Costa began the biblical criticism which also applied to Christianity as well as Judaism. However, Uriel da Costa, a member of the generation preceding Spinoza, was not yet an atheist. Spinoza continued da Costa's work in his critique of the Bible, but he not only criticized, he also created his own system. He began where Uriel da Costa left off, creating a synthesis of all preceding philosophy, building a new philosophical system.

The universal character of Spinoza's system represents the most grandiose expression, in the most metaphysical form, of the temper of mind of the seventeenth-century bourgeoisie. In this lies the uniqueness as well as the difficulty of the teaching of the philosopher of The Hague.

In analysing Spinoza's system it is customary, for some reason, to speak only of substance and attributes. The key to the enigma of Spinoza's philosophy is no doubt to be found in the doctrine of substance and attributes. But only the key. If Spinoza taught only about substance and attributes, why does his central work bear the title *Ethics?* Why does another of his works, perhaps no less important, bear the title *On the Improvement of the Understanding?* The *total unity* of Spinoza's thought must not be forgotten. We must not take merely the problem of substance and attributes and leave the rest outside our field of vision—not because such a procedure would be inadequate to establish Spinoza's materialism; no, in this, of course, lies the basis of his materialism, but because if we proceed thus we will not be able to answer a series of objections which our opponents may raise.

However strange it may seem, Spinoza set himself a practical problem: how to attain the true good. This harmonizes with and corresponds to the kind of problems that faced the bourgeoisie of his day in other areas of knowledge. Spinoza solved the problem as follows: the true good is true knowledge, and true knowledge is the knowledge of the unity of the mind with nature. Thus the ethical

THE SIGNIFICANCE OF SPINOZA'S PHILOSOPHY

problem of the true *good*, the theoretical or epistemological problem of true *knowledge*, and the ontological problem of the knowledge of the *unity of mind and nature*, are linked together.

If the true good can be attained only in the process of true knowledge then, Spinoza reasoned, we must face the problem: what are the sources of knowledge, and what are its forms? Spinoza did not discover imaginative, sensory perception, rational perception, or intuitive perception—they were present in Descartes's system. But what Spinoza contributed is a significant step forward from Descartes. Through imaginative perception, Spinoza taught, we perceive individual things and individual states, that is *modes*, which are contingent rather than necessary conditions of substance. By means of reason, *ratio*, we go further; we perceive the *attributes* of substance, that is, the essential properties of substance without which it could neither be nor be conceived. And only by means of intuitive perception, *scientia intuitiva*, according to Spinoza, do we perceive *substance* itself, the essence of a thing through itself. Thus Spinoza gives the structure of knowledge not in the form of a mere catalogue, but in the form of a hierarchy.

Spinoza was correct for his time in holding that we can understand individual manifestations of substance, individual things and objects, through sense perception, that we can reach an understanding of such categories as, say, extension and thought—Spinoza's attributes—only through a process of abstraction, a definite, rational, logical operation. But the case was much worse with intuitive perception, in which Spinoza's intellectualism is particularly apparent.

This is a point which we must examine in some detail. For here Spinoza was wrong; it was this rationalism that created the problem which Spinoza bequeathed to succeeding generations of materialists. In Spinoza's essentially rationalistic theory of knowledge there are a number of particular defects: there is no transition from imaginative perception to rational perception, nor from rational to intuitive perception. His criterion of truth, his criterion of the adequacy of ideas, is also purely rationalistic: to be convinced of the truth it is necessary only to possess the truth itself.

Thus Spinoza's substance is known only through intuition. What is this substance, and why did Spinoza solve the problem of cognition in just this way? Substance is an autonomous entity which is not reducible to any other entity whatsoever and is not dependent upon any other entity whatsoever. Descartes declared that body is a substance with the attribute of extension. But, according to Descartes's theory, mind too, with its attribute of thought, is a substance, and both of these substances were created by a primordial substance, God. This is not the place to discuss the part played by God in Descartes's system. But one thing is clear: in Descartes there is a dualism of God and nature, a dualism of mind and body. This was the heritage which Descartes left to Spinoza, who solved this central problem quite differently.

For Spinoza there exists only *one* substance, and this substance is *nature*. And God? 'God' is the concept without which it was still impossible to conceive life in seventeenth-century Holland among the bourgeoisie. Spinoza, as it were, addressed himself to his contemporaries and predecessors, to Christianity and Judaism, to scholasticism and Cartesianism with these words: 'You say, "God exists." Splendid! But do you know what your God is? God is nature!'

If we say that materialism assumes various forms depending upon the state of scientific knowledge, we are justified in saying the same thing with regard to atheism. The atheism of dialectical materialism is not the atheism of the French materialists, in whom it was bound up with a mechanistic materialism; and the atheism of the French materialists is not the atheism of the Renaissance or of seventeenth-century Holland. There is no doubt that for his own time, in his own language, and in the concepts and terminology of that time Spinoza provided an atheistic solution for the problem, destroying, drowning God, as it were, in nature.

Substance, then, is *one*. But, since substance is one, there is no transcendental essence beyond it; substance must be self-caused. This *infinite* substance has an infinite number of attributes. We know two of them: extension and thought. From this we should not conclude as the neo-Kantians do that Spinoza is an agnostic, that in affirming the existence of an infinite number of attributes he declares them to be unknowable. We have here a typical example of a philosophical conflict over the great thinkers of the past. Actually Spinoza's firm, rigorous logic is here in evidence. If substance is infinite he cannot limit it to two attributes, for every limitation of infinite substance would be its negation, a denial of the infinity of substance. But empirically he could point to only two attributes—extension and thought.

The schoolmen too understood that body is extended, so that in saying that matter is extended and that body is extended, Spinoza was not saying anything new. But Spinoza said: matter is extended,

THE SIGNIFICANCE OF SPINOZA'S PHILOSOPHY

extension is an attribute of matter, that is, an essential and necessary property of matter without which it can neither be nor be conceived; and this extended matter *thinks*. Thought is also an attribute of substance. In this lies Spinoza's materialism, in this his monism.

If Spinoza had said: extension is thought, this would have been a thoroughly idealistic philosophy of identity; it would have meant the annihilation of extension in thought. If Spinoza had said: thought is extension, this would have been a vulgarly materialistic solution of the problem; this would have meant that thought could be weighed out in kilograms and measured in metres. Spinoza assumed the *unity of extension and thought*. Spinoza's substance is not attributes plus some kind of carrier or substratum distinct from what it carries; Spinoza's God without his attributes is nothing, a concept without content, a scholastic fiction. The attributes do not flow out like some neo-Platonic emanation; rather they comprise substance. Consequently Spinoza says: '*Deus sive omnia Dei attributa*'—'God or all of God's attributes.'

However, Spinoza's substance is not empirical nature. It is nature and not something else, but it is nature metaphysically disguised, metaphysically inverted, metaphysically transformed in its separation from man. Marx wrote of this in *The Holy Family*.

What does this mean? Here the question arises of the relation of substance to its modes, of the relation of this single substance, all-embracing in its unity, to its separate manifestations and conditions, its separate modes. The problem of the relation of Spinoza's nature to man or, in more abstract, theoretical, philosophical language—the problem of the transition from the universal to the particular—is the weak point, the stumbling-block of all rationalists, Spinoza among them.

If there is no God, if substance is one, and if it is self-caused, how can we explain the transition from this single, indivisible substance (for one cannot speak of half of substance, a quarter of substance, or five per cent of substance) to particular, separate individuals? Spinoza does it as follows: substance is one, but it appears to us as *nature-producer* (*natura naturans*) and at the same time as nature-product (*natura naturata*). Nature as product is the world of modes, the world of separate particulars. Nature as producer is substance as such. If substance or nature as producer is the *essence* of things, the modes, nature as product, are their *existence*. We have two facets, two aspects of one substance, one nature. Neither of these dual aspects can be conceived without the other: substance and its modes, nature as producer and nature as product, essence and existence; yet they do not coincide logically. Nature as product, or the world of modes, is the actualization in time of that which is implicit in nature as producer. And here Spinoza's weakness is revealed, the weakness of his materialism which was evident even to the materialists of the following generation. This neither debases nor minimizes Spinoza's materialism, but it explains his complicated and for his age unique, yet inadequate, solution of this problem.

The world of modes, nature as product, is the actualization *in time* of what is implicit in substance, substance itself being *eternal*. The modes, taken in their totality, are also eternal. But in what sense? They are eternal in the sense of continuousness, of *infinite duration in time*. But substance is eternal in the sense of *timelessness*. Spinoza's substance may be contemplated only '*sub specie æternitatis*.' And this comprises the metaphysical costume of Spinoza's substance and of Spinoza's nature.

Did Spinoza solve the problem?—He solved it in the sense that he gave his contemporaries whose thinking lay within the orthodox church tradition or, if heretical, still kept within the boundaries of religion, an answer sufficient for the philosophy of his day. But he did not solve this problem, any more than one-sided rationalism in general, which can never furnish a transition from the universal to the particular, has solved it. Spinoza did not provide a transition from substance to modes, from essence to existence.

Substance as nature-producer explains all the apparent diversity of things. This apparent diversity results from motion. The concept is present in Spinoza, but *motion for Spinoza exists only in the world of modes*. Descartes had said: motion is a mode, not merely a mode of thought, but a genuine, actually existing mode. However, it is only a *mode* on a level with rest, not an attribute—that is, a necessary condition of substance. Spinoza went further; he said: motion is an *infinite* mode, because everything may be in motion. Nevertheless, motion and rest are infinite *modes*, that is, they appertain to nature as product rather than to nature as producer, to substance. Motion is not an attribute of substance. Hence results the static and metaphysical character of Spinoza's system, which caused Marx to say that the French materialists struggled against the metaphysics of Descartes, Malebranche, Leibniz, and Spinoza. Herein likewise is the metaphysical disguise of Spinoza's nature.

Extremely important conclusions follow from this: nature as product is not the historical *effect* of nature as producer, but its

THE SIGNIFICANCE OF SPINOZA'S PHILOSOPHY 173

logical *consequence*, following from the latter as it follows from the nature of a triangle that the sum of its interior angles is equal to two right angles.

And it is here that we must seek the key to the enigma of Spinoza's hylozoism, a problem about which much could be said and for which many incorrect solutions have been advanced. Spinoza is indeed a hylozoist. Dialectical materialism, however, is not in any sense hylozoistic. Spinoza reasons thus: What exists? Nature. Nature is substance. This substance is extended. What thinks? This same substance thinks, not some God, not some vital force which, although present in material substance, is not subject to it but acts and lives according to other laws. No. The same extended matter is what thinks. And this was a correct solution of the problem for the seventeenth century. But it was correct only within the framework of Spinoza's account of time and motion, according to which time applies only to the world of modes, and motion as an infinite mode exists only in the world of modes.

However, when later materialists said: Spinoza is right in principle—substance is material and extended and it is substance that thinks, *but time is a form of the existence of matter* (the French materialists said this quite clearly and articulately as early as the eighteenth century); when the materialists of the generation following Spinoza said: Spinoza is right in principle—substance is extended and it thinks, *but motion is also an attribute of substance*, that is, there can be no substance without motion; given matter, motion is given at the same time; motion is also an attribute of substance in the sense that it represents an essential and necessary property without which matter can neither be nor be conceived; when materialism reached a higher level than that of Spinoza—only then did the problem arise, only then could it arise: *does all matter think?*

As soon as men began to operate with the category of motion and the category of time, the question arose: matter thinks now, but did it think eighty million years ago? (Buffon and the French materialists operated with such periods.) And it is clear that the eighteenth century answered: only matter organized in a certain way thinks. The nineteenth century answered: matter at a certain stage of evolution thinks. Lenin said: at the foundation of the very structure of matter we may assume the presence of a capacity analogous to sensation.

Was this the sort of philosophical tradition that would have repudiated Spinoza and proceeded in a different direction?—This was the further development of what was implicit in Spinoza, but a development in which the result was in no sense identical with the embryo, the original point of departure. Accordingly, the eighteenth century characteristically spoke not of thought but of sensitivity as a property of matter. Robinet said: all matter is sensitive, which means that all matter is organic. Holbach objected: not all matter is sensitive, but only that which is organized in an appropriate manner.

And so, there is no God, but there is a single substance with single laws. Hence it follows that there are no accidents, everything is conditioned; there is no freedom of the will, everything is necessary. The purposiveness of creation is rejected. Teleology is not scientific; Spinoza scoffs at it. Perhaps the most acute, rich, and vivid pages in the *Ethics* are devoted to the refutation of teleology and the battle against it.

I said at the beginning that, according to Spinoza's doctrine, true knowledge is the perception of the unity of the mind with nature. This perception of the unity of the mind with nature is achieved through intuition. Why? Because Spinoza's substance is metaphysical and there is no other way to reach it. What was the task of subsequent materialists? Was it to find a new path, a new ladder that would lead them to this metaphysical substance? No, this would have been a most disserviceable and thankless task. Why? Because the object was thankless in the sense that it was metaphysical. It was not necessary to find some kind of new path to Spinoza's substance which would replace intellectual intuition; rather it was necessary to strip this substance of its theological trappings and metaphysical envelope. It was necessary to free it from its metaphysical costume, to unveil it, and reveal it as empirical nature. And this was done by means of the extension to substance of time and motion.

For Spinoza the perception of the unity of the mind with nature, which is true knowledge, is also the true good. He thus integrates his solution of ethical problems into his philosophical system. When objects act on me, on my sense organs, when they affect my senses, the result will be, as Descartes had said earlier, the passive states of the subject which were called in medieval Latin '*passiones*.' These emotions are passive conditions of the mind. But there is—as we know even from grammar—both a passive voice and an active voice. Similarly in Spinoza there are active conditions of the mind—'*actiones*'—as well as passive conditions of the mind.

An active condition of the mind, in Spinoza's terminology, is produced by rational cognition, when I do not simply perceive under the influence of an object outside myself, but act logically, reason deductively. Active conditions of the mind, arising as a result of the rational form of cognition, lead to an understanding of the attributes of substance, which is accompanied by a feeling of pleasure. The highest degree of pleasure, according to Spinoza, is attained in intuitive perception in which substance is revealed and the unity of the mind with nature is realized; this is the *amor Dei intellectualis*, the intellectual love of God.

If we strip the metaphysical garments from the intellectual love of God and strike off its theological trappings, there is revealed nothing other than man's cognitive love of nature, that is, man's comprehension of his unity with nature, which is accompanied by a feeling of delight. According to Spinoza's teaching, it is precisely here in the feeling of unity with material nature that man should seek and find his pleasure, and not in some world of religion beyond the grave, or some transcendental realm of metaphysics.

The defects of Spinoza's materialism, which resulted from the historical conditions of his time, were evident to the very next generation of materialists. I cannot go into this matter in any detail. It is well known that Toland in one of his 'Letters to Serena' criticized Spinoza's doctrine of motion—not the foundations of Spinozism, i.e. the doctrine of a single extended and thinking substance, but the fact that his substance was not in motion. The French materialists declared time a form of the existence of matter and motion a property of matter on a level with extension. In so doing they stripped off the metaphysical wrappings from Spinoza's substance, although they themselves remained metaphysicians, as is well known, in the sense of non-dialecticians.

Classical German idealism developed along a different path, but if we read Marx's *Holy Family* carefully we will see how elements of Spinozism penetrated even into nineteenth-century German philosophy. Marx says that Fichte's self-consciousness is metaphysically transformed, disguised mind in its separation from nature. And in Hegel we have a metaphysically inverted, transformed unity of Spinoza's nature and Fichte's mind. The Hegelian absolute mind is Spinoza's substance with the comprehension of Fichte's subject. Strauss started out from substance, from the Spinozistic element in Hegel's philosophy, and thus ended in materialism in his *Life of Jesus*. And Bauer, starting from self-consciousness, from the Fichtean element, ended in idealism. In Feuerbach there is a unity of subject and object—materialism, but it is a contemplative, passive, unproductive materialism.

Dialectical materialism completely solved the problem of the unity of subject and object—concretely, historically, actively, and practically. And it is dialectical materialism rather than bourgeois philosophy that represents the further historical development of historically given Spinozism, through all the stages of development which make up the glorious materialist tradition of Toland, Holbach, Diderot, and Feuerbach. It should be noted that dialectical materialism is the highest stage in this development.

To say that Marxism is a variety of Spinozism would be quite incorrect. But it is precisely in dialectical materialism that Spinoza's materialism has found its historical and logical fulfilment. And that is why on this tercentenary of Spinoza's birth we revive with such regard and interest the figure of this great materialist.

BIBLIOGRAPHY

LITERATURE ON SPINOZA IN RUSSIAN

Part I: Non-Marxist

ALEKSEYEV, N. N., *Nauki obschchestvennyie i yestyestvennyie v istoricheskom vzaimootnosheni ikh metodov*. Otd. I. 'Mekhanicheskaya teoriya obshchestva,' (*The Social and Natural Sciences in the Historical Interrelation of their Methods*, Sec. I. 'The Mechanistic Theory of Society'), pp. 1-80; Moscow, 1912. Spinoza: *passim*.

BELYAYEV, V. A., *Leibnits i Spinoza* (*Leibniz and Spinoza*), St. Petersburg, 1914.

CHICHERIN, B. N., *Istoriya politicheskikh ucheni* (*History of Political Theories*), Part II, Moscow, 1872. Spinoza: pp. 104-36.

FATEYEV, A. N., *Ocherk razvitiya individualisticheskikh napravleni v istori filosofi gosudarstva* (*An Outline of the Development of Individualistic Tendencies in the History of the Philosophy of the State*), Part II, 1907. Spinoza: pp. 278-91.

FRANK, S. L., *Predmet znaniya* (*The Object of Knowledge*), St. Petersburg, 1915. Spinoza: pp. 480-4.

—— 'Ucheniye Spinozy ob attributakh' ('Spinoza's Doctrine of Attributes'), *Voprosy filosofi i psikhologi*, No. 4 (1912), pp. 523-67.

GALICH, A. I., *Istoriya filosofskikh sistem* (*A History of Philosophical Systems*), Vol. II, St. Petersburg, 1819. Spinoza: pp. 39-49.

GAVRIIL, Archimandrite, *Istoriya filosofi* (*History of Philosophy*), Kazan, 1839, Part III. Spinoza: pp. 143-51.

GILYAROV, A. N., *Filosofiya, v yeyo sushchestve, znacheni i istori* (*Philosophy: its Nature, Meaning and History*), Kiev, 1916. Spinoza: pp. 169-71, 515-27.

GOGOTSKI, S. S., *Filosofski leksikon* (*Philosophical Lexicon*), Vol. IV, Kiev, 1872. Spinoza: pp. 388-99.

GROT, N. Ya., 'Osnovnyie momenty v razviti novoi filosofi, III, Spinoza,' ('Basic Stages in the Development of Modern Philosophy, III, Spinoza'), *Voprosy filosofi i psikhologi*, No. 10 (1891), Special Section, pp. 1-18.

IVANTSOV, N. A., 'Spinoza,' *Vestnik vospitaniya*, No. 9 (1906), pp. 49-88.

KECHEKYAN, S. F., *Eticheskoye mirosozertsaniye Spinozy* (*Spinoza's Ethical World-View*), Moscow, 1914.

KIRILOVICH, A., 'Ontologiya i kosmologiya Spinozy v svyazi s yevo teoriyei poznaniya' ('Spinoza's Ontology and Cosmology in Relation to his Theory of Knowledge'), *Vera i razum*, 1894, No. 3, pp. 119-50; No. 5, pp. 220-38; No. 6, pp. 255-86.

KORKUNOV, N. M., *Istoriya filosofi prava* (*History of the Philosophy of Law*), Fifth Edition, St. Petersburg, 1908. Spinoza: pp. 159-67.

KOVALEVSKI, M. M., *Ot pryamovo narodopravstva k predstavitelnomu i ot patriarkhalnoi monarkhi k parlamentarizmu. Rost gosudarstva i yevo otrazheniye v istori politicheskikh ucheni (From Direct to Representative Democracy and from Patriarchal Monarchy to Parliamentarianism. The Growth of the State and its Reflection in the History of Political Theories)*, Moscow, 1906, Vol. II. Spinoza: pp. 425–92.

KOVNER, S., 'Spinoza, yevo zhizn i sochineniya' ('Spinoza: His Life and Works'), *Kiev. Univ. Isvestiya*, No. 11–12 (1862), pp. 1–87.

—— *Spinoza, yevo zhizn i sochineniya (Spinoza: His Life and Works)*, Warsaw, 1897.

KROPOTKIN, P. A., Prince, *Ethics*, New York, 1924. Spinoza: pp. 157–62.

LAPSHIN, I. I., *Zakony myshleniya i formy poznaniya (The Laws of Thought and the Forms of Knowledge)*, St. Petersburg, 1906. Spinoza: App. II, 'O misticheskom poznani i "vselenskom chuvstve" ' ('On Mystical Knowledge and "Cosmic Feeling" '), pp. 62–5, 81, 91.

LINITSKI, P. I., *Obzor filosofskykh ucheni (Survey of Philosophical Doctrines)*, Kiev, 1874. Spinoza: pp. 78–9, 172–5, 177.

—— *Ocherki istori filosofi drevnei i novoi (Outlines of the History of Ancient and Modern Philosophy)*, Kiev, 1902. Spinoza: pp. 195–204.

LOPATIN, L. M., *Istoriya novoi filosofi (History of Modern Philosophy)*, Moscow, 1902 (hectograph edition). Spinoza: pp. 209–72.

—— *Polozhitelnyie zadachi filosofi (The Positive Tasks of Philosophy)*, Part I, Moscow, 1911. Spinoza: pp. 290–322.

PAPERNA, G. A., *Spinoza: Yevo zhizn i filosofskaya deyatelnost (Spinoza: His Life and Philosophical Activity)*, St. Petersburg, 1895.

POLOVTSOVA, V. N., 'K metodologi izucheniya filosofi Spinozy' ('On the Method of Studying Spinoza's Philosophy'), *Voprosy filosofi i psikhologi*, Vol. 24, No. 118 (1913), pp. 317–98.

—— Review of Dunin-Borkowski's *Der Junge de Spinoza*, 1910, *Voprosy filosofi i psikhologi*, No. 105 (1910), pp. 325–32.

POSSE, V. A., *V poiskakh smysla zhizni (In Quest of Life's Meaning)*, Voronezh, 1922.

RADLOV, E. L., 'Neskolko zamechani o Spinoze' ('Some Remarks on Spinoza'), *Severny vestnik*, No. 6 (1891), pp. 199–218.

—— 'Spinoza,' *Entsiklopedicheski slovar Brokgaus i Efron.*, Vol. 61, St. Petersburg, 1900, pp. 214–21.

—— 'Spinoza,' *Filosofski slovar*, Moscow, 1913, pp. 590–1.

SHERSHENEVICH, G. F., *Istoriya filosofi prava (History of the Philosophy of Law)*, St. Petersburg, 1907, Second Edition. Spinoza: pp. 322–42.

SHESTOV, LEO, 'Synovya i pasynki vremeni (Istoricheski zhrebi Spinozy)' ('Children and Stepchildren of the Time (Spinoza's Historic Fate)'), *Sovremennyie zapiski* (Paris), Bk. 25 (1925), pp. 316–42.

—— 'Kinder und Stiefkinder der Zeit (Das historische Los Spinoza's),' *Die Kreatur* (Berlin), Vol. 2 (1928), pp. 369–96. [A German translation of the above, by Hans Ruoff.]

SHILKARSKI, V. S., 'O panlogizme u Spinozy' ('On Spinoza's Panlogism'), *Voprosy filosofi i psikhologi*, No. 3 (1914), pp. 213–67.

SLIOZBERG, G. B., *Mest Spinozy za 'kherem' (Spinoza's Revenge for his Excommunication)*, Paris, 1933.

SOLOVYOV, V. S, 'Ponyatiye o Boge. (V zashchitu filosofi Spinozy),' ('The Concept of God. (In Defence of Spinoza's Philosophy)'), *Voprosy filosofi i psikhologi*, Bk. 38 (1897), pp. 383–414.

SPEKTORSKI, E. V., 'Fizitsizm i svoboda v ratsionalnoi psikhologi XVII v.' ('Physicism and Freedom in the Rational Psychology of the Seventeenth Century'), *Voprosy filosofi i psikhologi*, No. 5 (1915), pp. 461–98. Spinoza: *passim*.
—— *Ocherki po filosofi obshchestvennykh nauk* (*Essays in the Philosophy of the Social Sciences*), Part I, Warsaw, 1907. Spinoza: pp. 142–57, 165–87, 200–2.
—— *Problema sotsialnoi fiziki v XVII stoleti* (*The Problem of Social Physics in the Seventeenth Century*), Vol. I, Warsaw, 1910. Spinoza: pp. 91, 94–100, 245–8, 301–5, 456–7, 465–6, 470–3, 485–7, 562–3. Vol. II, Kiev, 1917. Spinoza: pp. 267–8; neo-Spinozism: pp. 316–44.
SPERK, F. F., *Sistema Spinozy* (*Spinoza's System*), St. Petersburg, 1893.
STRAKHOV, N. N., *Ocherk istori filosofi* (*An Outline of the History of Philosophy*), Kharkov, 1907. Spinoza: pp. 73–7.
TARNOPOL, I., 'Spinoza i spinozizm' ('Spinoza and Spinozism'), *Vestnik russkovo yevreya*, No. 30 (1871).
TRUBETSKOI, YE. N., *Istoriya filosofi prava* (*A History of the Philosophy of Law*), Kiev, 1899. Spinoza: Pt. II, pp. 51–9.
VOLYNSKI, A., 'Teologiko-politicheskoye ucheniye Spinozy' ('Spinoza's Theologico-Political Theory'), *Voskhod*, 1885, No. 10, pp. 114–36; No. 11, pp. 125–46; No. 12, pp. 122–49.
VVEDENSKI, A. I., 'Ob ateizme v filosofi Spinozy' ('On the Atheism in Spinoza's Philosophy'), *Voprosy filosofi i psikhologi*, Bk. 37 (1897), pp. 157–84.
—— 'The Atheism of Spinoza's Philosophy,' New York, 1949 (typescript in Columbia University Library). [An abridged translation of the above by G. L. Kline.]
YAROSH, K., *Kurs istori filosofi prava* (*A Course in the History of the Philosophy of Law*) (hectograph edition), Kharkov, 1907. Spinoza and Hobbes: pp. 106–11.
—— *Spinoza i yevo ucheniye o prave* (*Spinoza and his Theory of Law*), Kharkov, 1877.
ZALESKI, V. F., *Lektsi istori filosofi prava* (*Lectures on the History of the Philosophy of Law*), Kazan, 1902. Spinoza: pp. 227–37.

PART II: MARXIST

AKSELROD (ORTODOKS), L. I., 'Nadoyelo!' ('Enough!'), *Krasnaya nov*, No. 3 (1927) pp. 171–81.
—— 'Spinoza i materializm' ('Spinoza and Materialism'), *Krasnaya nov*, No. 7 (1925), pp. 144–68.
ALEKSANDROV, G. F., *Istoriya zapadnoyevropeiskoi filosofi* (*History of Western European Philosophy*), Moscow, 1946. Spinoza: pp. 244–61.
ASMUS, V. F., 'Dialektika neobkhodimosti i svobody v etike Spinozy' ('The Dialectics of Freedom and Necessity in Spinoza's Ethics'), *Pod znamenem marksizma*, No. 2–3 (1927), pp. 22–55.
—— *Dialekticheski materializm i logika* (*Dialectical Materialism and Logic*), Kiev, 1924. Spinoza: pp. 61, 122, 125, 167–9, 208, 213.
—— 'Spornyie voprosy istori filosofi' ('Controversial Questions in the History of Philosophy'), *Pod znamenem marksizma*, No. 7–8 (1926), pp. 206–25. Spinoza: pp. 210–11.
BASKIN, M. P. and Chudnovtsev, M. I., *Sistematicheskaya khrestomatiya po marksizmu* (*A Systematic Anthology of Marxism*), Moscow, 1925. Spinoza: pp. 30–43.

BOGDANOV, A. A., *Filosofiya zhivovo opyta* (*The Philosophy of Living Experience*), Moscow, 1920. Spinoza: pp. 200-1.
—— *Vera i nauka* (*Faith and Science*), Moscow, 1910. Spinoza: pp. 205-7.
BOSHKO, V. I., *Ocherki razvitiya pravovoi mysli* (*Outlines of the Development of Legal Thought*), Kiev, 1925. Spinoza: pp. 192-204.
BRUSHLINSKI, V. K., 'Spinozovskaya substantsiya i konechnyie veshchi' ('Spinoza's Substance and Finite Things'), *Pod znamenem marksizma*, No. 2-3 (1927), pp. 56-64.
—— Review of Dunin-Borkowski's *Spinoza nach dreihundert Jahren* (Berlin, 1932), *Pod znamenem marksizma*, No. 11-12 (1932), pp. 227-9.
BYKHOVSKI, *Byl li Spinoza materialistom?* (*Was Spinoza a Materialist?*), Minsk, 1928.
CHELPANOV, G. I., *Spinozizm i materializm* (*Spinozism and Materialism*), Moscow, 1927.
—— *Vvedeniye v filosofiyu* (*Introduction to Philosophy*), Riga, 1923. Spinoza: pp. 156-8, 485-9.
CHUCHMAREV, V. I., *Materializm Didro* (*Diderot's Materialism*), Moscow, 1925. Spinoza: pp. 63-5.
—— *Materializm Spinozy: k pereotsenke idealisticheskoi traditsi* (*Spinoza's Materialism: Toward a Revaluation of the Idealistic Tradition*), Moscow, 1927.
DEBORIN, A. M., 'Benedikt Spinoza' ('Benedict Spinoza'), *Pod znamenem marksizma*, No. 2-3 (1927), pp. 5-21.
—— 'Mirovozzreniye Spinozy' ('Spinoza's World-View'), *Vestnik kommunisticheskoi akademi*, Bk. 20 (1927), pp. 5-29.
—— 'Die Weltanschauung Spinozas,' in *Spinozas Stellung in der Vorgeschichte des dialektischen Materialismus*, Berlin, 1928, pp. 40-74. [German translation of preceding article.]
—— *Ocherki po istori materializma XVII–XVIII vv.* (*Essays in the History of Seventeenth and Eighteenth-Century Materialism*), Moscow, 1930. Spinoza: pp. 41-89. [Reprint of earlier articles.]
—— 'Spinozizm i marksizm' ('Spinozism and Marxism'), *Letopisi marksizma*, Bk. 3 (1927), pp. 3-12.
—— Above, reprinted in Chronicon Spinozanum, Tomus Quintus (1927), pp. 140-50, with German translation: 'Spinozismus und Marxismus.'
DMITRIEV, G., 'Filosofiya Spinozy i dialekticheski materializm' ('Spinoza's Philosophy and Dialectical Materialism'), *Pod znamenem marksizma*, No. 9-10 (1926), pp. 26-42.
DYNNIK, M., 'Benedikt Spinoza i yevo yubileinyie kommentatory' ('Benedict Spinoza and his Jubilee Commentators'), *Pod znamenem marksizma*, No. 6 (1927), pp. 191-203.
FARBER, G., 'Benedikt Spinoza' ('Benedict Spinoza'), *Nastupleniye*, No. 12 (1932), pp. 36-44.
GLUKHOV, I. K., *Mirovozzreniye B. Spinozy* (*Spinoza's World-View*) [dissertation], Moscow, 1947.
GNEZDILOV, M., *Ateizm Benedikta Spinozy* (*The Atheism of Benedict Spinoza*), Poltava, 1934.
ISAKOV, P., 'K voprosu o "teologicheskom priveske" v ucheni Spinozy' ('On the Question of the "Theological Trappings" in Spinoza's Teaching'), *Antireligioznik*, No. 11-12 (1932), pp. 13-23.

BIBLIOGRAPHY   181

KAMMARI, M. and YUDIN, P., 'Spinoza i dialekticheski materializm' ('Spinoza and Dialectical Materialism'), *Bolshevik*, No. 21 (1932), pp. 39–60.
KAREV, N., 'O deistvitelnom i nedeistvitelnom izucheni Gegelya' ('On the Valid and Invalid Study of Hegel') *Pod znamenem marksizma*, No. 4–5 (1924). Spinoza: pp. 248–51.
—— 'Spinoza i materializm' ('Spinoza and Materialism'), *Krasnaya nov*, June (1927), pp. 190–207.
KAZARIN, A., 'Benedikt Spinoza' ('Benedict Spinoza'), *Molodaya gvardiya*, No. 12 (1932), pp. 147–9.
KIBOVSKI, N., 'Teoriya substantsi, attributov, i modusov Spinozy,' ('Spinoza's Theory of Substance, Attributes and Modes'), [written in 1922], published in *Istoriko-filosofski sbornik* (foreword by Deborin), Moscow, 1925, pp. 47–74.
KRYVELEV, I., 'K voprosu o gilozoizme' ('On the Question of Hylozoism'), *Antireligioznik*, No. 21–2 (1932), pp. 36–42.
KUNOV, G., 'Ucheniye Spinozy o proiskhozhdeni prava' ('Spinoza's Theory of the Origin of Law') in *Istoriya filosofi v marksistskom osveshcheni*, ed. B. Stolpner and P. Yushkevich, 1925, pp. 143–6.
LENIN, V. I., 'Zametki na knigu Shulyatikova *Opravdaniye kapitalizma v zapadnoyevropeiskoi filosofi*' ('Notes on Shulyatikov's Book, *The Justification of Capitalism in Western European Philosophy*'), *Pod znamenem marksizma*, No. 6 (1937), pp. 1–13. Spinoza: pp. 6–7.
LENINGRADSKI, M., 'Menshevistvuyushchi idealizm v roli apologeta iudaizma' ('Menshevising Idealism in the Role of an Apologist for Judaism'), *Voinstvuyushchi ateizm*, No. 11 (1931), pp. 124–30. [On Rakhman's 'Spinoza and Judaism.']
LEVANTOVSKI, I. L., *Spinoza v marksistskom myshleni* (*Spinoza in Marxist Thought*), Moscow, 1947.
LIPENDIN, P., SITKOVSKI, E., and TAGANSKI, G., 'Spinoza i dialekticheski materializm' ('Spinoza and Dialectical Materialism'), *Izvestia*, Nov. 24, 1932, p. 3.
LUNACHARSKI, A. V., 'Barukh Spinoza i burzhuaziya' ('Baruch Spinoza and the Bourgeoisie'), *Novy mir*, Bk. 1 (1933) pp. 167–8. [Also published in booklet form, Moscow, 1933.]
—— *Ot Spinozy do Marksa* (*From Spinoza to Marx*), Moscow, 1925. Spinoza: pp. 13–21.
LUPPOL, I. K., 'Filosofskaya sistema Spinozy' ('Spinoza's Philosophical System'), in *Istoriko-filosofskiye etyudi*, Moscow, 1935, pp. 58–92.
—— 'Istoricheski smysl sistemy Spinozy' ('The Historical Meaning of Spinoza's System'), *Izvestia*, Nov. 24, 1932 (No. 324), p. 3.
—— 'Istoricheskoye znacheniye filosofi Spinozy' ('The Historical Significance of Spinoza's Philosophy'), *Pod znamenem marksizma*, No. 11–12 (1932), pp. 180–9.
—— 'K voprosu o tselostnom ponimani filosofskoi sistemy Spinozy' ('On the Question of the Unity of Spinoza's Philosophical System'), *Byulleten zaochnoi konsultatsi*, No. 10 (1930), pp. 11 ff.
—— 'Neskolko slov o neratsionalnom metode v istori filosofi' ('A Few Words on the Irrational Method in the History of Philosophy'), *Voinstvuyushchi materialist*, No. 3 (1925).

LUPPOL, I. K., 'O sinitse, kotoraya ne zazhgla morya' ('The Titmouse that Failed to Set the Sea on Fire'), *Pod znamenem marksizma*, No. 11 (1926), pp. 221-33.

'M', 'O prazdnovani 250-letiya smerti B. Spinozy' ('On the Celebration of the 250th Anniversary of Spinoza's Death'), *Pod znamenem marksizma*, No. 4 (1927), pp. 228-9.

MANKOVSKI, L. A., *Spinoza i materializm (Spinoza and Materialism)*, Moscow, 1930.

MILNER, YA. A., *Benedikt Spinoza (Benedict Spinoza)*, Moscow, 1940.

MITIN, M. B., 'Spinoza i dialekticheski materializm' ('Spinoza and Dialectical Materialism'), *Pod znamenem marksizma*, No. 11-12 (1932), pp. 153-79.

—— 'Spinoza i marksizm' ('Spinoza and Marxism'), *Pravda*, Nov. 24, 1932, p. 2.

MITIN, YUDIN, MILNER, et al., *Istoriya filosofi (History of Philosophy)*, Vol. II (15th-18th centuries), Moscow, 1941. Spinoza: pp. 166-200.

OBICHKIN, G., 'O materializme Spinozy' ('On Spinoza's Materialism'), *Antireligioznik*, No. 23-4 (1932), pp. 6-9.

PLEKHANOV, G. V., 'Bernshtein i materializm' ('Bernstein and Materialism'), *Collected Works*, Vol. XI, Moscow, 1923, pp. 9-22. Spinoza: pp. 12, 19-22.

—— Foreword to Deborin's 'Vvedeniye v filosofiyu dialekticheskovo materializma' ('Introduction to the Philosophy of Dialectical Materialism'), *Collected Works*, Vol. XVIII, pp. 315-17.

—— 'Osnovnyie voprosy marksizma' ('Fundamental Problems of Marxism'), *Collected Works*, Vol. XVIII, Spinoza, pp. 188f. (Also published in English translation by International Publishers, New York.)

—— 'Ot idealizma k materializmu' ('From Idealism to Materialism'), *Collected Works*, Vol. XVIII, pp. 166-8.

—— 'Truslivy idealizm' ('Faint-hearted Idealism'), *Collected Works*, Vol. XVII, pp. 122-9.

POZNER, V., 'Benedikt Spinoza' ('Benedict Spinoza'), in *Kratki ocherk istori filosofi*, ed. Shcheglov, Moscow, 1940, pp. 79-83.

—— 'Prichinnost i tseloobraznost v ucheni Spinozy' ('Causality and Teleology in Spinoza's Doctrine'), [written in 1922], published in *Istoriko-filosofski sbornik* (with foreword by Deborin), Moscow, 1925, pp. 75-85.

RAKHMAN, D., 'Spinoza i yudaizm' ('Spinoza and Judaism'), *Trudy instituta krasnoi professury*, I, Moscow, 1923, pp. 85-95.

RALTSEVICH, V., 'Ideolog peredovoi burzhuazi XVII veka' ('An Ideologist of the Progressive Bourgeoisie of the Seventeenth Century'), *Problemy marksizma*, No. 11-12 (1932), pp. 12-40.

RANOVICH, A. B., 'B. Spinoza kak rodonachalnik bibleiskoi kritiki' ('B. Spinoza as the Founder of Biblical Criticism'), *Antireligioznik*, No. 21-2 (1932), pp. 22-7.

RAZUMOVSKI, I. P., 'Spinoza i godudarstvo' ('Spinoza and the State'), *Pod znamenem marksizma*, No. 2-3 (1927), pp. 65-75.

ROSANOV, YA., 'Literatura o Spinoze' ('Literature on Spinoza'), *Pod znamenem marksizma*, No. 11 (1926), pp. 234-44.

SAVELYEV, M. A., 'K yubileyu Spinozy' ('On Spinoza's Jubilee'), *Pod znamenem marksizma*, No. 11-12 (1932), pp. 146-52.

SHULYATIKOV, V., *Opravdaniye kapitalizma v zapadnoyevropeiskoi filosofi (The Justification of Capitalism in Western European Philosophy)*, Moscow, 1908. Spinoza: pp. 34-42.

SITKOVSKI, E., 'E. L. Feierbakh ob ateizme Spinozy' ('E. L. Feuerbach on Spinoza's Atheism'), *Pod znamenem marksizma*, No. 9 (1937), pp. 75–80.
—— 'Kritika metafiziki XVII v. "Traktate o sistemakh" Kondilyaka' ('The Critique of Seventeenth-Century Metaphysics in Condillac's "Treatise of Systems" '), *Pod znamenem marksizma*, No. 6 (1937), pp. 68–97. Spinoza: pp. 68–71, 73–82, 84–6, 89, 91–6.
SKURER, K., 'Spinoza i dialekticheski materializm' ('Spinoza and Dialectical Materialism'), *Vestnik kommunisticheskoi akademi*, Bk. 20 (1927), pp. 50–74.
'Spinoza,' *Bolshaya sovetskaya entsiklopediya* (*Large Soviet Encyclopedia*), Vol. 52, Moscow, 1947, pp. 419–23.
'Spinoza,' *Kratki filosofski slovar* (*Short Dictionary of Philosophy*), Moscow, 1940, pp. 257–8. Also an article on the *Ethics*, pp. 324–5. (An adaptation of this article on Spinoza appears in the *Handbook of Philosophy*, ed. by Howard Selsam, New York, 1949, pp. 115–16.)
SPOKOINY, A., 'Materializm i ateizm Spinozy' ('Spinoza's Materialism and Atheism'), *Partrabotnik*, No. 21–2 (1932), pp. 75–9.
STOLYAROV, A., 'Etika Spinozy' ('Spinoza's Ethics'), [written in 1922], published in *Istoriko-filosofski sbornik* (with foreword by Deborin), Moscow, 1925, pp. 86–103.
THALHEIMER, A., 'Sootnosheniye klassov i klassovaya borba v Niderlandakh pri zhizni Spinozy' ('Class Relations and the Class Struggle in the Netherlands during Spinoza's Lifetime'), *Vestnik kommunisticheskoi akademi*, Bk. 20 (1927), pp. 30–49.
—— 'Die Klassenverhältnisse und die Klassenkämpfe in den Niederlanden zur Zeit Spinozas' in *Spinozas Stellung in der Vorgeschichte des dialektischen Materialismus*, Berlin, 1928, pp. 11–39. [German version of the above.]
TOKMAKOV, V., 'Materializm Spinozy' ('Spinoza's Materialism'), *Kulturny front*, No. 1–2 (1933), pp. 50–7.
TOPORKOV, A. K., Introduction to Russian edition of Spinoza's *Ethics*, Moscow, 1932, pp. v–xix.
TSEITLIN, Z. A., 'Karl Marks o spinozizme i istochnikakh frantsuzskovo materializma XVIII veka' ('Karl Marx on Spinozism and the Sources of French Eighteenth-Century Materialism'), *Pod znamenem marksizma*, No. 11 (1926), pp. 214–20.
TYMYANSKI, G. S., 'Spinozizm v Germani i Fridrikh Vilgelm Stosh' ('Spinozism in Germany and Friedrich Wilhelm Stosch'), *Pod znamenem marksizma*, No. 8–9 (1925), pp. 73–91.
—— Russian edition of Spinoza's 'Principles of Descartes's Philosophy' translated and with an introduction by G. S. Tymyanski, Moscow, 1926.
—— 'Spinoza i nauka XVII veka' (Spinoza and Seventeenth-Century Science'), *Priroda*, No. 1 (1933), pp. 6–15.
—— 'Teoriya poznaniya Spinozy' ('Spinoza's Theory of Knowledge'), introduction to Russian edition of Spinoza's *On the Improvement of the Understanding*, Moscow, 1934, pp. 11–94.
VAINSHTEIN, I., 'Sistema Spinozy v osveshcheni burzhuaznoi filosofi' ('Spinoza's System as interpreted by Bourgeois Philosophy'), *Vestnik kommunisticheskoi akademi*, No. 11–12 (1932), pp. 91–105.
—— 'Spinoza i materializm' ('Spinoza and Materialism'), *Pod znamenem marksizma*, No. 3 (1926), pp. 85–97.

VALENTINOV, N. V., *Filosofskiye postroyeniya marksizma* (*The Philosophical Constructions of Marxism*), Moscow, 1908. Spinoza: pp. 88–92.

VANDEK, V., and TIMOSKO, V., 'Kritika otsenki mekhanistami i menshevist-vuyushchimi idealistami filosofi Spinozy' ('Critique of the Appraisal of Spinoza's Philosophy by the Mechanists and Menshevising Idealists'), *Pod znamenem marksizma*; No. 1–2 (1932), pp. 128–59.

—— *Ocherk filosofi B. Spinozy* (*An Outline of Spinoza's Philosophy*), Moscow, 1932.

VARYASH, A. I., *Istoriya novoi filosofi* (*History of Modern Philosophy*), Moscow, 1926. Spinoza: Part I, pp. 129–220, 327; Part II, pp. 225–7.

VOLFSON, S. YA., *Dialekticheski materializm* (*Dialectical Materialism*), Fourth Edition, Moscow, 1924. Spinoza: pp. 35–9.

—— *Eticheskoye mirosozertsaniye Spinozy* (*Spinoza's Ethical World-View*), Minsk, 1927.

VYDRA, P., 'K voprosu ob ideologicheskom proiskhozhdeni Spinozy' ('On the Question of Spinoza's Ideological Lineage'), [written in 1922], published, in *Istoriko-filosofski sbornik* (with foreword by Deborin), Moscow, 1925. pp. 33–46.

INDEX

Abrabanel, Judah, *see* Leo Hebraeus
Absolute truth, *see* Truth
Akselrod, L. I. (Ortodoks), 15, 17, 30, 34, 37; cited, 22, 35; quoted, 29, 38
Aleksandrov, G. F., quoted, 31, 33, 42, 44
All-Union Philosophical Conference (1930), 2
'Amor Dei intellectualis,' 6, 9, 65, 156, 175
Anarchism or Socialism (Stalin), 26
Animism, 38
Anti-Dühring (Engels), 14
Aristotle, 43, 88, 136, 150, 164; cited, 39
Ashkenazim, 167
Asmus, V. F., 2
Auerbach, Berthold, 4
Avenarius, Richard, 24
Averroes, 52
Avicebron, *see* Ibn Gabirol

Baal-Shem, Rabbi, 58
Bacon, Francis, 20, 22, 39, 71*n*., 133
Basso, Sebastian, 100
Bauer, Bruno, 175
Bazarov, V. A., 18, 45
Belyayev, V. A., cited, 14
Berdyaev, N. A., quoted, 28
Bernoulli, Johann, 124
Bernstein, Eduard, 113
Boccaccio, Giovanni, 164
Bogdanov, A. A. (A. A. Malinovski), 37, 46; quoted, 17, 21, 45
Brahmanism, 7
Bruno, Giordano, 20, 71*n*., 104, 164
Buddhism, 7
Burg, Albert, 147
Bykhovski, B., 15

Cabala, 3, 49, 53, 55, 56, 57, 97, 98, 168
Campanella, Tommaso, 100
Capital (Marx), 14
'Causa sui,' 13, 33, 70, 75, 107
Chelpanov, G. I., quoted, 28
Chicherin, B. N., quoted, 5
Christ, Jesus, 152
Chronicon Spinozanum, 2
Chuchmarev, V. I., quoted, 29
Cogitata Metaphysica (Spinoza), 126
Colerus, J., 4
'Concluding Critical Remarks of 1847' (Feuerbach), 1
Condé, Prince de, 147
Copernicus, Nikolaus, 33, 163
Cordovero, Moses, quoted, 54
Correspondence (Spinoza), Russian translation (1932), 1
Crescas, Hasdai, 57; quoted, 52–3
Crown of the .Kingdom, The (Ibn Gabirol), 51
Crusades, 162
Curtius, J., 95

Da Costa, Uriel, 58, 167–8
Deborin, A. M. (A. M. Ioffe), 2, 3, 26, 27, 34, 37; cited, 19, 35, 40; quoted, 15–16, 25, 32
Decameron (Boccaccio), 163
De Corpore (Hobbes), 101
De Hooch, Pieter, 167
De Medigo, Joseph, 58
Democritus, 88, 132
De Roy, Henry (Regius), 98–100, 167
Descartes, René, 7, 23, 57, 167; and mathematics, 20, 66, 122; and religion, 152; dualism, 29, 132; influence on Spinoza, 59, 71*n*., 97, 99, 162, 169–70; methodological doubt, 22, 26; cited, 33, 174; cited by Spinoza, 112

186 INDEX

Des Périers, Bonaventure, 104, 164
Deutsche Ideologie, Die (Marx), 18
Dewey, John, 45
De Witt, Jan, 19
Dialectics of Nature (Engels), 14, 28n., 33, 46, 113
Dialoghi d'Amore (Leo Hebraeus), 55
Diderot, Denis, 1, 15, 24, 28
Dittes, Friedrich, quoted, 139, 146
Dmitriev, G., 15; cited, 29
Dunin-Borkowski, S. von, 98, 101-2; quoted, 100

Einstein, Albert, 33
Empiriocriticism, 24, 45, 92
Empiriomonism, 45, 92
Engels, Friedrich, 14, 24, 27, 28, 78, 91, 112, 133; cited, 15, 33, 42-3; quoted, 25, 34, 107, 111, 113-14, 120
'En Sof' (The Infinite), 53
Epicurus, 88, 133
Ethics (Aristotle), 150
Ethics (Spinoza), 14, 58, 59, 60, 67, 68-9, 72, 76-7, 81, 82, 97, 101, 133, 150; Russian translation (1860, 1886), 4n.; Russian translation (1933), 1

Faust (Goethe), quoted, 73-4
Feuerbach, Ludwig, 15, 24, 25, 62, 75, 77, 91, 113, 133, 152; quoted, 70, 132
Fichte, Johann Gottlieb, 4, 92, 175
Fischer, Kuno, cited, 4, 159; quoted, 59
Fountain of Life, The (Ibn Gabirol), 50
Frank, Semyon, 13, 31; quoted, 11-12
Freedom and necessity in dialectical materialism, 84
Free-Masonry, 23
Fundamental Problems of Marxism (Plekhanov), 61-2

Galich, A. I., quoted, 3-4
Galileo, 33, 163
Garden of Pomegranates, The (Cordovero), 54
Gassendi, Pierre, 100, 101

Gavriil, Archimandrite, quoted, 4
Gebhardt, Carl, quoted, 43
German idealism, influence on Russian philosophy, 3n.
Gershon, Rabbenu, cited, 49
Gersonides, quoted, 52
Glisson, Francis, 100
Goethe, Johann Wolfgang von, 73-5
Grot, N., quoted, 6
Grotius, Hugo, 154
Grundsätze der Philosophie der Zukunft (Feuerbach), 62-3

Harris, J., 101
Hasidism, 58
Hegel, Georg Wilhelm Friedrich, 1, 3n., 24, 25, 112; and Feuerbach, 113; Soviet controversy concerning, 91; Spinoza's influence on, 32, 108, 175
Heidelberg, University of, 147
Heine, Heinrich, quoted, 149, 160
Helvetius, Claude, 24
Hobbes, Thomas, 9, 40, 139, 146, 155; and mathematics, 20, 66; influence on Spinoza, 71n., 137, 159; social-contract theory, 6,154-5; quoted, 101
Höffding, Harald, 29; quoted, 71n.
Holbach, Paul, 24, 79-81, 133, 174
Holy Family, The (Marx), 171, 175
Hosea, quoted, 55
Huyghens, Christian, 33, 166
Hylozoism; of Plekhanov, 27; of Lenin, 27-8

Ibn Ezra, 22, 55
Ibn Gabirol (Avicebron), quoted, 50-1, 55
Improvement of the Moral Qualities of the Soul, The (Ibn Gabirol), 51
Inquisition, 64, 164
Ioffe, A. M.: *see* Deborin, A. M.
Isakov, P., quoted, 25-6, 36, 37
Ivantsov, N. A., quoted, 10
Izvestia, 2

James, William, 45
Jeremiah, 68

INDEX

Jhering, Rudolf von, quoted, 157
Jodl, Friedrich, cited, 142
Judah Demodines, 58
Judah the Pious, quoted, 56
Judaism, 162

Kant, Immanuel, 3n., 4, 135, 152; cited, 8
Karev, N., 15
Kazarin, A., quoted, 22
Kechekyan, S. F., quoted, 136, 139, 146
Kellermann, B., quoted, 114
Kepler, Johannes, 33, 163
Kireyevski, I. V., 4n.
Kirilovich, A., cited, 6
Korkunov, N. M., 9
Koshelev, A. I., 4n.
Kovalevski, Maxim, quoted, 10
Kovner, S., quoted, 4–5
Kropotkin, Prince P. A., cited, 142; quoted, 144
Kryvelyev, I., 16

La Mettrie, Julien de, 24, 28, 77, 79, 80, 139, 146; quoted, 78
Lapshin, I. I., cited, 9
League of Nations, 90
Le Clerc, Jean, 102
Leeuwenhoek, Anton van, 166
Leibniz, Gottfried Wilhelm von, 14, 20, 57, 60, 66; quoted, 124, 127
Lenin, V. I. (V. I. Ulyanov), 17, 18, 32, 149; hylozoism, 27–8; theory of absolute truth, 45; theory of knowledge, 42–3
Leo Hebraeus, quoted, 55
Lepeshenski, P. N., 27
Lessing, Gotthold E., 139
Linitski, P. I., quoted, 5
Lion's Roar, The (Demodines), 58
Lippershey, Johann, 166
Locke, John, 82
Logic (Hegel), 108
Logical positivists, 43
Lopatin, L. M., quoted, 9
Louis XIV, 147
Lucas, Maximilian, 101–2
Lucretius, 88

Luppol, I. K., 2, 15; cited, 23; quoted, 25, 31–2, 37
Lunacharski, A. V., 18, 36, 37, 39; quoted, 143
Lyken, Kaspar, 104

Mach, Ernst, 24
Machiavelli, Niccolo, 40
Maimonides, defence of teleology, 57; influence on Spinoza, 22, 36, 97; Spinoza's attitude toward, 5n.; quoted, 51, 55
Mankovski, L. A., 15, 25; quoted, 36
Marx, Karl, 24, 133, 149; historical determinism, 82; interpreted as hylozoist, 27–8; interpreted as Platonic realist, 44; on Spinoza, 14–15; quoted, 18, 25
Marx-Engels-Lenin Institute, 46
Materialism and Empiriocriticism (Lenin), 17, 18
Mechanists' interpretation of Spinoza's philosophy, 15–16
'Menshevising idealists'' interpretation of Spinoza's philosophy, 15
Menzel, A., cited, 160
'Methodological doubt' of Descartes, 26
Metzu, Gabriel, 167
Milner, Ya. A., 2; cited, 34; quoted, 24–5, 42
Mitin, M. B., 2, 16; cited, 34; quoted, 41
Mohammed, 163
Montaigne, Michel de, cited, 164–5
Montesquieu, Charles Louis de Secondat, 40, 161
Morteira, Saul, 22, 56
Moses, 68, 152, 155, 163

Nathan the Wise (Lessing), 163
'Natura naturans' and 'natura naturata,' 13, 32, 128, 171
Newton, Sir Isaac, 20, 66, 108
Nirvana, 6
Nominalism, 43–4

Odoyevski, Prince V. F., 4n.
Oldenburg, Henry, 112, 149

'Omnis determinatio est negatio,' 32
On the Improvement of the Understanding (Spinoza), 66, 67, 68, 133; Russian translation (1934), 1

Panlogism, 13
Pantheism, a self-contradictory notion, 37
Pentateuch, 50, 54
Philo Judaeus, 55
'Philosophers' Society,' 4
Philosophia naturalis (de Roy), 99
Philosophical Notebooks (Lenin), 42
Plato, 43, 81, 88, 135, 136
Platonic realism in Soviet philosophy, 43–4
Plekhanov, G. V., 23, 25, 133; and Spinoza, 14–15, 61–3; definition of matter, 47; definition of religion, 37–8; hylozoism, 27–8; quoted, 91, 113
Pod znamenem marksizma (Under the Banner of Marxism), 1, 2
Pogodin, M. P., 4*n*.
Political Treatise (Spinoza), 86–7, 157; Russian translation (1910), 1
Polovtsova, V., 30*n*., 67; cited, 12–13
Pragmatism, 45
Pravda, 2
Principles of Descartes's Philosophy (Spinoza) Russian translation (1926), 1

Rabelais, François, 164
Radlov, Ernst, quoted, 8
Reductive materialism, 24
Regius, *see* de Roy, Henry
Religion, social and economic function of, 35
Rembrandt van Rijn, 167
'Res extensa' and 'res cogitans,' 24
Revisionist Marxists, 15*n*.; interpretation of Spinoza's philosophy, 17
Robinet, J. B., cited, 174
Rousseau, Jean Jacques, 10, 40, 154, 159
Rudas, L., quoted, 46
Rudayev, B., quoted, 44

Saadia, quoted, 55
Savelyev, M. A., 2
Schelling, Friedrich Wilhelm von, 3*n*., 4; quoted, 84
Scholasticism, 9, 97
Schopenhauer, Arthur, 3*n*., 6, 9
Semanticists, 43
Sephardi, 167
Shershenevich, G. F., cited, 9
Shevyrev, S. P., 4*n*.
Shilkarski, V. S., 13, 14
Short Treatise (Spinoza), 43; Russian translation (1929), 1
Shulyatikov, V., 16; quoted, 21
Societas Spinozana, 90
Socrates, 88
Solovyov, Vladimir, cited, 7
Somerville, John, 16*n*.
Spektorski, E. V., 10–11
Spinoza, Benedict, and Christianity, 4, 5, 35, 48–9, 90, 105, 145, 146; and democracy, 155; and Descartes, 7, 22, 23–4, 71*n*., 97, 162; and Judaism, 5, 21, 22, 48–60, 63–5, 97, 149, 154, 162; and mathematics, 20, 49, 122; and organized religion, 20, 34–5, 66–8, 95–6, 152–3; and seventeenth-century materialism, 98–100, 104; and seventeenth-century science, 10, 49; and the Dutch bourgeoisie, 19, 21, 22, 40–1; and the Enlightenment, 25, 94; atheism of his philosophy, 3, 7, 9, 10, 14, 16, 34, 35, 42, 75; Bible criticism, 34, 67–8, 94, 96; concept of chance, 39, 174; concept of matter, 46–7; concept of causality, 8, 9, 71; concept of God, 6, 7, 9, 35*n*., 37, 62–3, 69–70, 71–5, 101–3, 121, 127; concept of motion, 23, 32, 41, 172; concept of substance, 7, 9, 12–13, 21, 23, 24, 29, 70–1, 107–8, 120–30, 169–71; concept of time, 23, 121; concepts of essence and existence, 126, 172; critique of anthropocentrism and anthropomorphism, 38, 50, 69–70, 80, 133; critique of

free will, 135; critique of teleology, 34, 37, 68-9, 93-4, 157, 174; deductive method, 14, 20, 31, 67; defence of logical realism, 12, 13, 14, 43-4; defence of political and intellectual freedom, 5, 10, 35, 96, 159; denial of act of creation, 34, 108-9; determinism, 5, 38, 42, 71, 77, 79, 83, 93, 122, 132, 135; dialectical elements in his system, 26, 32, 108-10, 123; doctrine of infinite attributes, 8, 12, 13, 36-7, 170; doctrine of man, 86-7, 112, 114, 133-4, 154; doctrine of modes, 13, 23, 120-30, 171; ethical theory, 4, 11, 38-9, 81, 85, 97, 114-19, 133-48, 155-6; excommunication, 5, 20, 49, 96, 99, 147; fatalism, 14, 38-9, 82-3; his religious nature, 7, 35, 65, 72-3, 75; hylozoism, 27, 41, 100-1, 173; identification of real and logical relations, 6, 9, 13; inappropriate terminology of, 12, 36, 103; jubilee years: 1927 and 1932, celebrated in Soviet Union, 2; materialism of his philosophy, 6, 7n., 9, 14, 16, 17, 20, 25, 29, 34, 37, 41, 76-7, 102; monism of his philosophy, 6, 7, 9, 20, 42, 132, 136, 170-1; mysticism, 6, 9, 12, 22, 39, 85; naturalism, 5, 14, 24, 41, 132; neglect of process and development, 8, 28, 32; overcoming of Cartesian dualism, 5, 132; pantheism, 4, 6, 7, 8, 9, 14, 37; psycho-physical parallelism, 30, 75-7; rationalism, 5, 10, 12, 30-1; relativism of ethical and æsthetic values, 44, 81, 138, 140, 141, 155-6; social and political philosophy, 4, 6, 10, 39-40, 86-7, 115-17, 154-61; Stoicism, 38-9, 83-4; subverter of religious belief, 4; theory of knowledge, 8, 11-12, 13, 29-30, 66-7, 92-3, 106, 151, 169; unity of his thought, 168-9, 174; universe as interconnected whole, 33, 110-11, 124; works about, published in pre-Revolutionary Russia, 3-14; works about, published in Soviet Union, 1; works by, published in Soviet Union, 1

Stalin, Joseph (J. Dzhugashvili), 16n.; quoted, 26, 33
Stevin, Simon, 166
Stoicism, 60
Strauss, David, 24, 25, 175
Swammerdam, Jan, 166
System of Nature (Holbach), 79

Talmud, 9, 49, 50, 51, 53, 54, 55, 56, 97, 168
Telesius, 100
Terburg, Gerard, 167
Thales of Miletus, 116
Thalheimer, A., 2
Theologico-Political Treatise (Spinoza), 10, 34-5, 53, 63, 66, 67, 68, 94, 96, 133; Russian translation (1935), 1
Theophrastus redivivus, 104
Three Impostors, legend of, 163
Timosko, V., 16, 22; quoted, 30
Toland, John, cited, 175
Toporkov, A. K., quoted, 30n., 37
Torah, 52
Truth, theory of, 44-6
Tschirnhaus, E. W. von, 112
Tseitlin, Z. A., 15, 23, 27
Tymyanski, G. S., 15; quoted, 19-20, 31

Ueberweg, Friedrich, quoted, 43
Ulyanov, V. I., *see* Lenin, V. I.
Universe infinite and eternal, 33

Valentinov, N. V. (N. V. Volski), quoted, 16, 24
Vandek, V., 16, 22; quoted, 30
Van den Enden, Francis, 59
Vanini, Lucilio, 104
Varyash, A. I., 15, 17, 30; quoted, 22
Vestnik kommunisticheskoi akademi (*Bulletin of the Communist Academy*), 2
Volfson, S. Ya., 2, 34; quoted, 38
Volski, N. V., *see* Valentinov, N. V.

Volynski, A., quoted, 5–6
Vvedenski, A. I., 7

Wars of the Lord, The (Gersonides), 52
Wetter, Gustavo A., 16*n*.
Worms, René, quoted, 137, 139, 146

Yudin, P., 16

Zaleski, V. F., cited, 8
Zanser, Zacharias, 166
Zevi, Shabbetai, 58

For Product Safety Concerns and Information please contact our EU representative GPSR@taylorandfrancis.com
Taylor & Francis Verlag GmbH, Kaufingerstraße 24, 80331 München, Germany

www.ingramcontent.com/pod-product-compliance
Lightning Source LLC
Chambersburg PA
CBHW052120300426
44116CB00010B/1731